P9-EMD-922

DISCARDED

Reforming Middle Level Education

Considerations for Policymakers

A volume in
The Handbook of Research in Middle Level Education
Series Editor: Vincent A. Anfara, Jr.

The Handbook of Research in Middle Level Education Series

Vincent A. Anfara, Jr., Series Editor

Reforming Middle Level Education

Considerations for Policymakers

Edited by

Sue C. Thompson
University of Missouri, Kansas City

NMSA

National Middle School Association
Westerville, Ohio

INFORMATION AGE
PUBLISHING

80 Mason Street • Greenwich, Connecticut 06830 • www.infoagepub.com

Library of Congress Cataloging-in-Publication Data

Reforming middle level education : considerations for policymakers /
edited by Sue C. Thompson.
    p. cm. – (Handbook of research in middle level education)
 Includes bibliographical references and index.
 ISBN 1-59311-118-5 (pbk.) – ISBN 1-59311-119-3 (hardcover)
 1. Middle school education–United States. 2. Educational
change–United States. I. Thompson, Sue Carol, 1946- II. Handbook of
research in middle level education series.
 LB1623.5.F42 2004
 373.236–dc22

                                        2004002895

Copyright © 2004 Information Age Publishing Inc.

All rights reserved. No part of this publication may be reproduced, stored in a
retrieval system, or transmitted, in any form or by any means, electronic, mechanical,
photocopying, microfilming, recording or otherwise, without written permission
from the publisher.

Printed in the United States of America

MIDDLE LEVEL EDUCATION RESEARCH
SPECIAL INTEREST GROUP

The Handbook of Research in Middle Level Education is endorsed
by the Middle Level Education Research Special Interest Group,
an affiliate of the American Educational Research Association.

As stated in the organization's Constitution, the purpose of MLER is
to improve, promote, and disseminate educational research
reflecting early adolescence and middle level education.

The Handbook of Research in Middle Level Education

EDITORIAL ADVISORY BOARD

P. Gayle Andrews	The University of Georgia, Athens
Dave F. Brown	West Chester University
Kathleen M. Brown	University of North Carolina at Chapel Hill
Micki M. Caskey	Portland State University
Kimberly J. Hartman	University of North Carolina at Charlotte
Richard P. Lipka	Pittsburgh State University
Robert J. Mahar	Temple University
Kathleen F. Malu	William Patterson University
Steven B. Mertens	Center for Prevention Research and Development
Nancy B. Mizelle	Georgia College and State University
Kathleen Roney	University of North Carolina at Wilmington
Sandra L. Stacki	Hofstra University
Sue C. Thompson	University of Missouri, Kansas City

CONTENTS

FOREWORD

Sue Swaim

Why should policymakers become involved in developing policy that guides the educational opportunities and expectations for 10 through 14 year olds? What is so unique about this age span that requires a special focus on their schools, curriculum, community opportunities, family, and caregiver relations? Why is there a call for specific teacher and principal preparation and licensure to work at this particular level? John Lounsbury, considered one of the founding fathers of middle level education, begins to answer these questions in *Understanding and Appreciating the Wonder Years* by saying, "No other age level is of more importance to the future of individuals, and, literally, to that of society; because these are the years when youngsters crystallize their beliefs about themselves, and firm up their self-concepts, their philosophies of life and their values—the things that are the ultimate determinants of their behaviors."

Everyday over twenty million diverse, rapidly changing 10 through 14 year olds arrive at our nation's schools. Each young adolescent is wrestling with critical and complex life choices and focused on his or her own journey towards adulthood. These young people undergo more changes during this developmental period than at any other time except for their first three years of life. Significant transitions occur intellectually, physically, emotionally, socially, and morally during these critical years. These changes prove to be a challenge to the young adolescents, themselves, as well as to their parents, teachers, and communities in which they live.

Reforming Middle Level Education: Considerations for Policymakers, pages ix–xi
Copyright © 2004 by Information Age Publishing
All rights of reproduction in any form reserved.

The challenges of "growing up" are hard enough work in and of themselves. But today's young adolescents also face the challenge of accomplishing this incredible work in a rapidly and ever changing world. Unprecedented changes in family structures and transitions, economic decisions that impact not only their personal finances but their schools' budgets, influences of electronic and print media, changing gender roles and role-models, increasingly diverse, multi-cultural communities, and the impact of international events on individual lives are things they encounter on a daily basis. At the same time, each young adolescent is striving to figure out who he or she is becoming and what special contribution each has to offer to his or her family and community. When one considers the impact of all these factors, it becomes easier to understand why a quality education for young adolescents must become a national priority and why the role of policymakers is so important to ensuring it truly happens.

The National Middle School Association (NMSA) advocates that every young adolescent deserves equal access to educational opportunities that engage him or her in meaningful, relevant, and challenging curriculum and does so in an environment that fosters respectful and supportive relationships among students, faculty, families, and the community. Middle level schools that are academically challenging in a developmentally responsive way for every student must become the norm, rather than the exception.

To accomplish this, NMSA believes middle schools must be staffed with teachers and administrators who are specifically prepared and committed to working with this age level so they understand the unique needs and opportunities of young adolescent learners. These educators must have access to ongoing professional development to assure they have the content knowledge and the instructional strategies appropriate for this age level based on the most current research and experiences. Furthermore, multiple accountability and evaluation strategies that promote quality student learning should be put into place. Teaching and learning decisions need to be based on data that goes beyond a single test result and reflect the many aspects of a student's development, such as critical, self-evaluation, and growth towards becoming a life-long learner.

NMSA also believes parents, caregivers, and families play a key role in helping young adolescents build positive attitudes toward education and in supporting the work of schools. We recognize that an educational partnership between parents, students, educators, and community members is important in expanding the educational opportunities of all students. Bottom line, our common goal must be to give our students a quality education that develops their unique skills and talents to the fullest. To do less is not acceptable.

This volume of *The Handbook of Research in Middle Level Education* is a significant contribution to the literature on middle level schools because it is written specifically with policymakers in mind. Middle level scholars have illuminated the most important issues concerning the education of young adolescents of which policymakers must be knowledgeable. It is only by having informed policymakers that middle level schools can truly thrive and provide the kind of education that every young adolescent deserves. The future of our country depends on it.

—Sue Swaim
Executive Director of NMSA

REFERENCE

Lounsbury, J. (2003, October). *Understanding the appreciating the wonder years: Month of the young adolescent.* Westerville, OH: National Middle School Association. Retrieved October 20, 2003 from, http://www.nmsa.org.

INTRODUCTION: POLICYMAKERS, PLEASE THINK ON THESE "THINGS"

John H. Lounsbury

With a fever pitch, federal and state politicians and policymakers have gone headlong into efforts to make public education—and *all* of its students—accountable by testing them regularly with the results tightly tied to various sanctions. The inadequacies of this limited approach have become increasingly apparent, particularly when coupled with the confusion that has plagued implementation efforts. It is time for all persons who are genuinely concerned with the improvement of middle level education to stop, reflect, and reconsider before taking further action.

In the paragraphs below are a number of closely related points that, I believe, warrant serious consideration by policymakers, politicians, principals, and all leaders if more successful middle level reform efforts are to be instituted. These points should spark thoughtful discussion by readers and reformers and help move middle school reform off the dead-end street it currently occupies.

- American impatience has played into the hands of politicians who are demanding overnight school reform. Real school improvement, however, is, and has to be, a long-term proposition. It is slow, tedious, almost always frustrating, and cannot be otherwise; for to be meaningful and lasting, changes proposed have to become integrated into

Reforming Middle Level Education: Considerations for Policymakers, pages xiii–xvii
Copyright © 2004 by Information Age Publishing
All rights of reproduction in any form reserved.

the school's culture and the beliefs of those who will implement them. A good dose of realism is needed by all who would seek to improve schools.

- A fundamental premise that underlies the process of making changes at the classroom level has long been overlooked but should be acted on. This truth was perhaps expressed best by Alice Meil in the 1940s. Alice had completed a rather voluminous dissertation on the process of changing the curriculum. She subsequently wrote a small book based on her study and was then asked to condense further her research to a six- or seven-page article. Alice complied. The editor, on receipt, indicated the article, while excellent, needed a good title. Could she, the editor asked, boil down all she had discovered about this issue in a title of less than ten words? No small task, but Alice said she would try. A few days later she called up the editor and said triumphantly, "I've got the title—Changing the Curriculum Means Changing People."

  And so it is. Millions and millions of dollars have literally been wasted over the last half century because that reality has been ignored. New courses of study have been compiled, but classroom practices remained much the same. Millions more are currently being wasted because reformers bypass the time-consuming and sometimes frustrating processes that involve people. Then, to make matters worse, in recent days funds for professional development, the best means of changing teachers, have been cut to the nub. John Goodlad (1983) made these still very relevant statements 20 years ago:

  > We have practiced for so long bad habits in regard to promoting school improvement that we tend to fall into them almost automatically. Ideas in hand, we need only legislate, mandate, dictate, or otherwise pass along the word that they are to be implemented by those in schools. We forget or deliberately ignore even the simplest principles regarding human motivation (p. 7).

  And so we continue to do.

- In a concerted effort to prepare students for standardized tests, in state after state the curriculum to be covered is being prescribed. These prescriptions, while seemingly sensible as a way to ensure accountability actually hinder middle level teachers in meeting the *intellectual* needs of their pupils. Courses of study with aligned and mandated curriculum are most likely to be counterproductive when presented to young adolescents. Teachers who know their students as individuals ought not be hampered unduly in exercising their professional judgment about what, when, and how to teach. In the current climate they are relinquishing much of their judgment and creativity and knuckling under narrowly conceived and highly specific objectives that are purported to yield improved test scores. The best middle school teachers, however, are more nearly artists than technicians. They adjust teaching strategies constantly in recognition of the varying needs and abilities of their diverse, in-transition students. One lesson for all simply doesn't fit the diversity of young adolescents. And those who would try to bully underachievers by demanding improvement need to come to grips with this reality: Underachievement is far more likely to be the result of deficiencies in the heart rather than in the head. The underachievement of students is more the result of attitude and self-perceptions than native ability.

- Human beings vary tremendously. It is a condition that is inevitable, inherent, and, in fact, highly desirable, although teachers on occasion would wish otherwise. The stubborn facts of individual differences show up in maturity, general ability, readiness to learn, and in preferred ways of learning. They also show up in all other aspects of human life. The degree that students vary one from another reaches its peak during the middle level years as young adolescents, each in his or her own time and rate, mature physically, socially, emotionally, intellectually, and morally. No scheme of school organization or federal mandate for uniform achievement can wash away human variability. In fact one wonders if all the provisions of No Child Left Behind as presently set could ever be met.

- Current reform efforts are aimed at making schools, as they are currently organized, better by imposing additional requirements and regulations. These impositions only increase the already excessive reliance on extrinsic measures. What is needed instead are serious efforts to make schools *different,* to bring them more in harmony with what we know about learning and human development, and to capitalize on intrinsic motivation.

    Learning, after all, is natural, God-given. Individuals inherently want to learn. Teacher-directed lessons from a textbook are perhaps acceptable at the elementary level. But when youth move into the middle grades and begin the extensive physical, social, emotional, and to be sure, the intellectual maturation that characterize this key phase of life, the continued use of extrinsic motivation and a canned curriculum become far less effective. The golden opportunity that Mother Nature now provides to move learning to a new level and exploit the possibilities for intellectual engagement is not only ignored, but directly countered by the perpetuation of traditional practices. The increasing incidents of behavior problems and the nearly universal judgments about the curriculum being boring that occur at this level are, for the most part, the direct result of failing to take advantage of the changes young adolescents undergo.

- Any thoughtful, honest assessment of contemporary society would lead one to recognize that formal education must deal with more than the acquisition of information and the limited skills needed to achieve acceptable scores on a paper and pencil test, whether teacher-made or standardized. Such objectives are valid, and tests to measure them should be used. But using test scores as the sole measure of school success is both unfair and invalid. Schools must be about the business of improving the behaviors of our youth, guiding their development as responsible, able persons. Inescapably, teaching is a moral enterprise, and an education in its fullest sense has to involve heart as well as head, attitude as well as information, spirit as well as scholarship, and conscience as well as competence.

  Our nation's problems, with rare exceptions, are the result of the consciously chosen behaviors of individuals. The ultimate goal of all education after all is changed behavior. John Ruskin claimed: "Education does not mean teaching people to know what they do not know, it means teaching them to behave as they do not behave." And it is during the middle years that students acquire the dispositions and attitudes that will direct their behavior in the years ahead. Alfred North Whitehead was sensitive to the importance of the early adolescent years, for he declared, "These are the years when the lines of character are graven." If middle schools do not fulfill their rightful role in developing ethical, responsible, self-motivated, thinking individuals, they will have failed at what ultimately is their most important responsibility. Middle schools must be concerned about what students are becoming not just about what test scores they are making.

- The Fortune 500 Companies have been reported as seeking in their employees these three traits as priorities: ability to work as a part of the team, ability to solve problems, and possession of good, interpersonal skills. None of these traits is fostered or developed by the rigid, narrow instruction now becoming even more common in the push to be "accountable." All of these important traits would, however, be very much part of an instructional program in a school that practiced what we know about learning and human development.

A FINAL CHALLENGE

Public education, once the pride of all Americans, is floundering. It seems to have lost its soul. Yet its continuance as a unifying element is critical to our overly fractured society. There are elements in our society that would like to see public education fail. They must not succeed. Those who would seek to improve education must be cognizant of the realities of educational reform, the findings of research, and the big picture. The all too often fisted minds of policymakers have to be opened so they can address thoughtfully essential questions about public education beginning with "What are schools for?" This volume provides appropriate food for thought as more deliberate and valid efforts to improve the critically important middle level schools are formulated. Read and be guided by its lessons.

REFERENCE

Goodlad, J. (1983). Improving schooling in the 1980s. *Educational Leadership, 40*(7), 7.

CHAPTER 1

CREATING HIGH-PERFORMANCE MIDDLE SCHOOLS

Recommendations from Research

Vincent A. Anfara, Jr.

INTRODUCTION

By the 1960s much of the literature on the junior high noted that such schools had turned into "miniature high schools" (Johnson, Dupuis, Musial, & Hall, 1994), albeit "pale imitations of senior high schools" (Grooms, 1967). Aided by sociological and psychological research during the 1950s and 1960s (Bossing, 1954; Gruhn & Douglass, 1956; Lounsbury, 1960), educators judged the junior high school organization as inappropriate for young adolescents (ages 10–15) who are psychologically, socially, emotionally, intellectually, and physically at a very different place than adolescents. Eventually, in the early 1960s the call to reform the junior high evolved into a call for the creation of the middle school. This call was supported with the publication in 1965 of W. M. Alexander's "The Junior High: A Changing View" in *Readings in Curriculum*, edited by Hass and

Reforming Middle Level Education: Considerations for Policymakers, pages 1–18
Copyright © 2004 by Information Age Publishing
All rights of reproduction in any form reserved.

Wiles; D. H. Eichhorn's *The Middle School* (1966); and W. M. Alexander's *The Emergent Middle School* (1969). Eventually, the middle school movement would grow to be characterized as "one of the largest and most comprehensive efforts at educational reorganization in the history of American public schooling" (George & Oldaker, 1985, p. 1).

Recent articles dealing with middle level education have been replete with indictments of what is happening, especially in reference to curriculum and student academic performance. As an example, the Southern Regional Education Board in March 1998 concluded that middle schools are a "weak link" in the K–12 education chain (cited in Bradley, 1998). Additionally, *Education Week* published two articles attacking middle schools; one was titled "A Crack in the Middle" (Killion & Hirsh, 1998) and the other was "Muddle in the Middle" (Bradley, 1998). As a result, the middle school model has come under attack for supplanting academic rigor with a focus on students' social, emotional, and physical needs.

In response to these attacks and the recent passage of the federal *No Child Left Behind Act*, I intend in this chapter to trace the recommendations offered by various professional organizations and foundations dedicated to the reform of middle level education and to look critically at these recommendations in light of the desired outcomes—improved student academic and socioemotional performance. During this process of construction and deconstruction I discuss issues related to implementation and present the research that is available to support middle school reform as delineated by these organizations. To conclude, I reveal what should capture our attention, energies, and resources in order that all of America's middle schools can become high-performing educational institutions.

THE RECOMMENDATIONS OF PROFESSIONAL ORGANIZATIONS AND HIGH-PERFORMING MIDDLE SCHOOLS

Many professional organizations and foundations authored reports which offered recommendations for creating exemplary middle schools that would be responsive to the needs of young adolescents and result in improved academic and socioemotional development. The assumption behind these reports was that by implementing the recommendations school improvement would occur. In 1969 the Association for Supervision and Curriculum Development (ASCD) established the Council on the Emerging Adolescent Learner. In 1974 after much work by formal and informal working groups, the Executive Council of ASCD appointed a group and charged them with "developing a paper for the Association identifying the rationale and significance of the American middle school and stressing the kinds of programs appropriate for emerging adolescent learners" (1975, p. v). In 1975, ASCD published *The Middle School We Need* that reasserted the need to develop schools around the needs and characteristics of young adolescents. Recommendations included practices like team teaching, individualized instruction, and flexible scheduling.

In 1982 the National Middle School Association (NMSA) published *This We Believe*. This position paper set forth the essential characteristics of the middle school:

1. Educators knowledgeable about and committed to young adolescents,
2. A balanced curriculum based on the needs of young adolescents,
3. A range of organizational arrangements (flexible structures),
4. Varied instructional strategies,
5. A full exploratory program,
6. Comprehensive counseling and advising,
7. Continuous progress for students,
8. Evaluation procedures compatible with the nature of young adolescents,
9. Cooperative planning, and
10. Positive school climate. (1982, p. 19)

In 1995, the original position paper was revised and given the subtitle, Developmentally Responsice Middle Level Schools.

In 2003, NMSA again revised *This We Believe*, now subtitled *Successful Schools for Young Adolescents*. Eight characteristics and six program components are offered to practitioners interested in creating "successful schools for young adolescents." The eight characteristics include:

1. Educators who value working with this age group and who are prepared to do so;
2. Courageous, collaborative leadership;
3. A shared vision that guides decisions;
4. An inviting, supportive, and safe environment;
5. High expectations for every member of the learning community;
6. Student and teachers engaged in active learning;
7. An adult advocate for every student; and
8. School-initiated family and community partnerships.

The six program components include:

1. Curriculum that is relevant, challenging, integrative, and exploratory;
2. Multiple learning and teaching approaches that respond to the students' diversity;

3. Assessment and evaluation that promote quality learning;
4. Organizational structures that support meaningful relationships and learning;
5. School-wide efforts and policies that foster health, wellness, and safety; and
6. Multifaceted guidance and support services.

This We Believe has become the most widely used document about middle level education ever published. Schools have employed this position statement as criteria for evaluation, self-studies, and school improvement initiatives.

In 1985 the National Association of Secondary School Principals (NASSP) released *An Agenda for Excellence at the Middle Level.* Focused on 12 areas (i.e., core values, culture and climate, student development, curriculum, learning and instruction, school organization, technology, teachers, transition, principals, connections, and client centeredness), this document aimed at creating school programs responsive to the needs of students. In order for middle schools to achieve academic productivity, they should be organized:

- so that decisions are made at the lowest possible level in the organization . . . by teams of teachers working closely together with students and other school personnel.
- so that the effects of size are minimized, large schools should be broken into smaller units or families. Schools should be organized around teaching teams that plan and work with clearly identified groups of students, thereby ensuring that every student is well known by a group of teachers.
- with a class schedule that allows the greatest amount of uninterrupted learning time for teams of teachers working with groups of students. Teachers should be given maximum control over how instructional time is allocated and used.
- with advisory groups of teachers and parents participating in important decisions about building goals, budget priorities, and school climate. (excerpted from NASSP, 1985, pp. 10–11)

In 1989, the Carnegie Council on Adolescent Development issued *Turning Points: Preparing American Youth for the 21st Century.* This document noted that:

"A volatile mismatch exists between the organization and curriculum of middle grade schools and the intellectual and emotional needs of young adolescents" (pp. 8–9). Carnegie challenged middle schools to be places where close, personal relationships with adults and peers create a climate for personal growth and intellectual development. To meet this challenge, middle schools were to:

1. create small learning communities,
2. teach a core academic curriculum,
3. Empower teachers and administrators,
4. staff middle schools with teachers who are expert at teaching young adolescents,
5. improve the academic performance of students,
6. reengage families in the educational process, and
7. connect schools with communities. (excerpted from Carnegie Council on Adolescent Development, 1989, p. 9)

According to *Turning Points*, these seven components would work collectively to ensure the success of all students. (It is important to note that "ensure the success for all students" was originally listed third in Carnegie's list of components. This helped to conceal the holistic, ecological nature of the reform, contributing to practitioners' beliefs that it was acceptable to pick and choose only the components they were interested in implementing.)

Most recently, in 2000 the Carnegie Corporation of New York published *Turning Points 2000: Educating Adolescents for the 21st Century* (Jackson & Davis, 2000). Ten years after the release of the original document this report asserted as core values the following beliefs: the primary purpose of middle grades education is to promote young adolescents' intellectual development; adolescents' intellectual, ethical, and social development requires strong, supportive relationships; and successful middle grades schools are equitable with high outcomes for every student. Jackson and Davis (2000) noted that the most important changes from the 1989 report included: ensuring the success of every student, placing a greater emphasis on teaching and learning, grounding curriculum in academic standards, and inspiring families and communities that are inextricably linked to the work of schools. While the original *Turning Points* provided a framework and the philosophy for middle grades educational reform, *Turning Points 2000* provided valuable guidance to practitioners interested in implementing the model.

After having quickly reviewed the recommendations of ASCD, NMSA, NASSP, and Carnegie, it should be obvious that a very consistent collection of ideas about what constitutes a good middle school has emerged. But as with any educational initiative or policy, it became a matter of implementation.

IMPLEMENTING THE RECOMMENDATIONS TO CREATE HIGH-PERFORMING MIDDLE SCHOOLS: "IF YOU BUILD IT, THEY WILL COME"

In an increasingly turbulent policymaking environment—amidst tough international competition, declining resources, a renewed emphasis on accountability, and an increasingly impoverished and ethnically diverse population—schools are under intense pressure to produce results (Reyes, Wagstaff, & Fusarelli, 1999). In this section of this chapter I focus on an often overlooked aspect of reform initiatives and educational policymaking—implementation. Some policy scholars have observed a tendency in the public's imagination, fueled by the popular press, to assume that once a policy is enacted or a reform initiated, things change (Fischer, 1995). Others have noted the very uneven nature of implementation, with great variance in what constitutes teacher teams, advisories, or transition programs. However, as Peters (1986) noted, "Once enacted, laws do not go into effect by themselves" (p. 84). Policies, like laws, are neither self-explanatory nor self-executing. Policies and reform initiatives, no matter how well designed, must be implemented with a high degree of fidelity to their original design to achieve the intended effects.

In *Field of Dreams*, Kevin Costner was told, "If you build it, they will come." With the publication of *Turning Points* (Carnegie Council on Adolescent Development, 1989) and *This We Believe* (NMSA, 1982, 1992, 1995) interest in the junior high waned and the number of middle schools increased. According to the *Digest of Education Statistics* (Department of Education Statistics, 1995), there were 9,573 middle schools in 1993–1994. The most recent figures (Bradley & Manzo, 2000) document the existence of 16,000 middle schools and only 2,000 junior highs. But all too often the change was in name only, and many middle schools continued to operate as "miniature high schools" (Johnson et al., 1994) or "transitional schools" (Manning, 1993).

While it seems common sense to assume that schools would respond to the needs of their students and create developmentally appropriate learning environments, it is evident from the history of middle-level reform that schools are slow to change. Capelluti and Stokes (1991) reminded us of this fact, "Although there is considerable knowledge about the characteristics and interests of early adolescents, this information has not at all times been reflected in what and how we teach these students" (p. iii).

As early as 1975, ASCD revealed that "the available research indicated a significant gap between the main tenets of the theoretical middle school concept proposed by leading middle school authorities and actual educational practices in most middle schools" (p. 3). In similar fashion, Jackson, project director for *Turning Points*, noted that "recent studies show that few of the recommended actions, though frequently proposed, are actually practiced in schools" (1990, p. 1).

Discussing obstacles to the implementation of middle school reform, Manning (1993) noted that many middle schools continue to operate as "transitional schools"—merely housing students between elementary and high school. Additionally, while many middle schools place a major emphasis on school organization and grade configurations, what remains lacking are appropriate educational environments and curricula. Other obstacles include: (1) the lack of understanding regarding the reform initiative with practitioners picking the parts of the reform they want to implement rather than ensuring fidelity to the model and adopting it in a holistic fashion, and (2) the lack of preparation and professional development for both teachers and administrators who are charged with implementation efforts. While obstacles to middle school reform are not the focus of this chapter, they are important for understanding the inability of most middle schools to effectively implement the reform.

Issues surrounding the implementation of middle school reform are sufficient enough that middle schools now find themselves on the defensive. The most recent attacks cite evidence from studies like the Third International Mathematics and Science Study (TIMSS) and the National Assessment of Educational Progress (NAEP). Among the findings drawn from TIMSS are the following:

- eighth-grade mathematics classes in the United States are not as advanced and not as focused as those in Japan and Germany;
- topics taught in U.S. eighth-grade mathematics classrooms are at a seventh-grade level by international standards;
- the content of U.S. mathematics classes requires less high-level thought than classes in Germany and Japan;
- U.S. mathematics teachers' typical goal is to teach students how to do something, while the Japanese teachers' goal is to help their student understand mathematical concepts. (excerpted from *A Sourcebook of 8th-Grade Findings: TIMSS*, Mid-Atlantic Eisenhower Consortium for Mathematics and Science Education, 1997)

Organizations like the National Middle School Association are feeling more pressured now than ever to demonstrate that the philosophy they promote works; that it produces the results it promised—improved intellectual and socioemotional development of young adolescents. Along with their 2003 publication of *This We Believe: Successful Schools for Young Adolescents*, a companion volume, *Research and Resources in Support of This We Believe* (Anfara, Andrews, Hough, Mertens, Mizelle, & White, 2003), was released. It is the hope of the National Middle School Association that this companion volume will provide advocates with the research base they need in the struggle to move middle level reform forward.

Few question that middle schools are at a crossroads. We must step back and evaluate where we have previously invested and are currently focusing our energies. We need more than ever to answer some of the ever-present questions that have haunted the middle school movement: Does the middle school concept work? Does it achieve the desired results of improved student academic and socioemotional performance? As a first step to answering these questions, let's turn now to the research that has been conducted on the relationship between the recommendations of *Turning Points* and improved student academic and socioemotional development.

RESEARCH THAT SUPPORTS THE REFORM OF MIDDLE SCHOOLS UTILIZING TURNING POINTS' RECOMMENDATIONS

Four major studies exist that examine the middle school concept and its effects on student academic and/or socioemotional performance. These studies include research conducted by Lee and Smith (1993), Felner, Jackson, Kasak, Mulhall, Brand, and Flowers (1997), the Center for Prevention Research and Development (CPRD) (1998), and Backes, Ralston, and Ingwalson (1999).

In 1993 Lee and Smith evaluated how middle school policies and practices influenced the students who attend them, focusing specifically on achievement, engagement, and equity issues. The sample for this study was drawn from the National Education Longitudinal Study (NELS) of 1988. Because of the nature of this database, Lee and Smith acknowledged that they are "not sure whether the sample of students in schools that reported that they engage in practices like heterogeneous grouping and team teaching actually encountered instruction in this way" (p. 180). Neither did they know the level of implementation of these practices. Specifically, they looked at reduced departmentalization, heterogeneous grouping, and team teaching as a "composite measure" of restructured middle schools.

Lee and Smith's (1993) findings indicated that the elements of restructuring were positively associated with academic achievement and engagement with schooling of eighth graders. Students who attended schools that encourage team teaching evidenced higher achievement. Additionally, less grouping by ability and a less rigid departmental structure appeared to promote social equity in achievement among students. In relation to engagement, Lee and Smith found that "although attending restructured schools may positively influence academic engagement, this engagement may coexist with higher levels of at-risk behaviors" (p.180).

Felner et al. (1997) conducted significant and compelling research that acknowledges the necessity of implementing *Turning Points'* recommendations as a comprehensive reform initiative. This team of researchers studied a network of 31 Illinois middle schools during the 1991–1992 school year. These schools represented a range of geographic, demographic, and size characteristics, including rural, suburban, and urban schools.

Felner et al. (1997) sought to "assess and evaluate the process of implementation of the recommendations of *Turning Points* for middle grade reform, as well as their impact on students' academic achievement, socioemotional development, and behavioral adjustment" (p. 42). Of particular concern was the association between the levels of implementation of the reform that participating schools attained and relevant student outcomes. The researchers obtained data on sets of schools that were at different levels of maturity (high, partial, or low) in reform implementation. The primary source of data was a set of annual surveys, the High Performance Learning Communities Assessments (HiPLaCes-A). These surveys were administered to teachers, staff members, students, administrators, and selected parents. Additional data were obtained from student records, attendance, and scores (reading, mathematics, and language arts) on local and state achievement tests.

Results of this longitudinal study indicated, "...across subject areas, adolescents in highly implemented schools had higher achievement (as measured by the Iowa Test of Basic Skills and the California Test of Basic Skills) than those in nonimplemented schools and substantially better than those in partially implemented schools" (p. 55). Felner et al. (1997) concluded, "...broad-range enhancements and adjustment are not obtained until implementation is quite mature, comprehensive, and conducted with a high degree of fidelity" (p. 67).

Researchers at the Center for Prevention Research and Development (CPRD) looked at 155 Michigan middle schools that were participating in the Michigan Middle Start Initiative funded in 1994 by the W.K. Kellogg Foundation. Surveys (the School Improvement Self-Study) were administered to principals, teachers, and students in 1994/95 and in 1996/97 by the Center for Prevention Research and Development. This Self-Study uses 24 scales to measure progress in dimensions of reform including, for example, curriculum, school climate, instruction, family involvement, professional development, and school organization.

Specifically, Mertens, Flowers, and Mulhall (1998) focused on trends related to teaching practices and learning environments and the relationship of this environment to student achievement, behaviors, and attitudes. By design the researchers compared and contrasted the progress of two groups of Middle Start schools: grant schools and non-grant schools. The "grant" schools group consisted of 21 schools that received intensive comprehensive school reform services, including individual school grant, onsite technical assistance, professional development, and networking opportunities. The "non-grant" group contained 134 schools that participated in the Self-Study but did not receive any other school reform services. Their findings indicate that the 21 Middle Start grant schools improved in both reading and math achievement scores over the two-year period, as measured by the Michigan Educational Assessment Program (MEAP). "Compared to the non-grant schools, the Middle Start grant schools showed dramatic gains in both 7th grade reading (+10 %) and math (+6 %) MEAP scores from 1994/95 to 1996/97" (p. 92).

Students reported higher levels of stress to succeed academically but felt safer at the school in 1996/97 than they did in 1994/95. Additionally, Middle Start grant schools displayed several positive improvements in the areas of student adjustment, behavior, and substance use (a decrease in the reported use of alcohol). Students reported a more positive self-esteem and academic efficacy. Lastly, teachers reported working more effectively to serve the needs of early adolescents and having more contact with parents and guardians. Schools implementing the Middle Start Initiative are showing improved school capacity for continuous improvement.

CPRD is also a partner in the expansion of this project with the Foundation for the Mid South's Middle Start Initiative. Middle schools in Louisiana, Arkansas, and Mississippi began participating in this project in 1998. In the area of academic achievement, the Arkansas Middle Start schools (80 schools) scored slightly higher on the 1998 reading and language achievement tests (SAT9) than the statewide group of middle-level schools (CPRD, 1999a). In Louisiana, Middle Start schools (68 schools) scored about the same on ITBS achievement tests as the statewide group of middle schools (CPRD, 1999b). Mississippi Middle Start schools (67 schools) had slightly higher student achievement scores (CTBS/5) in language arts, reading, and mathematics as compared to the statewide group of middle level schools (CPRD, 1999c). In short, these findings seem to suggest that Middle Start schools, despite their higher percentages of economically disadvantaged students, are keeping pace with the state averages (state averages include a higher percentage of more affluent schools).

Finally in 1999, Backes et al. examined the impact of middle school practices on student achievement in North Dakota's Middle Grade School State Policy Initiative (MGSSPI) schools (called BRIDGES schools). The major question asked was, What effect has the implementation of middle level practices by BRIDGES Project schools had on student achievement in grades 6 though 8 compared to non-BRIDGES schools in North Dakota? The authors of this study admit that they "...assumed that each of the recommended middle school practices had been implemented, [and] that students in BRIDGES Project systemic change schools should have measurable gains in student achievement because of the implementation of these practices..." (p. 49).

The findings of the Backes et al. (1999) study indicated that the composite grade equivalent score from grades 6 to 8 was higher in BRIDGES Project schools than in non-BRIDGES schools in the areas of reading vocabulary, language mechanics, study skills, science, and social studies.

There was no difference in composite grade equivalent scores in reading comprehension and spelling. Non-BRIDGES students outperformed BRIDGES students in the areas of language expression, math computation, and math concepts and applications.

The results of these four studies are promising. They provide middle level practitioners, scholars, advocates, and policymakers with a tentative foundation that links the middle school concept to improved student academic and socioemotional development. These studies also provide a point of departure for the design and conduct of future research.

But it should be troubling that I have summarized the results of only four studies. Other attempts, and they are numerous, to ascertain the relationship between middle-level reform (specifically *Turning Points'* recommendations) and student achievement have yielded ambiguous and conflicting results. There are an insufficient number of studies, a lack of longitudinal studies, weak research designs, difficulties with comparing studies with conflicting designs, and problems with the effects of extraneous variables on outcomes (Van Zandt & Totten, 1995). Indeed, the landscape of this corpus of research is painted utilizing many different brushes and diverse styles with the resulting product being very confusing. But, as mentioned earlier, there is an urgency regarding research in this area. As noted by Felner et al. (1997), "Although a more well-developed research base does not, by itself, ensure more successful reform efforts, without such a foundation the progress and fruits of reform efforts will continue to be disappointing" (p.41).

But before we accept the recommendations of *Turning Points* (Carnegie Council on Adolescent Development, 1989) and *This We Believe* (NMSA, 2003) and call for more empirical data to support the research base of the middle school movement as delineated in these two documents, we need to look at what a handful of researchers have been investigating—the "black box" that exists between the recommendations and the desired outcomes. I now turn to looking at the recommendations of *Turning Points* as "necessary but not sufficient" in the creation of high-performing middle schools.

WHAT SEEMS TO MATTER IN CREATING HIGH-PERFORMING MIDDLE SCHOOLS: RECOMMENDATIONS AS "NECESSARY BUT NOT SUFFICIENT"

Some important questions need to be addressed. Is there a direct, causal link between the recommendations offered in *Turning Points* and *This We Believe* and the desired results of improved academic and socioemotional performance? Have we misunderstood the nature of the reform, implementing it in a very mechanistic manner and not understanding the reasons (asking why and for what purpose?) for such practices as teaming and advisory? Have we simply looked for a quick fix and jumped on another of those infamous educational bandwagons? Responding to her reading of *The Exemplary Middle School* by Alexander and George (1981), Russell (1997) noted that there is the assumption that "...according to middle-level theory, if the middle level philosophy is implemented, the outcomes of enhanced personal development, group citizenship, and achievement will be attained" (p. 170). This assumption was thought to be true by many practitioners and policymakers who implemented the reform with a wide degree of fidelity and variability.

A small group of researchers (Felner et al., 1997; Roney, Anfara, & Brown, 2002; Stevenson & Erb, 1998) acknowledge the establishment of intermediate outcomes that result from the implementation of *Turning Points'* recommendations. These intermediate outcomes include, among others, improvement in teacher quality of life and job satisfaction; school and classroom climate; and student and school supports, stressors, and resources. When implemented well, *Turning Points'* recommendations facilitate improvement in these intermediate outcomes which in turn have a more direct impact on the desired outcomes (see Figure 1.1).

In Figure 1.1, *Turning Points'* recommendations are found in the ellipse on the left while the desired results are located in the box, labeled "student outcomes," on the far right. The three boxes in the center of Figure 1.1 contain the intermediate outcomes researchers have been investigating. Again, it is believed that these "intermediate outcomes" have a more immediate impact on student learning than do the initial recommendations offered to middle level practitioners in *Turning Points* (Carnegie Council on Adolescent Development, 1989) and *This We Believe* (NMSA, 1995, 2003). This is what is meant by "necessary but not sufficient" to result in improvement in student outcomes. In short, the reform recommendations cannot and do not directly cause the desired results. Looking at these intermediate outcomes allows us to shed some light on the "black box" of schooling and middle level reform.

Brown, Roney, and Anfara (2003), building on this conceptualization of the reform recommendations as "necessary but not sufficient" and utilizing the scholarship of Hoy and Hannum (1997) as a theoretical framework, looked at both high and low-performing middle schools and concluded that what seemed to matter most in high-performing middle schools could be classified into five areas: (1) academic emphasis, (2) teacher affiliation, (3) collegial leadership, (4) resource support, and (5) institutional integrity (see Table 1.1).

Additionally, the research of Brown et al. (2003) revealed that low-performing and high-performing middle schools actually implemented *Turn-*

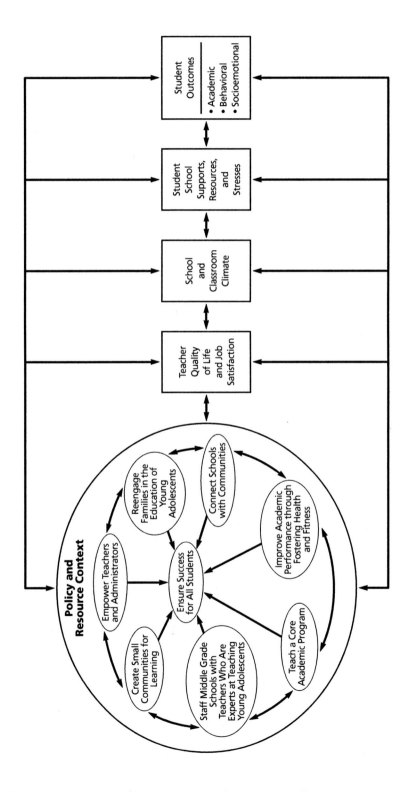

Figure 1.1. The "necessary but not sufficient" quality of turning points' recommendations.

Source: Stevenson, C., & Erb., T. O. (1998). How implementing Turning Points improves student outcomes. *Middle School Journal 30*(1), 49–52. Adapted from Felner, R.D. (1993). Understanding the impact of Turning Points on the adjustment and educational experiences of young adolescents. *Journal of Adolescent Medicine, 14,* 172–189.

Table 1.1.   Five Focus Areas for High-Performing Middle Schools

Area	*Description*
Academic	The extent to which the school is driven by a quest for academic excellence. High but achievable academic goals are set for students, the learning environment is orderly and serious, teachers believe in their students' ability to achieve, and students work hard and respect those who do well academically.
Teacher Affiliation	A sense of friendliness and strong affiliation with the school. Teachers feel good about each other, their job, and their students. They are committed to both their students and their colleagues and accomplish their jobs with enthusiasm.
Collegial Leadership	Principal behavior that is friendly, supportive, open, and guided by norms of equality. But, at the same time, the principal sets the tone for high performance by letting people know what is expected of them.
Resource Support	Refers primarily to the availability of classroom supplies and instructional materials. Sufficient materials are readily available; indeed, extra materials are supplied if requested.
Institutional Integrity	The degree to which the school can cope with its environment in a way that maintains the educational integrity of its programs. Teachers are protected from unreasonable community and parental demands.

Source: Based on the work of Hoy & Hannum (1997). Middle school climate: An empirical assessment of organizational health and student achievement. *Educational Administration Quarterly, 33*(3), 290–311.

ing Points' recommendations with about the same degree of fidelity. Interestingly, none of the 12 middle schools in their study were implementing exploratory curriculum or advisory programs, and flexible scheduling was not utilized in the high-performing schools. These findings pushed this team of researchers to then look more seriously at the "*not* necessary and not sufficient" nature of middle-level reform recommendations in the process of creating high-performing schools. In short, they concluded that there are multiple means that may be used to reach the desired result of improved student academic and socioemotional performance. What schools must concern themselves with are issues of teacher satisfaction, teacher and student sense of efficacy, high but achievable academic goals, an orderly learning environment, collegial leadership on the part of the principal, a strong sense of mission and vision, the availability of instructional materials and supplies, and parent and community involvement.

DISCUSSION

So where does this leave us? I see two possibilities. First, we can accept the recommendations of the Carnegie Council on Adolescent Development and the National Middle School Association and continue to travel forward in pursuit of more empirical evidence to support the connection between the reform (as they define and structure it) and the intended outcomes—high-performing middle schools. Or, second, we can admit that there are multiple methods that can be employed in creating high-performing middle schools and focus primarily on the intermediate outcomes (see Figure 1.1), implementing practices that are designed to improve them. We must not fool ourselves into believing that if we implement the components of the reform that the desired results will automatically happen. If implemented well (and that is a very important adverb), the intermediate outcomes discussed will result and improved student achievement and socioemotional development will be evidenced. Unfortunately there is too much evidence that implementation has not been faithful to the model. What constitutes advisory or teaming at one school is something far different at another school. Unlike Kevin Costner in *Field of Dreams*, we may implement teaming, advisory programs, and exploratory curriculum and realize none of the desired results.

In traveling either path we must also remind ourselves that what needs to be done to create high-performing middle schools was not first introduced in 1982 with *This We Believe* or in 1989 with *Turning Points*. The correlates of high-performing schools were first identified as part of the Effective Schools research—a body of literature (Brookover & Lezotte, 1977; Edmonds, 1979, 1986) that began to grow after Coleman et al. issued the famous report, *Equality of Educational Opportunity* (1966) and Jencks et al. (1972) published *Inequality: A Reassessment of the Effect of Family and Schooling in America*. This body of research grew out of social science research arguing that home background had a far greater influence on a child's development than the school.

According to the Association for Effective Schools (1996), there are seven correlates related to high-performing schools:

1. A clear school mission,
2. High expectations for success,
3. Instructional leadership,
4. Frequent monitoring of students' progress,
5. Opportunity for students to learn and time on task,
6. A safe and orderly environment, and
7. Home-school relations. (p. 2)

Firestone (1991) noted that "the work on effective schools is no longer trendy. Educators and policymakers have moved on to new 'fixes' for American education" (p. 8). But I contend that we must look at these elements. We must ensure that we have high expectations for our students, that there is a positive school climate, that curriculum is rigorous, that teachers have a high sense of job satisfaction and efficacy, and the like. We must recognize that these variables are more closely linked to improved student performance than teaming, or advisory, or transition programs. In the end, it comes down to a matter of implementation. Fortunately, schools DO have some control over some of the things that have been shown to correlate with high student achievement.

REFERENCES

Alexander, W.M. (Ed.). (1969). *The emergent middle school.* New York: Holt, Reinhart, Winston.

Alexander, W.M. (1965). The junior high: A changing view. In G. Hass & K. Wiles (Eds.), *Readings in curriculum* (pp. 29–42). Boston: Allyn and Bacon.

Alexander, W.M., & George, P.S. (1981). *The exemplary middle school.* New York: Holt, Reinhart, Winston.

Anfara, V.A., Jr., Andrews, P.G., Hough, D.L., Mertens, S.B., Mizelle, N.B., & White, G.P. (2003). *Research and resources in support of This We Believe.* Westerville, OH: National Middle School Association.

Association for Effective Schools. (1996). *What is effective schools research?* Retrieved July 19, 2003, from http://www.mes.org/esr.html

Association for Supervision and Curriculum Development. (1975). *The middle school we need.* Washington, DC: Author.

Backes, J., Ralston, A., & Ingwalson, G. (1999). Middle level reform: The impact on student achievement. *Research in Middle Level Education Quarterly, 22*(3), 43–57.

Bossing, N. (1954). A junior high designed for tomorrow. *The Clearing House, 9.*

Bradley, A., & Manzo, K. (2000, October 4). This weak link. *Education Week* (supplement), 3–8.

Bradley, A. (1998). Muddle in the middle. *Education Week on the Web.* Retrieved July 19, 2003, from http://www.edweek.org/ew/vol-17/31middle.h17

Brookover, W.B., & Lezotte, L.W. (1977). *Changes in school characteristics coincident with changes in student achievement.* East Lansing: Michigan State University, College of Urban Development.

Brown, K.M., Roney, K., & Anfara, V.A., Jr. (2003). Organizational health directly influences student performance at the middle level. *Middle School Journal, 34*(5), 5–15.

Capelluti, J., & Stokes, D. (Eds.). (1991). *Middle level education: Programs, policies, & practices.* Reston, VA: National Association of Secondary School Principals.

Carnegie Council on Adolescent Development. (1989). *Turning points: Preparing American youth for the 21st century.* New York: Carnegie Corporation.

Center for Prevention Research and Development. (1999a, September). *1998/99 Arkansas Middle Start: An executive summary.* Champaign, IL: Author. Retrieved July 19, 2003, from http://www.cprd.uiuc.edu/schools/AR4-pg exec summ.pdf

Center for Prevention Research and Development. (1999b, September). *1998/99 Louisiana Middle Start: An executive summary.* Champaign, IL: Author. Retrieved July 19, 2003, from http://www.cprd.uiuc.edu/schools/LA4-pg exec summ.pdf

Center for Prevention Research and Development. (1999c, September). *1998/00 Mississippi Middle Start: An executive summary.* Champaign, IL: Author. Retrieved July 19, 2003, from http://www.cprd.uiuc.edu/schools/MS4-pg exec summ.pdf

Coleman, J.S., Campbell, E.Q., Hobson, C.J., McPartland, J., Mood, A.M., Weinfield, F.D., & York, R.L. (1966). *Equality of educational opportunity.* Washington, DC: U.S. Office of Education, National Center for Educational Statistics.

Department of Educational Statistics. (1995). *Digest of education statistics.* Washington, DC: National Center for Educational Statistics.

Edmonds, R.R. (1979). Effective schools for the urban poor. *Educational Leadership, 37*(1), 15–24.

Edmonds, R.R. (1986). Characteristics of effective schools. In E. Neisser (Ed.), *The achievement of minority children* (pp. 93–104). Hillsdale, NJ: Erlbaum.

Eichhorn, D. (1966). *The middle school.* New York: The Center for Applied Research in Education.

Felner, R., Jackson, A., Kasak, D., Mulhall, P., Brand, S., & Flowers, N. (1997). The impact of school reform for the middle grades: A longitudinal study of a network engaged in Turning Points-based comprehensive school transformation. In R. Takanishi & D.A. Hamburg (Eds.), *Preparing adolescents for the twenty-first century: Challenges facing Europe and the United States* (pp. 38–69). Cambridge: Cambridge University Press.

Firestone, W.A. (1991). Introduction. In J. R. Bliss, W.A. Firestone, & C.E. Richards (Eds.), *Rethinking effective schools: Research and practice* (pp. 1–11). Englewood Cliffs, NJ: Prentice Hall.

Fischer, F. (1995). *Evaluating public policy.* Chicago: Nelson-Hall.

George, P.S., & Oldaker, L. L. (1985). *Evidence for the middle school.* Columbus, OH: National Middle School Association.

Grooms, M. (1967). *Perspectives on the middle school.* Columbus, OH: Merrill.

Gruhn, W., & Douglass, H. (1956). *The modern junior high* (2nd ed.). New York: Ronald Press.

Hoy, W.K., & Hannum, J.W. (1997). Middle school climate: An empirical assessment of organizational health and student achievement. *Educational Administration Quarterly, 33*(3), 290–311.

Jackson, A., & Davis, G.P. (2000). *Turning points 2000: Educating adolescents in the 21st century.* New York: Teachers College Press.

Jencks, C., Smith, M., Acland, H., Bane, M., Cohen, D., Gintis, H., Hetnes, B., & Michelson, S. (1972). *Inequality: A reassessment of the effect of family and schooling in America.* New York: Harper & Row.

Johnson, J., Dupuis, V., Musial, D., & Hall, G. (1994). *Introduction to the foundations of American education.* Needham Heights, MA: Allyn and Bacon.

Killion, J., & Hirsh, S. (1998, March 19). A crack in the middle. *Education Week,* 44–48.

Lee, V.E., & Smith, J.B. (1993). Effects of school restructuring on the achievement and engagement of middle-grade students. *Sociology of Education, 66*(3), 164–187.

Lounsbury, J. (1960). How the junior high school came to be. *Educational Leadership, 18*, 145–147.

Manning, M.L. (1993). *Developmentally appropriate middle level schools.* Wheaton, MD: Association for Childhood Education International.

Mertens, S.B., Flowers, N., & Mulhall, P. (1998). *The Middle Start Initiative, phase 1: A longitudinal analysis of Michigan middle-level schools.* (A report to the W.K. Kellogg Foundation). Urbana: University of Illinois. Retrieved July 19, 2003, from http://www/cprd.uiuc.edu/schools/Phase I report.pdf

Mid-Atlantic Eisenhower Consortium for Mathematics and Science Education. (1997). *A sourcebook of 8th-grade findings: TIMSS.* Philadelphia, PA: Research for Better Schools.

National Association of Secondary School Principals. (1985). *An agenda for excellence at the middle level.* Reston, VA: Author.

National Middle School Association. (1982, 1992, 1995). *This we believe: Developmentally responsive middle level schools.* Columbus, OH: Author.

National Middle School Association. (2003). *This we believe: Successful schools for young adolescents.* Westerville, OH: Author.

Peters, B.G. (1986). *American public policy: Promise and performance* (2nd ed.). London: MacMillan Education.

Reyes, P., Wagstaff, L.H., & Fusarelli, L.D. (1999). Delta forces: The changing fabric of American society and education. In J. Murphy & K. Seashore Louis (Eds.), *Handbook of research on educational administration* (2nd ed., pp. 359–383). San Francisco: Jossey-Bass.

Roney, K., Anfara, V.A., Jr., & Brown, K.M. (2002, April). *Revealing what's in the black box: The middle school movement and high student achievement.* Paper presented at the annual meeting of the American Educational Research Association, New Orleans, LA.

Russell, J.F. (1997). Relationships between the implementation of middle-level program concepts and student achievement. *Journal of Curriculum and Supervision, 12*(2), 152–168.

Stevenson, J.C., Jr., & Erb, T.O. (1998). How implementing *Turning Points* improves student outcomes. *Middle School Journal, 30*(1), 49–52.

Van Zandt, L.M., & Totten, S. (1995). The current status of middle level education research: A critical review. *Research in Middle Level Education Quarterly, 18*(3), 1–25.

CHAPTER 2

THE IMPORTANCE OF HAVING A HIGHLY QUALIFIED PRINCIPAL IN EVERY MIDDLE GRADES SCHOOL

Sue C. Thompson

The National Middle School Association and the National Forum to Accelerate Middle-Grades Reform speak with one voice by emphasizing the importance of creating high-performing middle schools that are academically excellent, developmentally responsive, and socially equitable. In the vision statement for the National Forum to Accelerate Middle-Grades Reform, academically excellent middle schools are defined as schools that "challenge all students to use their minds well, providing them with the curriculum, instruction, assessment, support, and time they need to meet academic standards." Developmentally responsive middle schools "create small learning communities of adults and students in which stable, close, and mutually respectful relationships support all students' intellectual, ethical, and social growth" and socially equitable middle schools "seek to keep their students' future options open. They have high expectations for all

Reforming Middle Level Education: Considerations for Policymakers, pages 19–31
Copyright © 2004 by Information Age Publishing
All rights of reproduction in any form reserved.

their students and are committed to helping each child produce work of high quality. These schools make sure that all students are in academically rigorous classes staffed by experienced and expertly prepared teachers" (National Form to Accelerate Middle-Grades Reform Vision Statement, 1999).

In response to the need to redesign leadership for the 21st century, the Interstate School Leaders Licensure Consortium (ISLLC), a program of the Council of Chief State School Officers, has worked at crafting model standards for school leaders. The standards present a common core of knowledge, dispositions, and performances that will help link leadership more forcefully to productive schools and enhanced educational outcomes. There is a real sense of urgency that leaders connect what they do to student learning. The following standards are:

> A school administrator is an educational leader who promotes the success of all students by:
> - *Standard 1:*   facilitating the development, articulation, implementation, and stewardship of a vision of learning that is shared and supported by a school community.
> - *Standard 2:*   advocating, nurturing, and sustaining a school culture and instructional program conducive to student learning and staff professional growth.
> - *Standard 3:*   ensuring management of the organization, operations, and resources for a safe, efficient, and effective learning environment.
> - *Standard 4:*   collaborating with families and community members, responding to diverse community interests and needs, and mobilizing community resources.
> - *Standard 5:*   acting with integrity, fairness, and in an ethical manner.
> - *Standard 6:*   understanding, responding to, and influencing the larger political, social, economic, legal, and cultural context.

But just being able to understand and demonstrate the above standards is not enough. High-performing middle grades principals must understand the research and literature on middle grades education. Creating the kind of middle school that is consistent with what is known about high-performing middle schools can be overwhelming to a middle level principal, and yet, in *Turning Points 2000,* Jackson and Davis (2000) assert that "no single individual is more important than the school principal" (p. 157).

According to the National Policy Board for Educational Administration (NPBEA), "Every educational reform report of the last decade concludes that the United States cannot have excellent schools without excellent leaders." Traditional preparation programs for school leaders no longer meet the needs of today's society. Schools are complex organizations where principals answer to multiple constituencies, e.g., students, teachers, support staff, parents, district office personnel, and community members. In order to lead such a complex and important organization where the responsibility for the welfare of young people is the most important priority, there has been a shift from the traditional knowledge base for school leaders. The NPBEA has identified five broad shifts required of educational leaders today compared to the traditional knowledge base (2002, pp. 3–4).

INTERPERSONAL SKILLS THAT BUILD RELATIONSHIPS

Highly qualified middle grades principals know the importance and power of having trustful and respectful relationships between administrators and teachers, teachers and teachers, administrators and students, teachers and students, and students and students and have the interpersonal skills to make these relationships work for the betterment of the school. "The degree of collaboration a staff is willing to engage in is directly related to trust, dialogue, new learning, time, and tangible support" (Doda & Thompson, 2002, p. 6). Lambert et al. (2002) claim that patterns of relationships form the primary bases for human growth and development. Middle grades principals, through their knowledge based on research and best practice for young adolescents, understand what kind of dialogue teachers should be having, what kinds of job-embedded professional development teachers need to improve student learning, and respect teachers' time to collaborate. They provide the tangible support teachers need to do the things they need to do to create truly meaningful learning experiences for their young adolescent learners. These principals know successful middle grades schools are organized for collaboration through team learning. The new knowledge base recognizes the importance of principals being able to work with people, rather than just focus on technical skills. Building collaborative work cultures must equate with becoming a professional learning community in order for everyone to be a learner, adult and student alike. Dufour and Eaker (1998) state that "the most promising strategy for sustained, substantive school improvement is developing the ability of school personnel to function as professional learning communities" (p. xi). They go on to say:

> Each word of the phrase "professional learning community" has been chosen purposefully. A "professional" is someone with expertise in a specialized field, an individual who has not only pursued advanced training to enter the field, but who is also expected to remain current in its evolving knowledge base. . . . "Learning" suggests ongoing action and perpetual curiosity. . . . The

school that operates as a professional *learning* community recognizes that its members must engage in ongoing study and constant practice that characterize an organization committed to continuous improvement. . . . In a professional learning *community*, educators create an environment that fosters mutual cooperation, emotional support, and personal growth as they work together to achieve what they cannot accomplish alone. (DuFour & Eaker, 1998, pp. xi–xii)

Little (1982) conducted case studies of four schools identified as successful on the basis of student achievement on standardized achievement scores and two schools identified as unsuccessful on the basis of the same criteria. She found that the successful schools were characterized by frequent teacher evaluation and feedback on them, teachers talking with one another about teaching, teachers working together to design their classes, and teachers teaching each other about teaching. All of these collaborative practices were conspicuously absent in the unsuccessful schools (as cited in Smith & Scott, 1990, p. 16).

According to Pounder (1998), "Interdisciplinary instructional teams appear almost exclusively in middle level schools and emerged in the late 1960s as a key component of the middle schools movement" (p. 71). The principal is ultimately responsible for the way the school is organized. Highly qualified middle grades principals understand that middle grades schools that are organized into interdisciplinary teams and small learning communities have the structure to support team learning, but structure is not enough. Team learning must focus on group interaction through dialogue and skillful discussion (Senge, 2000). According to Erb (1997), "Teams where teachers engage in dialogue about matters of mutual concerns do reflect new levels of teacher interaction leading to the creation of novel solutions to educational problems" (p. 39). According to Thompson (2002), there is a profound difference between dialogues and discussions.

Traditionally, we have had two different forms of conversation that can occur in schools—dialogue and discussion. Traditionally, we have had discussions in schools about a variety of different issues. Discussions result in one person's trying to convince another person that his or her way of doing business or solution to a problem is better. Much time and energy is spent in advocating for one's beliefs, but very little time is spent in listening to the other person or suspending one's mental model to gain an understanding of the other person's views. (p. 12)

Principals must be facilitators of dialogue and understand the processes to use that will engage small or large groups of people in effective ways to improve instruction, identify and solve problems, and create the kind of middle school that will be academically excellent, developmentally responsive, and socially equitable. Then principals must also teach teachers to dialogue in small groups without the assistance of the principal.

Whether teachers and teams have the authority to make decisions that directly impact their work is dependent upon the encouragement and support of the principal.

As Jackson and Davis (2000) emphasize:

> A successful team depends on leadership from within. The principal, no matter how supportive and involved, is not a team member and will not be there every day as a team gets down to business. Teams must lead and manage themselves, not only out of necessity, but also to deepen their sense of ownership and commitment to the work of the team. (p. 138)

CONSENSUS BUILDER AND MOTIVATOR

Highly qualified middle school principals understand the power of involving all constituencies in creating a vision for the school that will focus on the intellectual, social, emotional, and physical needs of the young adolescents they serve. Moving from consensus builder to a person that can help diverse groups of people find common ground is extremely important in today's world. The idea that any principal will find herself in a totally homogenized middle school is almost laughable. There is a strong need to acknowledge diversity, whether it is race/ethnicity, class, gender, sexual orientation, or differently abled people. The highly qualified principal not only welcomes diversity in her school, she values it. As Schein (1985) points out, the root of division in many groups is likely to be grounded in communication failures and cultural misunderstandings that prevent the parties involved from working together constructively. "Undiscussables" related to issues of race/ethnicity, gender, class, sexual orientation, and differently abled people must be at the heart of the dialogue concerning the creation and sustainability of a high-performing middle school.

One person, regardless of her knowledge, skills, and dispositions, cannot create the kind of middle school that will meet the criteria established by the National Middle School Association and the National Forum to Accelerate Middle-Grades Reform. Highly qualified middle grades principals understand the need to develop and nurture the leadership capabilities of every faculty member. They acknowledge that the work that is done in a middle grades school is too important and too overwhelming to leave to one or two people. According to Katzenmeyer and Moller:

> Within every school there is a sleeping giant of teacher leadership, which can be a strong catalyst for making change. By using the energy of teacher lead-

ers as agents of school change, the reform of public education will stand a better chance of building momentum. (2001, p. 2)

The highly qualified middle level principal "leads from the middle." Lambert et al. (2002) challenges the old definition of leadership as one or two people who have been given the formal title of leader. Crowther, Kaagan, Ferguson, and Hann (2002), define teacher leadership as:

A form of leadership suited to the imperative that schools transform themselves, and in so doing, demonstrate for communities how that transformation can be managed positively and effectively. Ultimately, teacher leadership is about action that transforms teaching and learning in a school, that ties school and community together on behalf of learning, and that advances social sustainability and quality of life for a community. (p. xvii)

Teachers are motivated to be contributors when they have the opportunity to create the future that they desire. Highly qualified middle grades principals understand that one must work with people, not do things do people.

RESULTS-DRIVE AND DATA-INFORMED

No longer can principals allocate resources to programs that have not been proven to be successful in improving instruction and assisting young adolescents in becoming all that they can become. Knowing how to look at data, teach others to look at data, and then collectively make decisions based on what the data says about what is actually happening in the school is an extremely important skill. Consequently, highly qualified middle grades principals must understand the kind of instruction that 10 to 14 year olds need to achieve at their highest level of competency, while maintaining the integrity of the characteristics and developmental needs of this age group.

In *Opportunities and Accountability to Leave No Child Behind in the Middle Grades: An Examination of the No Child Left Behind Act of 2001* prepared by Cynthia Brown for the Edna McConnell Clark Foundation (2002), the author states:

On January 8, 2002 President George W. Bush signed the *No Child Left Behind Act of 2001* (NCLB). This historical piece of education legislation reauthorized and significantly expanded the Elementary and Secondary Education Act, first enacted in 1965. Its most important title, Title 1, has focused federal government attention and money on students in high poverty schools for more than 35 years. Congress made significant changes to the law in 1994, and the most recent changes build upon them dramatically. It also provided significant funding increases. The new Act is the result of bipartisan leadership among five political leaders—President Bush, Senators Kennedy and Gregg, and Representatives Boehner and Miller—and a large majority of the U.S. Congress who were clearly fed up with inadequate learning among the groups of students that federal programs are most supposed to help. (Brown, 2002, p. 2)

Much of the rhetoric concerning No Child Left Behind (NCLB) has been focused on having a highly qualified teacher in every classroom. At the same time, although NCLB also states that there should be a highly qualified leader in every school, there has been much less discussion about what that would look like, especially for middle grades schools. Most people would agree that leadership is an extremely important component to the creation and sustainability of a successful middle grades school where all children are educated well.

According to George (2002), while it is the classroom teacher who directly affects student achievement, it is the principal who provides teachers with the necessary support to create a high-performing middle grades school. In the U.S. Department of Education No Child Left Behind: A Parents Guide, it stated that "Principals will have information they need to strengthen their schools weaknesses and to put into practice methods and strategies backed by sound, scientific results" (2003, p. 5).

INTEGRATOR OF SCHOOL AND COMMUNITY SERVICE

No longer can a principal find all the resources needed for students and their families by looking within the school system. Understanding the underlying tensions that families are facing today with the economy, changing roles in the families, demographic changes through an increasingly diverse population, and societal messages that aren't in the best interest of young adolescents but nevertheless influence their perceptions of themselves, is absolutely critical. Locating and collaborating with multiple organizations to better serve students and their families is another responsibility of the principal and staff of a high-performing middle school. The interpersonal skills and collaboration skills mentioned above, are absolutely necessary to create these kinds of partnerships.

POLICY DEVELOPER AND PARTICIPANT

Unfortunately, policies often are at odds with what recipients of those policies know are in the best interest of their constituencies. Highly qualified middle grades principals understand policies that best serve young adolescents and policies that are actually detrimental to the creation of a high-performing middle school.

Fowler (2000) tells the story of a group of practicing school administrators who had an opportunity to meet with a state department of education official, who was supposed to brief the group on policy trends. For 50 minutes he had inundated them with facts and figures about taxes, school finance formulas, and economic growth, interspersing these statistics with complaints about how much time it took to operate a large district that the state had recently taken over. Finally, he paused and asked, "Any questions?" After a silence, a principal in the group inquired, "What about kids?" The official explained that his own background was in economics and that he had never worked in a school. This fact, he said, made it hard for him to conceptualize how education policy affects children. (p. 1)

This story, and others like it, point out how important it is that informed middle level educators and policymakers learn how to communicate with one another.

Many principals are being asked to be site-based managers, and consequently, principals and assistant principals are working directly with state policy makers. The positive side of this is that educators can create a dialogue with policy makers that will hopefully result in policies that take into account the students. The good news is that there is an abundance of research to share with policymakers that is both high quality and user friendly. This research states that middle schools that implement the full range of the middle school concepts with fidelity will both improve student achievement and promote the healthy development of young adolescents (Felner, Jackson, Kasak, Mulhall, Brand, & Flowers, 1997; Flowers, Mertens, & Mulhall, 1999, 2000a, 2000b, 2002; Jackson & Davis, 2000).

Boards of Education (BOE) also need to understand the research on high-performing middle grades schools. Some Boards of Education have developed policies that are actually harmful to the very goal they desire, and that is higher achieving students. An example would be a district policy that supports tracking. Oakes (1985), long a proponent of detracking schools, has repeatedly pointed out the damage that tracking can do to children of poverty and African American children. Slavin (1987a, 1987b) states that tracking that begins in many middle grades schools can influence the access that students have in high school and beyond. Many classes, such as Algebra, is a "gateway" class to higher levels of mathematics that can ensure that a student who enters college has the prerequisite skills to be successful at the university level. Jackson and Davis (2000) state, "Along with intellectual development, at the heart of our definition of "middle grades education" is the requirement for equity in outcomes for all groups of students, regardless of their race, ethnicity, gender, family income, or linguistic background" (p. 11).

It takes a principal who has a strong belief that what is good for some students is good for all students. It is a fight that often occurs because of forces from powerful groups within the community, e.g., affluent parents who are often the power brokers in the community. Kohn (1998) states that this story is rarely told but shares examples of dismantling elitism:

> From Amherst, Massachusetts, where highly educated white parents have fought to preserve a tracking system that keeps virtually every child of color out of advanced classes, to Palo Alto, California, where a similarly elite constituency demands a return to a "skill and drill" math curriculum and fiercely opposes the more conceptual learning outlined in the National Council of Teachers of Mathematics (NCTM) standards; from an affluent suburb of Buffalo, where parents of honors students quashed an attempt to replace letter grades with standards-based progress reports, to San Diego, where a program to provide underachieving students with support that will help them succeed in higher-level courses has run "head-on into vigorous opposition from some of the community's more outspoken, influential members—the predominantly white, middle-class parents of high-achieving students. (p. 87)

Could a principal who had the knowledge about the importance of developmentally appropriate schools that are academically challenging and socially equitable have made a difference in the way that the above scenarios played out? If it is the responsibility of administration to "educate" board members with the research related to young adolescents and high-performing schools and the research on tracking, then possibly a different scenario could have been played out in Amherst, Palo Alto, Buffalo, San Diego and other places where vocal segments of the community have dictated policy that is, in fact, harmful to the young adolescents in the community.

District personnel who make hiring decisions must understand that being a middle grades principal is a goal in and of itself. Even more important than the lack of professional preparation is the fact that some superintendents see the middle grades school as a holding tank until a high school position becomes available. Some districts even require that high school principals serve as middle school assistant principals or principals before becoming a high school administrator. Middle schools have often been neglected or overlooked in the P–12 program of many school districts because board members and administrators in district office have not understood the critical importance of this stage of development. Early adolescence and the middle grades that serve them have been viewed as something to "get through" until students begin the important work of high school. Nothing could be further from the truth.

In addition to these five broad areas of competencies, skills, and dispositions that the highly qualified principal needs, is the understanding that principals at the middle level must have special preparation and professional development to understand what a high-performing middle level school looks like. Yet, as Little (2001) states "The middle level principal has a particularly significant role to play in developing a successful middle school" (p. 1). Unfortunately, according to the most recent National Association of Secondary Schools National Study of Leadership in Middle Level Schools conducted by Valentine, Clark, Hackman, and Petzko and cited in the *NASS Bulletin*:

> The results of this study show that most principals do not have academic preparation that specifically addresses middle level concepts. When asked how many classes they had taken that explicitly focused on middle level education, 37% of principals who responded stated that they had not taken any such courses, followed closely by 34% who had taken one or two courses, and 20% who had taken three to five courses. Although the percentage of principals with undergraduate degrees in middle level education has remained between 0% and 1% since 1992, a promising trend emerges when graduate degrees are examined. The number of principals with advanced degrees in middle level education has increased from fewer than 1% in 1992 to 11% in 2000. (Petzko et al., 2000, pp. 3–15)

While this increase is encouraging, it is still woefully lacking. Principal preparation programs must step up to the plate and demand that those aspiring administrators who wish to be middle level principals must be well grounded in the knowledge, skills, and dispositions necessary to create a high-performing middle grades school and be able to educate others about what this middle grades school should look like.

CONCLUSION

More than twenty-five years ago, the Ford Foundation commissioned a study entitled Growing Up Forgotten (cited in Lipsitz, Anthony, & Austin, 1997) that examined the status of research and programs that concerned young adolescents. According to Lipsitz, Anthony, and Austin, "The age group had been overlooked in research and services. Most professionals and policy makers were unaware of this void" (1997, p. 517). Since that report, many other reports concerning the education of young adolescents have been released. The Carnegie Corporation's report, *Turning Points: Preparing American Youth for the 21st Century* in 1989, and ten years later, *Turning Points 2000: Educating Adolescents in the 21st Century* supported the need for a different kind of education for young adolescents than the mini-high-school model that many adults had experienced.

There also needs to be a different kind of education for middle grades principals. This is absolutely imperative because to create a high performing middle grades school requires courage. Courage to support teachers in creating meaningful educational processes and experiences for young adolescents in the middle of cries for more standardization. Courage to challenge exclusionary programs where some young adolescents benefit from opportunities to participate, while other students find doors closed to them. Quite frankly, middle school principals must not allow tests to sort students into ability groups, leaving some students without exposure to certain knowledge and higher level problem solving and thinking skills. Courage to promote the middle school as an institution that not only accepts diversity but honors and values diversity. Courage to provide a safe haven for democracy to flourish because participating in democracy is a right for young adolescents, as well as adults.

It is the core values and beliefs of the middle grades principal, along with strong convictions and courage, that will determine whether there are supporting conditions evident in middle grades schools that will improve student learning for all students and, in turn, that all students have equal opportunities to be engaged in meaningful, high level learning experiences. As stated by Arnold and Stevenson (1998), "In our view there is no more challenging and heroic work than that of a principal who is committed to a responsible evolution of progressive student-centered educational practices and who leads that process by personal example" (p. 36).

REFERENCES

Arnold J., & Stevenson, C. (1998). *Teachers' teaming handbook: A middle level planning guide*. Fort Worth, TX: Harcourt Brace College Publishers.

Brown, C. (2002). *Opportunities and accountability to leave no child behind in the middle grades: An examination of the No Child Left Behind Act of 2001*. New York:Edna McConnell Clark Foundation.

Carnegie Council on Adolescent Development. (1989, June). *Turning points: Preparing American youth for the 21st century*. Washington, DC: Author.

Crowther, F., Kaagan, S., Ferguson, M., & Hann, L. (2002). *Developing teacher leaders: How teacher leadership enhances school success*. Thousand Oaks, CA: Corwin Press.

Doda, N., & Thompson, S. (2002). Introduction. In N. Doda & S. Thompson (Eds.), *Transforming ourselves, transforming schools: Middle school change* (pp. 3–8). Westerville, OH: National Middle School Association.

Dufour, R., & Eaker, R. (1998). *Professional learning communities at work: Best practices for enhancing student achievement*. Alexandria, VA: Association for Supervision and Curriculum Development.

Erb. T. (1997). Thirty years of attempting to fathom teaming. In T. Dickinson & T. Erb (Eds.), *We gain more than we give. Teaming in middle schools*. Columbus, OH: National Middle School Association.

Felton, R.D., Jackson, A.W. , Kasak, D., Mulhall, P., Brand, S., & Flowers, N. (1997). The impact of school reform for the middle years: Longitudinal study of a Network engaged in Turning Points-based comprehensive school transformation. *Phi Delta Kappan, 78*, 528–532, 541–550.

Flowers, N., Mertens, S.B., & Mulhall, P.F. (1999). The impact of teaming: Five research-based outcomes of teaming. *Middle School Journal, 32*(5), 57–61.

Flowers, N., Mertens, S.B., & Mulhall, P.F. (2000a). What makes interdisciplinary teams effective? *Middle School Journal. 31*(4), 53–56.

Flowers, N., Mertens, S., & Mulhall, P. (2000b). How teaming influences classroom practices. *Middle School Journal, 32*(2), 52–59.

Flowers, N., Mertens, S., Mulhall, P. (2002a). Four important lessons about teacher professional development. *Middle School Journal, 33*(5), 57–61.

Flowers, N., Mertens, S., Mulhall, P. (2002b). The relationship between middle-grades teacher certification and teaching practices. In V.A. Anfara, Jr., & S.L. Stacki (Eds.), *Middle school curriculum, instruction, and assessment*. Greenwich, CT: Information Age Publishing.

Fowler, F.C. (2000). *Policy studies for educational leaders: An introduction*. Upper Saddle River, NJ: Merrill.

George, P. (2002). *No child left behind: Implications for middle level leaders*. Westerville, OH: National Middle School Association.

Interstate School Leaders Licensure Consortium: Standards for School Leaders. (1996). Washington, DC: Council of Chief State School Officers.

Jackson, A.W., & Davis, G.A. (2000). *Turning points 2000: Educating adolescents in the 21st century*. New York: Teachers College Press.

Katzemeyer, M., & Moller, G. (2001). *Awakening the sleeping giant: Helping teachers develop as leaders*. Thousand Oaks, CA: Corwin Press, Inc.

Kohn, A. (1998). *What to look for in a classroom . . . and other essays*. San Francisco: Jossey-Bass.

Lambert, L., Walker, D., Zimmerman, D., Cooper, J., Lambert, M.D., Gardner, M., & Szabo, M. (2002). *The constructivist leader* (2nd ed.). New York: Teachers College Press.

Lipsitz, J., Jackson, A.W., & Austin, L.M. (1997). What works in middle-grades school reform. *Phi Delta Kappan, 78*(7), 517–519.

Little, A.L., & Little, S. (2001). *How to become an exemplary middle school principal*. Westerville, OH: National Middle School Association.

National Forum to Accelerate Middle-Grades Reform Vision Statement. (1999). Retrieved September 5, 2003 from http://www.mgforoum.org/about/vision.asp.

National Middle School Association. (1995). *This we believe: Developmentally responsive middle level schools*. Columbus, OH: Author.

National Policy Board for Educational Administration. (2002). *Instructions to implement standards for advanced programs in educational leadership for principals, superintendents, curriculum directors, and supervisors*. Retrieved September 15, 2003, from http://www.npbea.org

No child left behind act of 2001. Public Law 107-110.

No Child Left Behind: A Parents Guide. (2003). Washington, DC: Author.

Oakes, J. (1985). *Keeping track: How schools structure inequality.* New Haven, CT: Yale University Press.

Petzko, V.N., Clark, D.C., Valentine, J.W., Hackman, D.G., Nori, J.R., & Lucas, S.E. (2002). Leaders and leadership in middle level schools. *National Association of Secondary School Principals Bulletin, 86*(631), 3–15.

Pounder, D. (1998). *Restructuring schools for collaboration: Promises and pitfalls.* Albany: State University of New York Press.

Senge, P. (2000). *Schools that learn.* New York: Doubleday.

Schein, E. (1985). *Organizational culture and leadership: A dynamic view.* San Francisco: Jossey-Bass.

Slavin, R. (1987a). Ability grouping and student achievement in elementary schools: A best-evidence synthesis. *Review of Educational Research, 57*(3). 293–336.

Slavin, R. (1987b). Grouping for instruction. *Equity and Excellence, 23.* 31–36.

Smith, S., & Scott, J. (1990). *The collaborative school: A work environment for effective instruction.* Eugene, OR: ERIC Clearinghouse on Educational Management.

Thompson, S. (2002). Learning from past mistakes: Professional development "The old way." In N. Doda & S. Thompson (Eds), *Transforming ourselves, Transforming schools: Middle school change.* Westerville, OH: National Middle School Association.

CHAPTER 3

CREATING ACADEMICALLY CHALLENGING MIDDLE LEVEL SCHOOLS FOR EVERY CHILD

Ronald D. Williamson and J. Howard Johnston

INTRODUCTION

The execution of Socrates (c. 399 BC) for teaching the youth of Athens to question their government and the established religion is probably one of the first, and certainly among the most arresting, recorded incidents of educational accountability in western history. While more dramatic than contemporary events, the remarkable tale of teachers who suffer terrible consequences rather than recant their beliefs has been told in both history and legend throughout time. But despite his rejection of its beliefs, even Socrates accepted the authority of the State to punish him for his admittedly revolutionary curriculum and methods. Rather than succumb to the entreaties of his students to escape his fate and leave Athens, he chose to drink the hemlock and, instead, become a martyr to intellectual integrity and academic freedom.

Reforming Middle Level Education: Considerations for Policymakers, pages 33–48
Copyright © 2004 by Information Age Publishing
All rights of reproduction in any form reserved.

A BRIEF HISTORY OF EDUCATIONAL ACCOUNTABILITY

Apart from being a monument to intellectual censorship, the Athenian government's treatment of Socrates can also be seen as an early (if somewhat draconian) assertion of the state's duty to regulate what is taught and to assure that education properly serves public order and the common good, at least as the state sees it. Education in western culture, particularly state-sponsored education, has always accepted a measure of accountability to that public trust. In more recent times in Great Britain, the Newcastle Commission (1861) reported on strategies for providing the masses with "a sound and cheap education," concluding that teachers spent too little time teaching students the basic subjects. Thus, in its Revised Code of 1862, Parliament "stipulated exactly what children of each 'grade' should be able to perform in terms of reading, writing and arithmetic, and linked payment of grants to pupil performance in this narrow range of skills" (Lacey & Lawton, 1981, p. 26). Although payment for results gradually disappeared by the end of the 19th century, the standardized exams used to assess pupil performance became institutionalized in the elementary and later the secondary schools (Nixon, 1992).

Of course, testing is no stranger to American schools or students. Since the 19th century, students have been required to take tests to determine if they had mastered what they were taught, and those who had not were retained. Also, 19th century schoolteachers often were required to take tests of their knowledge before being hired, and were even questioned by the school board on matters of moral philosophy, religious beliefs and personal habits. However, after they were appointed, they were not subjected to further scrutiny of their suitability for the job, unless they committed some egregious offense. However, "the idea of accountability—holding not only students, but teachers, schools, even school districts, accountable for student performance—is a more contemporary invention" (Ravitch, 2002, p. 1).

Throughout the 19th and early 20th centuries, secondary education was reserved for those who were able to "handle the work." Just before the turn of the 20th century, fewer than 10% of adolescents were in school, and an even smaller handful of those sought college admissions. Colleges generally admitted anyone who applied, although the prestigious Ivy League schools usually required students to pass entrance exams that each faculty designed. The College Entrance Examination Board was formed in 1900 in response to complaints from principals and headmasters about the difficulty of preparing students for different exams, so, shortly after its formation, the Board prepared a single test for college admission. The College Board also published syllabi for each subject covered on the test, and teachers began to use these course syllabi to prepare their students for college entrance (Ravitch, 2002, p. 2). Thus began one of the earliest forms of accountability for curriculum coverage in the United States.

ACCOUNTABILITY AND U.S. SCHOOLS

In the United States, the roots of educational accountability can be traced to the "efficiency" and the "scientific management" movements of the late 19th and early 20th centuries. The strategies used by industrialists to organize their factories and make them most efficient began to influence public education. The roles of principals and teachers were prescribed as sets of principles for effective school operation (Kuchapski, n.d.). This movement was aligned with a focus on vocationalism that required "an exact statement of what [would] later be called accountability, functional literacy, career education, competency-based education, competency based career education, and more" (Wise, 1979). Kuchapski (n.d.) says that in this climate, a philosophy of "earning over learning" developed, as evidenced by this quotation from an educator speaking in 1909, "Ordinarily, a love of learning is praiseworthy. But when this delight in the pleasure of learning becomes so intense and so absorbing that it diminishes the desire, and the power of earning, it is possibly harmful" (cited in Bobitt, 1913, pp. 81–90).

The accountability movement was also fueled by the growth of the field of Educational Psychology, which was initially devoted to the reform of educational testing. Led by Robert L. Thorndike, educational psychologists were determined to demonstrate that education could become a precise science and sought to apply rigorous scientific methods to the measurement of academic performance. Housed in newly formed colleges of education, this new discipline brought a level of scientific respectability to the testing of students.

At virtually the same time, Progressive Education arose as a powerful philosophical force in American schools. Focused on the development and psychological well-being of children, Progressives sought to facilitate healthy growth and preparation for life in a democratic society. Testing, even scientifically generated testing, was seen as subordinate to the goals of individual development and the cultivation of social adjustment, although tests were seen to have some limited potential for helping to identify students' interests and talents.

The John Dewey Project at the University of Vermont (2002) summarizes the growing conflict between the by-now-entrenched scientific management movement and the progressives.

> Led by Dewey, progressive educators opposed a growing national movement that sought to separate academic education for the few and narrow voca-

tional training for the masses. During the 1920s, when education turned increasingly to "scientific" techniques such as intelligence testing and cost-benefit management, progressive educators insisted on the importance of the emotional, artistic, and creative aspects of human development–"the most living and essential parts of our natures," as Margaret Naumburg put it in *The Child and the World*. After the Depression began, a group of politically oriented progressive educators, led by George Counts, dared schools to "build a new social order" and published a provocative journal called *The Social Frontier* to advance their "reconstructionist" critique of *laissez faire* capitalism. A major research endeavor, the "eight-year study demonstrated that students from progressive high schools were capable, adaptable learners and excelled even in the finest universities." (John Dewey Project, 2002, p. 1)

Ironically, the Eight Year Study was, itself, an accountability effort. In the words of the Commission, one of the principal purposes of the investigation was "To find, through exploration and experimentation, how the high school in the United States can serve youth more effectively" (Aiken, 1942, p. 1). In this report, the Progressives introduced the notion that it was the school that was accountable for student success; accountability for performance was not entirely the responsibility of the student. It is an idea that would dominate American education until the present.

POST WORLD WAR II ACCOUNTABILITY

Through the 1940s and 1950s, World War II and the Cold War diverted America's attention from educational accountability. Even the publication of the Eight Year Study in 1942 went largely unnoticed. But in 1957, the Soviet Union launched a 183-pound basketball sized satellite into space, and the American school system was instantly in the spotlight once again. Suddenly, education was linked to national security, and with the success of America's space program in the 1960s, another model for school management was discovered. Chase (1971) suggested that "a union of research and development might be applied to education with results comparable to those achieved in aeronautics, atomic energy and medical science" (p. 182). This form of scientific management was essential, said Chase, because education "was too sluggish to respond promptly to the new demands or make good use of science and technology for the engineering of change" (Chase, 1971, p.182).

In 1966, *Equality of Educational Opportunity* (Coleman, 1966), more commonly known as the "Coleman Report," studied the distribution of resources and opportunities among children of different races and used achievement scores as outcome measures for educational effort. This study became important not only as a blueprint for the reforms initiated by the

Elementary and Secondary Education Act, but, as Ravitch (2002) says, "the study was significant for . . . its shift in focus from inputs to results, one of which followed the authors' decision to examine how school resources affected achievement" (p. 3). Ravitch continues, "This shift in focus from inputs (resources) to outputs (results) was facilitated by the increasing availability of test scores," especially "...cumulative new data and trend lines to document the educational achievement of American students" (p. 3). International comparisons of test scores placed American students well below those of other industrialized nations in mathematics and sciences, and the venerable College Board scores declined steadily through the 1970s and 80s. Despite technical analyses that showed rather stable performance for most student groups and improvements for many disadvantaged students (Berliner, 1993), elected officials came under increasing pressure to "do something" about low test scores.

By the time the U.S. Department of Education published these words in April 1983, educational accountability was no longer being touted as simply a cornerstone of national defense, but of economic prosperity as well.

> Our Nation is at risk. Our once unchallenged preeminence in commerce, industry, science, and technological innovation is being overtaken by competitors throughout the world. [T]he educational foundations of our society are presently being eroded by a rising tide of mediocrity that threatens our very future as a Nation and a people. What was unimaginable a generation ago has begun to occur—others are matching and surpassing our educational attainments. If an unfriendly foreign power had attempted to impose on America the mediocre educational performance that exists today, we might well have viewed it as an act of war." (National Commission on Excellence in Education, 1983)

While not as dramatic as the execution of Socrates, it is difficult to imagine a more ringing indictment of the public schools.

Many educators called "foul," claiming that in this simplistic condemnation no consideration was given to a host of other factors that affected a sagging economy. "This decline in competitive advantage was not attributed to outdated or ineffective management practices of business, or even to increased competition from Europe and Asia, but rather to public education" (Kuchapski, n.d.).

The release of *A Nation at Risk* launched a tremendous number of state and local initiatives to improve secondary education that came to be known collectively as the standards-based reform movement. "Education was to be improved through state legislation and mandates that would be implemented at the local level" (Kuchapski, n.d.). By 1989, forty states had passed standards legislation and called for testing requirements; by 1995, all states but one (Iowa) had mandatory achievement standards for students at the secondary level, including the middle school. Still, the focus remained on the high school, as graduation requirements were increased, vocational courses curtailed in favor of "academic" programming, and high school graduation tests introduced in many states.

CONTEMPORARY ACCOUNTABILITY APPROACHES

Through the 1980s, middle schools remained immune from the most strident calls for accountability, although at the local level parent concerns were sometimes expressed about the softening of academic requirements as districts converted their junior highs to middle schools. Also, as pressures were placed on high schools to prepare students to meet rigorous standards and perform on high stakes tests, additional attention was given to the middle school as a preparatory academy for the rigors of high school. Within communities, the middle school's most vocal critics were often found among their colleagues at the high school (Johnston & Williamson, 1998). Simultaneously, the media began to report low performance by middle school students on state-mandated achievement tests, and the National Assessment of Educational Progress (NAEP) continued to report relatively stable but uninspired trends in student performance in Reading, Mathematics, and Science over the twenty-year history of the test (National Center for Educational Statistics, 2003a).

In 1995, the results of the Third International Study of Mathematics and Science (TIMSS) were released, and the lens of accountability was focused directly on the middle level school. TIMSS included comparisons between the United States and other industrialized nations with large economies - particularly those that are viewed as major economic competitors, for example, the Group of Eight (G8) countries: Canada, France, Germany, Italy, Japan, the Russian Federation, the United Kingdom, and the United States. U.S. students, particularly 8th graders, scored poorly when compared with their G8 counterparts, and scored lower than students from many developing countries as well. Although less strident than the tone of *A Nation at Risk,* the language used to describe TIMSS intimated once again that the public schools were to serve as a cornerstone of America's preeminence on the world stage—and that they weren't doing a very good job of it.

With the emergence and growth of the global economy, policymakers and educators have turned to international comparisons to assess how well national systems of education are performing. These comparisons shed light on a host of policy issues, from access to education and equity of resources to the quality of school outputs. They provide policymakers with benchmarks to assess their systems' performances, and to identify potential strategies to improve student achievement and system outputs (National Center for Educational Statistics, 2003b).

This performance on TIMSS, combined with sluggish improvements on state assessments, led to the creation of a full program of accountability for middle schools in most states. High stakes testing became the norm, with many states requiring tests for grade promotion as well as graduation. Still other states linked school funding to school wide test performance, and a growing number began to explore the use of student test scores as a means for determining individual teachers' compensation and pay increases.

Then, in 1999, Hayes Mizell, Director of the Program for Student Achievement for the Edna McConnell Clark Foundation challenged one of the middle school movement's most fundamental values: its commitment to student centeredness.

> There has been a lot of loose talk about middle schools being 'student-centered.' If middle schools had truly been student-centered there would be more impressive evidence of student performance than is currently the case. In fact, most middle schools have been more adult-centered than anything else. It is, after all, the adults in the schools who have been the most resistant to change and who have been inclined to expect so little of themselves and their students. (Mizell, 2002a, p. 46)

In these remarks and throughout his writings, Mizell (2002b), a "critical friend" of the middle school, linked achievement with student centeredness and called upon schools to create programs that fostered academic rigor, developmental responsiveness, and social equity.

By 1997, middle school advocates were prepared to argue that the systematic implementation of middle level reforms, based on its Progressive ancestry and advocated by the Carnegie Corporation in *Turning Points* (1989), did precisely what Mizell sought—and more. Felner, Jackson, Kasak, Mulhall, Brand, and Flowers (1997), in Illinois and Missouri, found that comprehensive and intensive levels of implementation of recommended reforms produce major gains in all spheres of school functioning for middle grades students. Moreover, Felner et al. (1997) concluded:

> Our findings to date strongly support the view that high quality schooling, well implemented, can make profound contributions to the achievement, mental health and socio/behavioral functioning of students who are left behind and for whom there is often a sense that school cannot make a difference in their lives. These data also argue for resources to be used effectively in schools with high concentrations of at-risk students, and, in some instances, for resources to be increased significantly in order to create the necessary conditions for all children to be successful. (Felner et al., 1997, p. 528)

Despite this evidence, which bears striking similarity to the arguments advanced by the Eight Year Study, and a rising chorus of critics of high stakes testing as the engine of educational reform (AERA, 2000; Berliner, 1993; Biddle, 1997; Bracey, 2002; Comer, 2001; Cuban, 2001; Kohn, 2000; National Middle School Association, 2002; Schrag, 2000), in 2002 the U.S. Congress, at the urging of the Bush administration, passed the most sweeping test-intensive accountability requirements in history when it reauthorized the Elementary and Secondary Education Act, renaming it the No Child Left Behind Act (NCLB).

> Under the act's accountability provisions, states must describe how they will close the achievement gap and make sure all students, including those who are disadvantaged, achieve academic proficiency. They must produce annual state and school district report cards that inform parents and communities about state and school progress. Schools that do not make progress must provide supplemental services, such as free tutoring or after-school assistance; take corrective actions; and, if still not making adequate yearly progress after five years, make dramatic changes to the way the school is run. (U.S. Department of Education, 2001.

Among these "dramatic changes" are closing the school, reassigning staff, and changing school leadership. The Act also provides for public funds to be used to support a child's attendance at a school of choice if he or she wishes to leave a "persistently low performing school." While the full effect of this legislation remains to be seen, it will most certainly be far-reaching and dramatic. At the very least, it has placed "accountability" at the top of every educator's professional agenda.

The history of educational accountability in the United States is characterized by conflict, political maneuverings, and sometimes astonishing claims and counterclaims, all of which appear to be supported by research. However, the clearest picture that emerges is the inexorable march of accountability to the lowest levels of the school system—individual teachers and students. From the turn of the 20th century, when students alone bore the responsibility for their performance on tests, to the opening of the 21st century, in which individual students, teachers, principals and schools shoulder the accountability for student performance on standardized tests, we have witnessed a growing trend toward holding individuals, rather than systems, accountable for the performance of students. Ultimately, this may become the most defining school reform event of the 21st century.

THE HIGH-PERFORMING MIDDLE LEVEL SCHOOL

At the center of the debate about educational accountability lies the middle school. Described as both "the last best hope of American youth" (Carnegie Council, 1989) and as "education's weak link" (Southern Regional Education Board, 1998) the role and function of the middle school continues to be the center of dispute. Proponents of a strong academic program and advocates of a developmental approach debate the values on which middle level programs are based. Differing perspectives on the middle school often contribute to passionate debate about its role (Beane, 1999; Williamson & Johnston, 1999).

While the debate continues among advocates, individual schools and districts are faced with resolving these tensions in a local context (Johnston & Williamson, 1998). Demand for improved student achievement, greater accountability, improved test scores, and greater responsiveness to parents characterize the tensions.

Out of this milieu the discussion about middle level reform was altered. Several foundations committed to school reform funded efforts to make academic excellence the center of middle grades reform. Their efforts led to publication of a position paper, *Speaking With One Voice*, advocating a three-part agenda for middle school reform. The position paper argued that high performing middle schools must be academically excellent and socially equitable as well as developmentally responsive (Lipsitz, Mizell, Jackson, & Austin, 1997).

As part of this initiative, the foundations invited leading middle school researchers and advocates to participate in a conversation about the characteristics of high-performing middle schools. These conversations led to the founding of the National Forum to Accelerate Middle Grades Reform, a group advocating a middle school model patterned on the three characteristics described in the position paper.

The National Forum developed a set of detailed descriptors of high-performing middle schools and launched a project to identify middle schools that met the criteria. The descriptors, commonly known as the Schools to Watch criteria, emerged as the definition of a high-performing middle school. The complete list of descriptors is available at the National Forum's Schools to Watch website (http://www.schoolstowatch.org).

Concurrent with articulation of the characteristics of high-performing middle schools, a series of studies found a strong correlation between these characteristics and improved student learning. This empirical research found that where school personnel implemented a high fidelity middle school program there was a positive impact on student achievement and school climate (Balfanz & Mac Iver, 2000; Felner et al., 1997; Lee & Smith, 1993; Mertens & Flowers, 2003; Mertens, Flowers & Mulhall, 1998; Russell,

1997; Steffes & Valentine, 1996). Especially significant was that the positive benefits were identified for students attending high poverty schools as well as schools in other settings.

IMPLICATIONS FOR THE POLICY DEBATE

The demand for greater accountability for the achievement of all students reignited the debate about the middle school. Passionate debate continued about the focus of a quality middle grades program and how to balance the middle school's long standing commitment to providing an educational experience appropriate for middle school students with the expectations for academic achievement embedded in state and federal accountability models (Anfara & Lipka, 2003).

Embedded within the policy discussion about high performance in middle schools are several factors with broad policy implications. Each will be discussed in some detail.

The Uniqueness of the Middle Grades' Student

First, policy makers must recognize that students in the middle grades possess unique educational needs, needs that neither align with the needs of elementary age students nor with high school students. That is not to suggest that the sole focus of middle schools should be developmental issues, but it recognizes the evidence that to maximize the learning of middle grades' students, schools must respond to their diverse learning styles and assure that curriculum and instruction incorporate practices that are proven to maximize student learning with this age group (Tomlinson, 1998).

Be Clear about the Targets, Allow the Means to Vary

Early efforts to reform middle schools were characterized by the adoption of a set of programs, often those espoused by national advocacy groups (Williamson & Johnston, 1999). While these initiatives focused on organizational changes and reflected a commitment by middle level educators to align their practice more closely with the needs of students, impact on student learning was often a secondary concern.

Mounting evidence demonstrates that many of the recommendations for reformed middle schools contribute to improved achievement and a more positive school environment (Felner et al., 1997; Lee & Smith, 1993; Mertens

& Flowers, 2003; Russell, 1997). This same research confirms that there is no one organizational model for achieving the positive benefits for students.

The National Forum to Accelerate Middle Grades Reform's initiative to identify middle schools that meet the Forum's criteria for high performance found middle schools across the country that serve as exemplars of a high performance. The schools were located in rural, suburban and urban areas, in areas of high poverty and in middle-class communities.

Remarkably, examination of the programs offered in the schools revealed that they varied significantly. Organization and structure were less important than a shared commitment to "doing whatever it takes" to assure a high quality educational experience for their students. The greatest achievement gains occurred where teachers and administrators examined their own students' educational needs and adopted a set of educational practices to meet those needs.

The implication for policy makers is clear. The standards for high performance in the middle grades must be clear but the means to achieve those targets must be left to the discretion of the teachers, parents and administrators at each school site.

Accountability Must Focus on Individual Students

Recent accountability legislation shifted emphasis from a focus on "all children" to a focus on "each child." Schools are now accountable not only for achievement in the aggregate but also for identified subgroups, particularly those groups that were often underserved by schools (*No Child Left Behind*, 2001). The implications for schools are significant. No longer can a school emphasize the combined achievement of its students. Rather, attention must be paid to each child and their individual learning gains.

Implementation of these expectations will require policy makers to adjust current state approaches to monitoring school accountability. Most states currently aggregate student achievement data with a focus on the progress of a school from year to year. What is needed is a system to monitor the progress of individual children year to year. Comparing the aggregate results of groups, and subgroups, of students may distort real and significant achievement gains for individual students. For example, a year to year comparison of sixth grade test scores will not account for the gains an individual group of students may have from fifth to sixth grade.

Provide Professional Development to Support High-Performance

Models of high-performing middle schools have been identified by the National Forum to Accelerate Middle Grades Reform and through empirical research (Balfanz & Mac Iver, 2000; Mertens & Flowers, 2003; Mertens et al., 1998). At the same time, models of effective professional development to support high performance also emerged (Doda & Thompson, 2002; Doda & Williamson, 2002; Speck, 1996; Williamson & Galletti, 2003).

As schools strive to meet expectations for high performance from all students they must confront years of debilitating practice—low expectations for some students and instructional practices that fail many students. High-quality professional development that engages teachers and school leaders in authentic work, focused on the needs of their own students, can result in changes in both beliefs and behaviors. The National Staff Development Council identified specific, targeted professional development strategies that support high performance in the middle grades (Sparks & Hirsch, 1997) and those practices should be supported.

The Requirement for Self-Accountability

No Child Left Behind (2001) emphasized the responsibility of school personnel for high performance from all students. Even with this shift, current accountability models rely on external pressure, the label of a failing school, reduction of funding and sanctions on personnel, for motivation.

As long as the motivation remains external the debate will continue about the appropriateness of the current accountability model, about the standards imposed on schools and whether the goals, however laudable, are attainable. What is required is acceptance by school personnel of their own responsibility for the achievement of their students and a commitment to do "whatever it takes" (Williamson & Johnston, 1999) to assure their students' success.

Cynicism might lead some to argue that if educators were interested in such a level of accountability it would have emerged years ago. They also might question how such a model would assure similar standards across a state.

While past practice might warrant such cynicism, the culture of external accountability fails to adequately change norms in either districts, schools, or individuals in a way that will result in the long lasting changes that positively impact students. Current models reward schools for short-term compliance, for quick results rather than for aggressively examining what part of their operation needs to be jettisoned and replaced by more appropriate and effective practice. Schools must abandon the current "tinkering" at educational change and deeply examine the current educational model and make needed changes.

M. Hayes Mizell described a model of "self-accountability" when he spoke to a group of central office staff, principals, teachers and teacher union representatives from the Corpus Christi Independent School District (Mizell, 2002b). He suggested that educators need "to take control of their own destiny and their own schools, and . . . see themselves not as victims but as potentially powerful agents for change" (p. 186).

Mizell suggested that a shift to self-accountability requires accepting responsibility for student performance. It also requires acceptance of shared responsibility for working collaboratively to improve student learning. This responsibility requires that school personnel be willing to abandon practices that don't work and that they use a variety of means to measure whether or not their students meet the school's own high standards. Additionally, schools must be candid with themselves and with the public about the performance of their students and must be willing to hold themselves accountable for aligning professional development with the identified learning needs of their students. Finally, Mizell argued that the bottom line was to "take whatever actions are necessary to improve student performance" (p. 190).

Policymakers must support local initiatives to create "self-accountability" systems. Rather than discourage local policy and local responses, policymakers must recognize that only when middle school personnel hold themselves personally accountable for the high performance of each of their students will the needed break through in student learning occur.

CONCLUDING DISCUSSION

High performing middle schools, schools that provide a challenging academic experience for every student are possible. Schools that have achieved that goal have been located and empirical research has identified programs and practices that support such high performance.

What seems to be lacking is the will to take the steps necessary to assure that every child, in every middle school, is supported by a culture that believes they can learn at very high levels, and that they will thrive in an academically challenging setting. Too often policy inhibits the responsiveness and creativity that can lead to such results.

Policymakers are right to expect that middle school personnel will accept accountability for the learning of all students. But they also have a responsibility to assure that schools have the policy resources necessary to be successful. Such resources include flexibility in program design, access to appropriate high-quality professional development, and policy written in a way that it encourages "self-accountability," local creativity and responsiveness.

The potential is limitless. What is required is a desire by school personnel and policy makers to set aside narrowly focused agendas and replace them with strong efforts to create and sustain a culture of academic excellence in every middle school for every child.

REFERENCES

Aiken, W. (1942). *Adventure in American education, Volume I: The story of the eight year study.* New York: Harper Brothers. Retrieved October 12, 2003 from http://www.geocities.com/mr_br00ks/8year/chapter6.html.

American Educational Research Association. (2000). Position statement on high stakes testing in k–12 education. Washington, DC: Author.

Anfara, V., & Lipka, R. (2003). Relating the middle school concept to student achievement. *Middle School Journal, 35*(1), 24–32.

Balfanz, R., & Mc Iver, D. (2000). Transforming high poverty urban middle schools into strong learning institutions: Lessons from the first five years of the talent development middle school. *Journal of Education for Students Placed at Risk, 5*(1), 137–158.

Beane, J. (1999). Middle schools under siege: Points of attack. *Middle School Journal, 30*(4), 3–9.

Berliner, D. (February, 1993). Educational reform in an era of disinformation. *Educational Policy Analysis Archives. 1*(2). Retrieved October 14, 2003 from, http://epaa.asu.edu/epaa/v1n2.html

Biddle, B. (1997). Foolishness, dangerous nonsense, and real correlates of state differences in achievement. *Phi Delta Kappan. 79*(1), 8–13.

Bobitt, F. (1913). The supervision of big city schools: Some general principles of management applied to the problems of city school systems. *Twelfth yearbook of the National Society for the Study of Education.* Bloomington, IL: National Society for the Study of Education.

Bracey, G. (2002). *The war against America's public schools.* Boston: Allyn and Bacon.

Carnegie Council on Adolescent Development. (1989). *Turning points: Preparing American youth for the 21st century.* New York: Author.

Chase, F. (1971). Problems of autonomy and accountability in government contracts for research and development in education. In L. Bruce, R. Smith, & D. Hague. (Eds.), *The dilemma of accountability in modern government: Independence vs. control.* New York: St. Martin's Press.

Coleman, J.S. (1966). Equality of student educational opportunity. Washington, DC: U.S. Department of Health, Education and Welfare.

Comer, J. (2001). Schools that develop children. *The American Prospect. 12*(7). Retrieved October 14, 2003, from http://www.prospect.org/print/V12/7/comer-j.html

Cuban, L. (2001). Why bad reforms won't give us good schools. *The American Prospect. 12*(1). Retrieved October 14, 2003 from http://www.prospect.org/print/V12/1/cuban-l,.html.

Doda, N., & Thompson, S. (Eds.) (2002). *Transforming ourselves: Transforming schools*. Westerville, OH: National Middle School Association.

Doda, N., & Williamson, R. (2002). Principals make a difference: Learning and leading together. In N. Doda & S. Thompson (Eds.), *Transforming ourselves, Transforming schools*. Westerville, OH: National Middle School Association.

Felner, R., Jackson, A., Kasak, D., Mulhall, P., Brand, S., & Flowers, N. (1997, March). The impact of school reform for the middle years: Longitudinal study of a network engaged in Turning Points-based comprehensive school transformation. *Phi Delta Kappan. 78*(7). 528.

John Dewey Project. (2002). A *brief overview of progressive education*. Burlington, VT: John Dewey Project on Progressive Education. Retrieved October 14, 2003 at http://www.uvm.edu~dewey/articles/proged.html.

Johnston, J.H., & Williamson, R. (1998). Listening to four communities: Parent and public concerns about the middle level school. *NASSP Bulletin, 82*(597), 44–52.

Kohn, A. (2000). *The case against standardized testing*. Portsmouth, NH: Heinemann.

Kuchapski, R. (n.d.). *Conceptualizing accountability for education*. SSTA Research Centre, University of Saskatchewan, Saskatoon, Saskatchewan. Retrieved October 17, 2003, from http://www.ssta.sk.ca/research/evaluation_and_reporting/02-08.htm

Kuchapski, R. (1998). Accountability and the social good: Utilizing Manzer's Liberal Framework in Canada. *Education and Urban Society, 30*(4), 531–545.

Lacey, C., & Lawton, D. (1981). Introduction. In C. Lacey & D. Lawton (Eds.), *Issues in educational accountability*. New York: Methuen.

Lee, V., & Smith, J. (1993). Effects of school restructuring on the achievement and engagement of middle-grades students. *Sociology of Education, 66*(3), 164–187.

Lipsitz, J., Mizell, M.H., Jackson, A., & Austin, L. (1997). Speaking with one voice: A manifesto for middle-grades reform. *Phi Delta Kappan, 78*(7), 533–540.

Mertens, S., & Flowers, N. (2003). Middle school practices improve student achievement in high poverty schools. *Middle School Journal, 35*(1), 33–43.

Mertens, S., Flowers, N., & Mulhall, P. (1998). *The middle start initiative, phase 1: A longitudinal analysis of Michigan middle-level schools*. Urbana: University of Illinois.

Mizell, M.H. (2002a). What if there were no state test? In M.H. Mizell (Ed.), *Shooting for the sun: The message of middle school reform* (pp. 182–192). New York: Edna McConnell Clark Foundation.

Mizell, M.H. (2002b). *Shooting for the sun: The message of middle school reform*. New York: Edna McConnell Clark Foundation.

National Center for Educational Statistics. (2003a). *The nation's report card: National assessment of educational progress*. Washington, DC: Author. Retrieved October 15, 2003, from http://nces.ed.gov/nationsreportcard/

National Center for Educational Statistics. (2003b). *Education indicators: An international perspective*. Washington, DC: Author. Retrieved October 15, 2003, from http://nces.ed.gov/surveys/international/IntlIndicators/

National Commission on Excellence in Education. (1983, April). *A Nation at risk.* Washington, DC: U.S. Department of Education.

National Forum to Accelerate Middle-Grades Reform. (1999). *Schools to watch criteria, organizational supports.* Retrived October 15, 2003, from http://www.mgforum .org/Improvingschools/STWcriteria.asp

National Middle School Association. (2002). *Position statement on high stakes testing.* Columbus, OH: Author

Nixon, J. (1992). *Evaluating the whole curriculum.* Philadelphia, PA: Open University Press.

No child left behind act of 2001, Pub. L. No 107-110, 115 Stat. 1425 (2002).

Ravitch, D. (2002). A brief history of testing and accountability. *Hoover Digest, 2002*(04), 1–6. Retrieved October 12, 2003 from, http://www.hoover.stanford.edu/publications/digest/024/ravitch.html

Russell, J. (1997). Relationships between the implementation of middle level program concepts and student achievement. *Journal of Curriculum and Supervision, 12*(2), 152–168.

Schrag, P. (January, 2000). Too good to be true. *The American Prospect. 11*(4).

Southern Regional Education Board. (1998). *Education's weak link: Student performance in the middle grades.* Atlanta, GA: Author.

Sparks, D., & Hirsch, S. (1997). *A new vision for professional development.* Alexandria, VA: Association for Supervision and Curriculum Development.

Speck, M. (1996). Best practice in professional development for sustained educational change. *ERS Spectrum, 14*(2), 33–42.

Steffes, B., & Valentine, J. (1996). The relationship between organizational characteristics and expected benefits of interdisciplinary teams. *Research in Middle Level Education Quarterly, 19*(4), 83–106.

Tomlinson, C. (1998). Curriculum and instruction for gifted learners in the middle grades: What would it take? In. R. Williamson & J.H. Johnston (Eds.), *Able learners in the middle level school: Identifying talent and maximizing potential* (pp. 21–34). Reston, VA: National Association of Secondary School Principals.

Williamson, R., & Galletti, S. (2003). Leadership for results. In V. Anfara & G. Davis (Eds.), *Handbook of research in middle level education: Preparation & professional development of middle level teachers and administrators.* Greenwich, CT: Information Age Publishing.

Williamson, R., & Johnston, J. H. (1999). Challenging orthodoxy: An emerging agenda for middle level reform. *Middle School Journal, 30*(4), 10–17.

Wise, A.E. (1979). *Legislated learning: The bureaucratization of the American classroom.* Berkeley: University of California Press.

CHAPTER 4

CREATING QUALITY IN THE MIDDLE SCHOOL CURRICULUM

James A. Beane

INTRODUCTION

Little more than a decade after the first junior high schools opened their doors, leading reformers like Thomas Briggs (1920) and Leonard Kobos (1927) were already warning that the most difficult challenge facing the fledgling movement would be in working on the curriculum. Unless a curriculum was organized for the junior high school itself, not simply as a prelude to the high school, the institution would make little headway toward providing an appropriate education for young adolescents. As it turns out, they were partially, though not completely, correct in this forecast.

Though the evolution of middle level schools from the junior high school of those years to the middle schools of today has seen its shares of ups and downs, there can be little question that substantial progress has been made (Cuban, 1992). Improved understanding of young adolescents and the subsequent development of structural arrangements like team teaching have helped to make middle level schools in many places increasingly more appropriate for that age group (Lee & Smith, 1993; McEwin,

Reforming Middle Level Education: Considerations for Policymakers, pages 49–63
Copyright © 2004 by Information Age Publishing
All rights of reproduction in any form reserved.

Dickinson, & Jenkins, 1996). Yet the matter of the curriculum remains largely unsettled and unsettling (Beane, 1993; Dickinson, 2001; Powell & Skoog, 1995; Powell, Skoog, & Troutman, 1996). As those early reformers predicted, the lack of an appropriate curriculum continues to frustrate the lives of young adolescents and a great many of the adults who live and work with them in school and at home.

As we think about today's middle school curriculum, we must remember that the junior high school, at its roots, was created out of a rare alliance of competing cultural and political pressure groups (Kliebard, 1986). As momentum built to replace the 8–4 elementary to high school grade configuration with 6–3–3 plan, a variety of groups saw an opening for their interests. Higher education officials, for example, saw an opportunity to begin college preparatory courses earlier. Social reformers hoped to keep children in school, and thus diminish child labor abuses, by offering a curriculum more appealing to seventh and eighth graders than the elementary school offered. Industrial leaders sought to have trade skills and vocational guidance offered to young people who would leave school at the end of ninth grade to enter their factories. And developmentalists, by far the least influential of these groups, imagined this moment to be their opportunity to solidify a place for "early adolescence" in the psychological and educational structure. Unfortunately the academic and vocational aspects of the curriculum were cast according to the social and economic class backgrounds of students thus involving the junior high school in the long and continuing history of social inequity in schools in general (Beane, 1993).

Given this context we are reminded that the junior high school was intended to be what its name implied: a "junior" version of the high school. Thus the long struggle to create a curriculum specifically appropriate for young adolescents was bound to be complicated from the start for it has always been a struggle against the middle level's own history and those who remain loyal to it. This does not mean that no progress has been made on the curriculum question. In the middle of the 20th century many junior high schools across the United States and elsewhere centered the curriculum on "core" programs organized around problem-oriented issues and themes rather than the separate subject approach handed down from the high school (Bossing & Cramer, 1965; Faunce & Bossing, 1951; Vars, 1991).

Likewise in the 1990s, a new wave of interest brought the curriculum question to the forefront again and with it renewed interest in more integrative approaches. Although, for the most part, the curriculum of middle schools remains much the same as the one that dominated the junior high schools, namely a collection of academic and "exploratory" subjects named much like the ones offered in high schools and colleges and generally concerned with mastery of some portion of the content and vocabulary within each. Summarizing data from a national, one-day "shadow study" of sixth graders, Lounsbury and Johnston (1988) reported:

> The students' day is intellectually fragmented, and they are seldom called upon to utilize learning from one subject in another area . . . Much attention is given to coverage and retention of content; little instruction makes use of higher order thinking skills. (p. 41)

Fifteen years later, there is no evidence to suggest their description does not still apply. Nevertheless, contemporary middle school policy makers continue in their efforts to push for reform at the middle level. Most recently, high-profile groups such as the National Middle School Association have called for a middle school that is "academically challenging, developmentally responsive, and socially equitable." The purpose of this paper is to explore the question, "What kind of curriculum is academically challenging, developmentally responsive, and socially equitable? In answering that question, though, I first want to expand and clarify the way those conditions ought to be used.

The first condition, "academically challenging," typically refers to the presence of a curriculum (and teaching and assessment) that is "standards-based." But standards come in different forms including some that are merely a collection of facts and skills whose real challenge, often mistaken for intellectual rigor, lies in their remoteness from the personal or social needs, interests, problems, and concerns of middle school students who are, after all, young adolescents and not scholars or graduate students. The academic challenge in a middle school curriculum lies not in painful abstraction, but rather in its capacity to engage the intellectual imagination and curiosity of young adolescents. As such, it should encourage them to make good use of their minds in broadening their understanding of themselves and their world. A lesser kind of challenge created mainly out of academic ritual and resulting mostly in drudgery hardly seems like one worth pursuing. For this reason, I want to add "intellectually stimulating" to the condition of "academically challenging."

The second condition, "developmental responsiveness" typically means that arrangements within the school take account of the fact that young adolescents find themselves at or about puberty. In this moment, most experience increased concern for peer relationships, heightened attention to self-identity, desire for greater independence, and increasingly complex awareness of value and moral questions. Too often, though, middle level educators and others seem to view young adolescents not as real people experiencing a lifespan transition, but as rootless and superficial "hormones with feet." In this case the concept of developmental responsiveness is left open to narrow discussions of how to respond to what appears in school as short attention spans, preoccupation with peer acceptance, and lack of attention to homework and textbooks. For this reason I want to add the concept of "developmental respectfulness" to the understanding of "responsiveness." This means that middle level educators would want to know not just the generic and statistical descriptions of young adolescents in general, but also the personally and socially significant agendas and perspectives emerging in the lives of those in their own schools. As we will see, respecting these agendas and perspectives can provide important clues to a high quality curriculum.

The third condition, "socially equitable," is long overdue in a middle level discourse that has mainly focused on physical and psychological dimensions of young adolescents. The fact is that junior high schools often played a leading role in the school inequities as they sorted and selected young people into various academic and vocational tracks, mainly according to race, class, and gender. Yet forging a curriculum that rejects these practices in favor of more equitable ones does not push far enough since social inequities are not simply school matters. I want to stretch the concept of "socially equitable" to embrace the idea of "socially conscious." In this sense, we need to think about a curriculum that not only avoids internal inequities but which consciously engages young people in thinking about and working on social issues and problems. For the middle school, overcoming inequity should begin at "home," but it should not end there.

Reframed in this way, then, the contemporary version of a high quality middle school is one that is academically challenging and intellectually stimulating, developmentally responsive and respectful, and socially equitable and conscious. As we now turn to the question of what kind of curriculum such a school would have, it is important to remember that these three conditions might be met in a variety of ways. Thus the task is not to describe a single approach or "a curriculum," but to instead name some of the characteristics of any particular curriculum focused on these conditions.

A GENERAL EDUCATION

In the interest of equity and developmental responsiveness, a middle school curriculum should emphasize a general education for all young adolescents. Put another way, what is offered in the school program would be intended for all students and all students would be involved in it. This does not mean that all young adolescents would do exactly the same thing in the same way or be expected to derive the same meanings from various curriculum experiences. However, it does mean that the important ideas, content, skills, resources, and so on provided by the school, would be shared by all with the intention of enhancing and equalizing access to knowledge, outcomes, and offerings for all young adolescents.

A democratic society to some extent depends upon all citizens having some shared understandings and experiences regarding the persistent and critical ideas of democratic living. The kind of general education as necessary to meet the conditions outlined earlier would present just such an experience. As we will see later, it would involve exploring self and societal issues, collaborative problem-solving, authentic projects, and other activities associated with democratic living while also introducing and applying important content and skills from the disciplines of knowledge and popular culture (Beane, 1993).

A general education curriculum is also intended to avoid fragmenting young adolescents into various programs or tracks based on special interests, abilities, or talents. Young adolescents are not ready to make decisions about their futures, even though they may express early preferences or inclinations. Moreover, adults have a dismal record of predicting what those futures might be. To force young adolescents to make such decisions or, worse yet, to decide for them is one way in which some curriculum arrangements have been developmentally inappropriate for young adolescents.

The move toward more specialized curriculum offerings based upon individual differences or interests has also been one of the main ways by which social and economic inequities have been sustained in the school. To understand this we need look no further than limited Algebra sections in the eighth grade in schools with diverse populations. Too often, such sections are disproportionately filled with social and economically privileged students. Moreover, including these tracked courses as well as specialized performing musical groups and other single section classes in the regular school schedule usually interferes with diversity in class and team groupings across the whole school, disrupting the general education curriculum, differentiating access to knowledge, and unfairly judging the future possibilities and aspirations of young adolescents. A moral and ethical middle school curriculum simply cannot allow these kinds of inequities.

In examining existing curriculum arrangements or proposals for new ones, then, middle level educators and policymakers need to ask:

- Do all students have access to the important ideas, content, skills, and resources provided by the school?
- Does the curriculum encourage diverse, heterogeneous groupings or does it lead toward tracking?
- Do specialized arrangements for a few students tend to dominate the program and schedule or is priority given to those that are meant for all students?

- Does the curriculum encourage all students to have high aspirations or does it suggest some students have limited career opportunities?

FRAMED FOR YOUNG ADOLESCENTS

Young adolescents are neither children nor mature adolescents. Nor are they adults, scholars, graduate students, or paid laborers. They are young adolescents and they cannot be otherwise. Thus the curriculum of the middle school should be framed for them rather than as if they are one of those other groups. When we engage them with content, skills, values, social issues, or any other kind of knowledge, we have an obligation to do so in terms that are meaningful, appropriate, and accessible for them as young adolescents.

As described above, most young adolescents are experiencing considerable change in perspectives about themselves and the world around them (Eccles & Midgley, 1989). Among these is expanding awareness of self, especially in relation to others (Brinthaupt & Lipka, 2002). This is the time when the self becomes defined not so much as the "I am what I own" or "I am what I do" of childhood as the "I am who I am" of expanded awareness (Beane & Lipka, 1987). Arnold (1985) takes this one step further in saying that:

> Young adolescents are asking some of the most profound questions human beings can ever ask: Who am I? What should I be? What should I do? To respond to them effectively we must forge a curriculum that frequently deals with their own questions. (p. 14)

In addition to this expanding sense of self, young adolescents are also becoming increasingly aware of and concerned about value and moral issues. Teachers who have involved young adolescents in curriculum planning (Alexander, McAvoy, & Carr, 1995; Beane, 1997; Brodhagen, 1995) by asking what questions they have about themselves and the world have reported that they consistently ask questions like:

> What will happen to the earth in the future? Why are there so many crimes? Will racism ever end? Will the United States ever be out of debt? Will cures be found for cancer and AIDS? Why are schools the way they are? Will the rain forests be saved? Why is there so much prejudice? Why are there so many poor people? Will there ever be a time when no one is poor? When will gang violence stop? Will there ever be world peace? Why do people hurt/kill each other?

Moreover, when the same young adolescents are asked what themes their questions suggest, they again consistently name themes like: Jobs, Money, Careers, Living in the Future, Environmental Problems, Conflict and Violence, "ISMs" and Prejudice, Government and Politics, Outer Space, Economy, and Drugs, Diseases, and Health (Beane, 1997; Brodhagen, 1995).

Some teachers have used young adolescent questions and themes like these to plan their full curriculum. Others have used them to inform decisions within teacher planned units or even traditional subject area courses. The point is that young adolescents are concerned about significant self and societal issues and those ought to be taken into account in the middle school curriculum if it is to be intellectually stimulating, developmentally respectful, and socially conscious.

Two important points are suggested by the case for this kind of curriculum focus. First, the questions and themes just cited are obviously not those of people who are simply "hormones with feet" or "brain dead," two descriptors that are often applied to young adolescents. On the contrary, those questions and themes are significant enough to organize or at least play a major role in a curriculum that meets the three conditions we are considering here. Young adolescents will not answer such questions or deal with issues at the same technical level as scholars or graduate students, but they can and have dealt with them at sufficiently sophisticated levels to maintain academic integrity.

This observation leads to the second point which is that such questions and themes offer a sufficient purpose for a middle school curriculum. In keeping with the earlier point about the uniqueness of young adolescence, I want to argue that a middle school curriculum should be concerned with the here and now of young adolescent lives. We need look no further for a curriculum rationale. The purpose of the middle school curriculum should not be to prepare young adolescents for high school or college. Nor should the school be a farm team for the labor force needs of corporations. Rather the purpose of the middle school curriculum should be to help young adolescents explore life as they are living it and to have the best middle school experience possible.

In examining existing curriculum arrangements or proposals for new ones, then, middle level educators and policymakers need to ask:

- Do they provide space for the kind of self and societal questions that are on the minds of young adolescents?
- Do they emphasize themes, content, and skills appropriate for young adolescents?
- Do they frame knowledge in terms of what young adolescents are thinking about and experiencing at this time of their lives?

DEMOCRACY AND DIGNITY

The middle school is not some independent entity without obligation to the society of which it is a part. Therefore, it must take seriously the conditions of social equity and consciousness as well as the dignity of young adolescents. These are, after all, among the most important demands that democracy and democratic living make upon us. A curriculum that meets these conditions requires both content and process considerations.

With regard to content, we have already seen the possibilities for using significant personal and societal issues to organize themes, projects, and activities. A socially conscious curriculum cannot ignore these possibilities since one of the most important parts of democratic living involves the right and responsibility of citizens to participate in resolving such problems. Moreover, to the extent that such problems frequently involve social inequities, the use of problems and issues to organize the curriculum is the path by which the middle school might demonstrate its commitment to social equity.

In addition to content considerations, the obligation to democracy and democratic living requires that the middle school curriculum also emphasize at least two kinds of processes. One is the involvement of young adolescents in making decisions about matters that affect them. In a middle school, of course, this means including student voice in almost everything ranging from governance, to curriculum planning, to student-led conferences. The other kind of process is emphasis on collaborative learning through a variety of small and large group discussions, debates, and projects. In addition to their justification on democratic grounds, these kinds of collaborative arrangements also respond to the young adolescent urge for peer group connections (Beane & Lipka, 1987).

Finally, the conditions of democracy, equity, and respectfulness require the middle school curriculum to persistently emphasize and prize diversity. Too often the diversity among young adolescents in terms of physical, social, and intellectual development as well as race, class, gender, sexual orientation and other characteristics is seen as a problem or obstacle to overcome in order to create efficiency in the school. A democratic society prizes diversity because it is built partly upon the notion of individual rights, freedoms, and perspectives. For this reason the middle school curriculum is obliged to seek out and persistently use resources that prevent different views and perspectives on life. These may range from materials, to community resources, to the culturally based questions and concerns that diverse young people want considered in the curriculum. This obligation also speaks to the need for heterogeneous grouping in both large and small groups as well as diverse representation in governance groups and all school and classroom activities. This is extremely important as it is these arrangements that constitute much of the "hidden" curriculum from which young adolescents learn a great deal about themselves and others, frequently more than from the planned curriculum.

In examining existing curriculum arrangements or proposals for new ones, then, middle level educators and policymakers need to ask:

- Do they provide opportunities for young adolescents to participate in decision-making?
- Do they encourage collaborative learning and problem solving?
- Do they prize the diversities among young adolescents and across the larger society?

PROBLEMS AND PROJECTS

If the separate subject curriculum and lecture-worksheet regimen worked, middle level schools would have a very different history. For these have been the pedagogical bread and butter at this level from the earliest junior high schools to the more recent middle schools (Lounsbury & Marani, 1964; Lounsbury, Marani, & Compton, 1980; Lounsbury & Johnston 1988). Granted middle school literature and conference programs are full of alternatives, but these would not be given so much program space if they were not so unusual. In order for a curriculum to be intellectually stimulating it must first engage the attention and then the curiosity of young adolescents. To be academically challenging it must provide opportunities to actually apply content and skills to authentic tasks that require their authentic use (Newman & Associates, 1996).

A high quality middle school curriculum begins with the understanding that content and skills are not learned well by most young adolescents, and not at all by others, without a meaningful context. We have already seen that it is possible for curriculum contexts to be created by inviting young adolescents to identify their self and societal concerns through collaborative planning with teachers. They may also be created by teachers themselves out of significant social problems such as environmental conditions, community issues, and current events. Such problems and concerns, in turn, can be used to organize major integrative themes or as the content of writing experiences, science experiments, literature discussions, art projects, or musical programs. Either way, they offer the potential to give purpose and direction to content and skills that otherwise are much like a jumble of jigsaw puzzle pieces with no picture (Beane, 1997; Vars, 1996). In summarizing a "solid body of research [that] has been accumulating," Iran-Nejad, McKeachie, and Berliner (1990) concluded that:

> The more meaningful, the more deeply or elaboratively processed, the more situated in context, and the more rooted in cultural, background, metacognitive, and personal knowledge an event is, the more readily it is understood, learned, and remembered. (p. 511)

Within these contexts, a high quality middle school curriculum emphasizes the use of projects as a means for both learning about and applying content and skills. This means that young adolescents are constantly involved in making, creating, dramatizing—in other words, "doing." The application of content and skills in large and small projects in this way gives them the kind of authentic purpose and use through which they may actually be "learned" (Blumenfeld, Soloway, & Marx, 1991). Projects also provide excellent opportunities to "perform knowledge" so that it is publicly shared and demonstrated in authentic and meaningful ways rather than through the artifice of tests and worksheets.

The use of problem-centered themes and activities as well as projects and performances also serve as the springboard to take the middle school curriculum past the separate subject approach and toward more interdisciplinary and integrative arrangements (Beane, 1997; Nagel, 1996). Ample evidence tells us that moving in this direction is a crucial step for the middle school curriculum. From a review of research, Thomas (2000) concluded that project-based learning:

> Seems to be equivalent or slightly better than other models of instruction for producing gains in general academic achievement and for developing lower-level cognitive skills in traditional subject matter areas . . . [and] for enhancing the quality of students' learning in subject matter areas, leading to the tentative claim that learning higher-level cognitive skills via [project-based learning] is associated with increased capability on the part of students for applying those learnings in novel, problem-solving contexts. (Pp. 34–35)

Moreover, experience in middle level schools reminds us constantly that young adolescents are not graduate students or scholars. They do not see the world or their concerns in strictly disciplinary categories (nor do most scholars, of course). Though the content and skills found within the traditional disciplines of knowledge are important for young adolescents to encounter, presenting them through a separate subject program both limits the possibilities they will be learned and diminishes their importance in the minds of young people. It is important to remember, however, that to be academically challenging and intellectually stimulating, the interdisciplinary and integrative contexts for content and skills must be of explicit significance as in the personal and societal issues and problems I have described. Selecting a theme simply because it sounds fun or exciting, runs the risk of continuing to trivialize important content and skills and in doing so insufficiently challenging young adolescents.

In examining existing curriculum arrangements or proposals for new ones, then, middle level educators and policymakers need to ask:

- Do they involve questions and concerns that are on the minds of young adolescents?
- Do they involve issues of clear and compelling societal signi_cance?
- Do they engage a wide range of knowledge, skills, and resources?
- Do they pose opportunities for in-depth and extended projects?
- Do they present possibilities for a wide variety of activities, especially ones that involve collaborative problem solving?
- Do they present possibilities for personal and social action, both in school and outside the school?

PROSPECTS FOR A HIGH QUALITY MIDDLE SCHOOL CURRICULUM

Only a decade ago, we were in the midst of what seemed to be a renaissance of educational ideas like those I have described (Alexander et al., 1995; Beane, 1993; Brazee & Capelluti, 1995; Brodhagen, 1995; Pace, 1995; Stevenson & Carr, 1993; Vars, 1993). Around the country educators were talking about whole learning, democratic schools, interdisciplinary and integrative curriculum, detracking, problem-centered math and science, project-centered learning and many more ideas like them. In many cases these discussions were not simply about teaching methods. They were also about redirecting classrooms and schools toward more institutional equity, more meaningful learning, more culturally responsive content, more authentic assessments, and more socially conscious purposes. Conferences, journals, and workshops were full of these ideas and more than a few teachers and schools created projects and programs to bring them to life.

Ironically, though, that renaissance in schools was surrounded by a steady growth in the power of social and economic conservatives intent upon downsizing everything public and progressive and using legislative policy to move the schools a very different direction. Today, the progressive educational ideas so popular just a decade ago have fallen on hard times, marginalized in public and professional media, their advocates silenced by the language of the new accountability movement and censored by the growing authority of standards and testing.

In dismantling progressive initiatives, advocates of the new accountability have set up a convenient rhetorical contrast: their supposedly "rigorous" standards and tests versus the allegedly "soft" methods of progressives.

According to this argument, the quality of public education has been going steadily downhill since the 1960s. What is needed to make things right is a good dose of hard-nosed academic retrofitting. No matter, by the way, that the 1960s were actually a decade of some of the most conservative measures ever seen in education, including behavioral objectives, teaching machines, "structure of the disciplines," teacher-proof curriculum packages, and performance contracting for student achievement. What does matter is that in order to make the new accountability seem the road to salvation, progressive ideas had to be made to seem the enemy of educational progress. Flimsy as it is, the accountability "thesis" requires an "antithesis" to be believable.

This analysis might seem to have taken us away from the question of what constitutes a high quality middle school curriculum. However, it is exactly that political struggle over curriculum in general that makes the middle school question so difficult to pursue. Historically, its ambiguous position between the elementary and high school has made the middle level a favorite site for curriculum conflict. Attempts to satisfy competing pressures with a multipurpose program have done little to settle debates over such issues as general versus specialized education or separate subject versus integrative curriculum.

Today, the pursuit of a middle school curriculum that would satisfy the three conditions outlined earlier is further hindered by the emerging version of the standards movement that is less concerned with significant learning and more concerned with increased testing and centralized control through standardized curriculum and teaching methods. This movement suggests an ominous future for the possibility of a high quality middle school curriculum. As I have defined it, such a curriculum requires that teachers and other local educators have the flexibility to work with students to define relevant themes or topics, draw upon a wide range of knowledge, select worthwhile projects and activities, and create appropriate assessments. When externally imposed standards, tests, and methods eliminate that flexibility, the middle school curriculum is fundamentally corrupted, losing the potential to meet the conditions for high quality.

Now this would seem simply a wildly hypothetical argument were it not actually true in so many places, either because external mandates have had that effect directly or because local officials have insisted on standardized methods. Ironically, of course, there is substantial evidence to suggest that the structures and methods associated with the middle school concept generally have proved to be academically and affectively quite successful with young adolescents (Beane & Brodhagen, 2002; Felner et al., 1997). Whether this evidence has been ignored out of ignorance or political convenience, the net effect is that the middle school concept has been seriously downsized. Worse yet, middle school educators themselves seem afraid to say out loud that the emerging wave of standards, tests, and standardization is antithetical to the middle school concept. In some classrooms and schools the kind of curriculum I have described is still alive, but almost always under growing duress from the demands of national, state, and local authorities.

If current trends persist, we will soon be able to describe the middle school curriculum as a collection of test-driven content and skills isolated in separate subject classes and superficially covered by teachers using standardized methods and materials. In other words, we will have precisely the curriculum that has historically failed young adolescents so miserably, especially those who are poor and of color. It is time for middle school educators and policy makers to raise some serious questions about the kind of curriculum that seems to be emerging from the standardization movement. Whose interests are being served by this kind of curriculum? How is it that this kind of curriculum will challenge the intellect and curiosity of young adolescents when it never has before? In what way is this kind of curriculum responsive to the perspectives and developments that emerge in the lives of young adolescents? And how will it lead toward social equity now when historically it has lead in exactly the opposite direction?

REFERENCES

Alexander, W., McAvoy, K., & Carr, D. (1995). *Student-oriented curriculum: Asking the right questions.* Columbus, OH: National Middle School Association.

Arnold, J. (1985). A responsive curriculum for early adolescents. *Middle School Journal, 16*(5), 14–18.

Beane, J.A. (1993). A middle school curriculum: From rhetoric to reality (rev. ed.). Columbus, OH: National Middle School Association.

Beane, J.A. (1997). *Curriculum integration: Designing the core of a democratic education.* New York: Teachers College Press.

Beane, J., & Brodhagen,B. (2002). Teaching in middle schools. In V. Richardson (Ed.). *Handbook of research on teaching* (4th ed., pp.1157–1174). Washington, DC: American Educational Research Association.

Blumenfeld, P.C., Soloway, E., & Marx, R.W. (1991). Motivating project-based learning: Sustaining the doing, supporting the learning. *Educational Psychologist, 26,* (3&4), 369–398.

Bossing, N.L., & Cramer, R.V. (1965). *The junior high school.* Boston: Houghton Mifflin.

Brazee, E., & Capelluti, J. (1995). *Dissolving boundaries: Toward an integrative middle school curriculum.* Columbus, OH: National Middle School Association.

Briggs, T.H. (1920). *The junior high school.* Boston: Houghton Mifflin.

Brinthaupt, T., & Lipka, R. (2002). *Understanding early adolescent self and identity: Applications and interventions.* Albany: SUNY Albany Press.

Brodhagen, B.L. (1994). Assessing and reporting student progress in an integrative Curriculum. *Teaching and Change, 1*(3), 238–254.

Brodhagen, B.L. (1995). The situation made us special. In M.W. Apple & J.A. Beane (Eds.), *Democratic schools* (pp. 83–100). Alexandria, VA: Association for Supervision and Curriculum Development.

Cuban, L. (1992). What happens to reforms that last: The case of the junior high school. *American Educational Research Journal, 29*(2), 227–251.

Dickinson, T.S. (2002). Reinventing the middle school: A proposal to counter arrested development. In T.S. Dickinson (Ed.), *Reinventing the middle school* (pp. 3–21). New York: Routledge Falmer.

Eccles, J.S., & Midgley, C. (1989). Stage/environment fit: Developmentally appropriate classrooms for early adolescents. In R.E. Ames & C. Ames (Eds.). *Research on motivation in education* (pp. 139–186). New York: Academic.

Faunce, R.C., & Bossing, N.L. (1951). *Developing the core curriculum.* New York: Prentice-Hall.

Felner, R.D., Jackson, A.W., Kasak, D., Mulhall, P., Brand, S., & Flowers, N. (1997). The impact of school reform in the middle years. *Phi Delta Kappan, 78*(7), 528–550.

Iran-Nejad, A., McKeachie, W.J., & Berliner, D. C. (1990). The multisource nature of learning: An introduction. *Review of Educational Research, 60*(4), 509–15.

Kliebard, H. (1986). *The struggle for the American curriculum: 1893–1958.* Boston: Routledge and Kegan Paul.

Koos, L. (1929). *The junior high school.* New York: Ginn.

Lee, V., & Smith, J. (1993). Effects of school restructuring on the achievement and engagement of middle grades students. *Sociology of Education, 66*(3), 164–187.

Lounsbury, J.H., & Johnston, J.H. (1988). *Life in the three 6th grades.* Reston, VA: National Association of Secondary School Principals.

Lounsbury, J.H., & Marani, J. (1964). *The junior high school we saw: One day in the eighth grade.* Washington, DC: Association for Supervision and Curriculum Development.

Lounsbury, J.H., Marani, J., & Compton, M. (1980). *The middle school in profile: A day in the seventh grade.* Columbus: OH: National Middle School Association.

McEwin, C.K., Dickinson, T.S., & Jenkins, D.M. (1996). *America's middle schools: Practices and progress, a 25 year perspective.* Columbus, OH: National Middle School Association.

Nagel, N. (1996). *Learning through real-world problem solving.* Thousand Oaks, CA: Corwin.

Pace, G. (Ed.). (1995). *Whole learning in the middle school.* Norwood, MA: Christopher-Gordon.

Powell, R.R., & Skoog, G. (1995). Students' perspectives of integrative curricula: The case of Brown Barge middle school. *Research in Middle Level Education Quarterly, 19*(1), 85–114.

Powell, R.R., Skoog, G., & Troutman, P. (1996). On streams and odysseys: Reflections on reform and research in middle level integrative learning environments. *Research in Middle Level Education Quality, 19*(4), 1–30.

Stevenson, C., & Carr, J.F. (Eds.), (1993) *Integrative studies in the middle grades: Dancing through walls.* New York: Teachers College Press.

Thomas, J. (2000). *A review of research on project-based learning.* San Rafael, CA: Autodesk Foundation.

Vars, G.F. (1991). Integrated curriculum in historical perspective. *Educational Leadership, 49*(1), 14–15.

Vars, G.F. (1993). *Interdisciplinary teaching: Why & how* (2nd ed.). Columbus, OH: National Middle School Association.

Vars, G.F. (1996). The effects of interdisciplinary curriculum and instruction. In P.S. Hlebowitsh & W.G. Wraga (Eds.), *Annual review of research for school leaders, Part 11: transcending traditional subject matters lines: Interdisciplinary curriculum and instruction* (pp. 147–164). Reston, VA: National Association of Secondary School Principals.

CHAPTER 5

CREATING SOCIALLY EQUITABLE MIDDLE GRADES SCHOOLS

Nancy M. Doda

INTRODUCTION

Education for social justice is a noble and ambitious agenda for middle schools. It includes a vision for an inclusive school in which the distribution of opportunity is genuinely equitable, where all individuals are able to develop their full capacities, where young people are able to be both self-determining and interdependent, and can learn to live in and value a diverse, socially just, democratic community. A truly just middle school is an ideal bent on ultimately creating citizens who will perpetuate and extend social equity in their lives and in the world. It constitutes more than a hope for decent schools; it constitutes a hope for a better, more just world.

This is not only an ambitious agenda because social equity is a gigantic principle of great complexity and magnitude, but because it has not been a clearly developed agenda for middle schools in the past. The middle school movement's illustrious history has, for decades, centered on the goal of creating "developmentally responsive" schools for young adolescents, fashioning educational practices that respond to the unique devel-

Reforming Middle Level Education: Considerations for Policymakers, pages 65–84
Copyright © 2004 by Information Age Publishing
All rights of reproduction in any form reserved.

opmental characteristics of young adolescence (National Middle School Association, 1995). As such, the middle school's unique identity has been aligned with the physical, social, and intellectual changes of young adolescence. In 1989, the Carnegie Council on Adolescent Development (CCAD) Task Force produced its seminal report, *Turning Points: Preparing American Youth for the 21st Century*, in which the authors articulated this rationale for middle grades reform. There exists a volatile mismatch between the organization and curriculum of middle grades schools and the intellectual and interpersonal needs of young adolescents (Carnegie Council on Adolescent Development, 1989, p. 32).

Even the more recent belief statements included in *This We Believe-Now We Must Act* (NMSA, 2001) do not make explicitly clear the goal of social equity. Most recently, the National Forum to Accelerate Reform in the Middle Grades created a set of criteria to identify high-performing middle grades schools. Based on the Forum's original vision describing middle grades schools as "Developmentally responsive, academically excellent and socially equitable" (National Forum to Accelerate Reform in the Middle Grades Schools to Watch Criteria for Social Equity, 1999), criteria for social equitable schools were generated:

- High-performing schools with middle grades are socially equitable, democratic, and fair. They provide every student with high-quality teachers, resources, learning opportunities, and support. They keep positive options open for all students.
- Faculty and administrators expect high-quality work from all students and are committed to helping each student produce it. Evidence of this commitment includes tutoring, mentoring, special adaptations, and other supports.
- Students may use many and varied approaches to achieve and demonstrate competence and mastery of standards.
- The school continually adapts curriculum, instruction, assessment, and scheduling to meet its students' diverse and changing needs.
- All students have equal access to valued knowledge in all school classes and activities.
- Students have ongoing opportunities to learn about and appreciate their own and others' cultures. The school values knowledge from the diverse cultures represented in the school and our nation.
- Each child's voice is heard, acknowledged, and respected.
- The school welcomes and encourages the active participation of all its families.
- The school's reward system demonstrates that it values diversity, civility, service, and democratic citizenship.
- The faculty is culturally and linguistically diverse.

This, however, represents the first such public advocacy document to state directly the middle school's need to address social equity. Nonetheless, it only begins to challenge some of the most critical inequities in middle grades schools. It is possible, for example, to have students use many and varied approaches to study content that actually defiles certain kinds of students. Likewise, it is possible to adapt curriculum and instruction without ever making it stimulating, relevant and meaningful to the learners themselves. Finally, "keeping options open for students" is also not sufficient. Middle grades schools have to actively create equitable options that provide all of our young adolescents with classrooms that are meaningful, relevant, stimulating and purposeful. When special needs students are pulled out for extensive remediation, for example, they are destined to experience less stimulating learning environments.

This forthright critique is not to diminish the significant changes in middle schools that have implemented the core recommendations from *Turning Points 2000* (Felner, Jackson, Kasak, Mulhall, Brand & Flowers, 1997), those as Dickinson (2001) note "...that have taken the total ecological approach to the process of implementation" (p. 15) and have yielded profound growth for students (Felner et al., 1997). Nor should we undervalue the many rich examples of schools and classrooms that have successfully untracked and moved toward patterns and practices that approach equity (Oakes, 1990; Wheelock, 1992). During the 1990s, however, when some middle school advocates began to more aggressively push the equity agenda to the forefront, it became clear that the middle school concept did not have a well-developed equity ideology. As Beane (2001) explains:

> If middle schools were to provide more access to more knowledge to more children in a positive and nurturing climate, efforts would have to be made to emphasize collaborative learning, get rid of tracking, create heterogeneous grouping, develop curriculum integration, involve students in curriculum planning, celebrate diversity, respond to diverse learning styles, and connect schools to community life. (p. xix)

Social equity, though faintly articulated, is a part of the middle school's promise. The very nature of young adolescence cries out for attention to fairness, justice and civil rights (Quintana, 1998). Middle school students, when asked to generate questions and concerns they have about the world, repeatedly identify social inequities as the most disturbing of personal and world problems they hope to study and address (Beane, in press). Moreover, equity is fundamental to democracy. We have a rich national legacy of articulated ideals that espouse educational equality for all. In 1837, Horace Mann first spearheaded the "common school" movement as his proposed radical, great equalizer for all Americans. In present day, federal and state laws now affirm that every U.S. citizen has the right to a free, public school education:

> The Congress hereby declares it to be the policy of the United States to provide to every person an equal opportunity to receive an education of high quality regardless of his or her race, color, religion, sex, age, handicap, national origin or social class. (U.S. Congress, 1981)

Though not without dynamic tension, all Americans have been deemed equally worthy of the best schooling we can provide. As such we have an obligation to protect our children, and to provide them with promising futures; not just some of them, but all of them. As Deborah Meier said, "The question is not, 'Is it possible to educate all children well?' but rather, 'Do we want to do it badly enough?'"(Meier, 1995, p. 4). In the next generation of middle schools, this is indeed the question to be answered.

THE PERILS OF INEQUITABLE MIDDLE GRADES SCHOOLS

The majority of young adolescents from diverse life circumstances enter the years of preadolescence with grand aspirations for themselves and their social, and vocational futures (Gay, 1994; Ladson-Billings, 1994). The majority aspire to attend college (NELS, 1988), and, many dream of professions in law, medicine, education, business and government. For many young people, these aspirations often diminish or even vanish completely during the middle school years, as they find these dreams deferred in uninviting and discouraging school environments (Fullan, 2001; Goodlad, 1984).

Young adolescence is both a period of enormous opportunity and enormous risk. In 1989, the Task Force on Education of Young Adolescents, presented this challenge to the middle grades educational community:

> Depending on family circumstances, household income, language, neighborhood, or the color of their skin, some of these young adolescents receive the education and support they need to develop self-respect, an active mind, and a healthy body. They will emerge from their teen years as promising youth who will become the scientists and entrepreneurs, the educators, and health care professionals, and the parents who will renew the nation. These are the thoughtful, responsible, caring, ethical, robust young people the Task Force envisions. To them, society can entrust the future of the country with confidence.

> Under current conditions, however, far too many young people will not make the passage through early adolescence successfully. Their basic human needs—caring relationships with adults, guidance in facing sometimes overwhelming biological and psychological changes, the security of belonging to

constructive peer groups, and the perception of future opportunity go unmet at this critical stage of life. Millions of these young adolescents will never reach their full potential . . . early adolescence for these youth is a turning point towards a diminished future. (CCAD, 1989, p. 20)

Some thirty years later, although there have been significant, positive changes in middle grades education, we should take note that we have not yet profoundly altered this trajectory toward diminished futures for some of our children (Dickinson, 2001; Jackson & Davis, 2000).

The consequences of losing millions of young adolescents are grave and have enormous implications for our nation's economic and social future. When young people fall out of love with noble visions of their futures, when they enter schools that inadvertently create barriers to success, they can fall prey to many high-risk choices and behaviors. These behaviors reek havoc with their development and capacity to learn and succeed in and out of school. For example, in 1998, approximately 50 percent of eighth graders had engaged in alcohol, illicit drug and tobacco use. In spite of a recent decline in teenage sexual activity (i.e., approaching 50%), the United States still has the highest incidence of teenage births among developed countries in the world (Annie Casey Foundation, 1998). Many young adolescents choose to leave school, with a substantially higher dropout rate for minority, non-English speaking, and poor students (Levin, 1998). Young adolescents, particularly those with fewer developmental assets, or those with special education needs, lose ground rapidly when schools fail to serve them well.

In recent years, attention to the middle school has been heightened by data suggesting flat academic gains among the nation's middle grades students (Donahue, Voekl, Campbell, & Mazzeo, 1990; Reese, Miller, Mazzeo, & Dossey, 1997). While this attention has led to a number of questionable reform initiatives, it has gratefully illuminated and reconfirmed the disturbing gap in achievement among diverse populations of students. This has in turn nudged a reexamination of middle school practices with a critical eye on social equity in school programs, practices, and pedagogy. Perhaps the most significant conclusion from the research is that middle schools in the United States still fail to educate all students equally well. In fact, in spite of the middle school movement's long history of advocacy for all children, many middle schools remain entrenched in cultural patterns, practices, pedagogy, and beliefs that prohibit success for all learners (Wheelock, 1998).

Today, nearly 89% of America's middle grades schools still employ some form of tracking and/or ability grouping as a means of managing student diversity (Lounsbury & Clark, 1990). Regardless of the ongoing "tracking wars" (Loveless, 1999), this practice compromises the equity dream

(Oakes, 1990; Wheelock, 1992), by institutionalizing the perception that some students have what it takes to be successful while others do not (Wheelock, 1998). These perceptions in turn fuel teacher expectations which ultimately shape student learning. What is often overlooked in understanding the destructive nature of tracking is the powerful role class composition plays in determining the quality of classroom life. Classroom norms and teaching practices are inextricably linked to the student composition of those classes. The level of discourse, the degree of student freedom, the choices of literature, the nature of pedagogy, and so on, are all moderated by the class demographics.

Race, class, language, gender and learning disabilities, still engender inequitable schooling practices, which limit learning, opportunity, exposure, and achievement for minorities, special needs learners, and children of poverty. Children of color and children of poverty are disproportionately assigned to lower academic tracks, in which they are unintentionally fed a steady diet of low level, skill-based, cognitively undemanding tasks (Goodwin, 2000; Haberman, 1991; Singham, 1998). Similarly, African American, Native American, and low-income 8th graders are twice as likely as white or upper income students to be placed in remedial math courses taught by the least experienced teachers (McDonnell et al., 1990; NELS, 1988). Given that mathematics is deemed the contemporary great equalizer, this is a frightening finding with which to be reckoned (Oakes, 1990). Moreover, Lipman's (1998) ethnography of middle grades schools revealed that many middle school teachers view their African American students and other less advantaged students, as "at-risk," which led them to engage in pervasive labeling, lowered expectations and to offer those students less stimulating learning experiences. As Goodwin (2000) concludes:

> When one examines the literature on teachers' interactions with their students, an implicit hierarchy emerges. It appears that European American boys benefit the from most positive teacher interactions, followed by European American girls, then girls of color, particularly African American girls, with African American and Latino boys following. (Goodwin, 2000, p. 2)

While we have, as a national community, continually rearticulated the principle of equality in schooling, and have repeatedly been challenged to respond more fully to the increasing diversity in schools, we have yet to accomplish our dream of success for all. The middle school remains for many young adolescents a place of exclusion, disenfranchisement and even hostile learning conditions that dramatically impact educational and social outcomes for young people. As Wheelock (1998) observed, "The process of moving from the simple statement, 'all children can learn', to results that match that expectation involves hard work" (p. 4), and I would add, radical change.

THE KIND OF MIDDLE SCHOOLS WE NEED

There is considerable understanding of the variables that seem to characterize schools and classrooms in which students experience the most inequitable conditions. These settings share many common interdependent attributes:

- Belief in intelligence as a fixed, predetermined commodity;
- Notion of student diversity as a difficulty to be overcome;
- Grouping students homogenously (i.e., tracking and fixed ability grouping);
- A heavy dose of teacher-directed instruction;
- Reliance on paper and pencil; traditional forms of assessment over other more authentic means of assessment;
- Emphasis on content knowledge acquisition;
- Use of punitive approaches to discipline;
- Reliance on textbooks as a primary curriculum source;
- Impersonal school and classroom cultures;
- Pullout remediation for special needs learners;
- Competitive norms and related practices;
- Teacher isolation; and
- Eurocentric, fragmented curriculum. (Garcia & Pearson, 1994; Newman & Wehlage, 1995; Noguera, 2000; Sizer, 1996; Wheelock, 1998)

Schools with the above attributes fail to become safe, inviting, and just educational places for all our young people. Rather, they are intellectually dry and emotionally empty places, which further discourage the discouraged and even dull the compliant.

Sociologists have long argued that schools mirror the social inequities in society, and thus actually increase the gap between students who enter school with advantages and those who enter with less advantages. Indeed, our middle grades schools must aspire to create the kind of equity we hope for and not mirror the kind of inequity we are fighting to correct. If we are to have a quality middle school experience for every child in America, what must be done? What do we know about the nature of equitable middle grades schools and classrooms?

ELIMINATING STUDENT DISENGAGEMENT:
A NEW PEDAGOGY

Disengagement from learning is the key to our most dramatic school inequities. We leave students behind in America's middle schools because we fail to provide meaningful, relevant and engaging learning experiences for all of our students. Many middle school students describe schoolwork as mediocre and boring. Only one in four middle school students report being excited about something they are learning in school (Farkus & Johnson, 1997; Lounsbury & Clark, 1990). O'Loughlin (1995) observed that 95% of the time, students participate in passive learning environments where student voice is absent, and where "transmission of information" teaching dominates. This is the very kind of teaching we know places the heaviest burden on our disenfranchised or struggling students.

Students from supportive home cultures that apply themselves to schoolwork will often confess they do so not because what they are learning is meaningful, relevant or useful to them, but rather because they have the support needed to tolerate the school game (Clinchy, 1997). Sadly, many of these students whose grades reflect success, come to value completing work in compliance with regulations over the quality of the work itself (Haberman, 1997). Thus, even for our advantaged students, potential to grow in profoundly intellectual ways is compromised by the curriculum and instruction most encounter.

As Michael Fullan concludes:

> Only when schooling operates in a way that connect students relationally in a relevant, engaging and worthwhile experience that substantial learning can occur. That only a small proportion of students are so engaged is a measure of the seriousness of the problem. (Fullan, 2001, p. 152)

Middle school pedagogy must be transformed in substantive ways if we are to achieve the equity dream. First and foremost, our models of teaching and learning must guarantee that students have the right to be who they are (McDaniel, Necochea, Rios, Stowell, & Kritzer, 2001). Such a middle school would place students and their diverse development, language, race, disabilities, and culture at the center of all educational planning. Students bring to school unique cognitive maps they must use to make sense of the world and what they encounter in school. They have no choice in this, considering culture, class, and language shape cognition. Hence, we have never had the right, nor can we afford to ask learners to unlearn their cognitive maps in order to succeed in school. Middle school classrooms must structure learning in ways that allow for many cognitive styles and for cultural congruence in what and how students learn (Huber & Pewewardy, 1990; Neito, 1992).

This perspective on social equity implies that different ways of knowing are not deficits or difficulties to be overcome, but assets to be engaged in the way that schools design learning. Traditional notions of intelligence would have to be abandoned and replaced with a notion of intelligence as an expandable and flexible attribute. In socially equitable middle grades schools, "smart" would no longer be used to describe a student's innate condition. Instead, it would be an attribute used to describe learning behaviors that are taught, developed and nurtured. This shift in beliefs is enormously important in altering what students ultimately have the chance to learn.

In a study of student motivation, Henderson and Dweck (1990) found that what students believe about intelligence shapes their motivation to learn. Students who see intelligence as inborn associate their difficulty completing challenging tasks with the lack of innate ability. Those who view intelligence as flexible and expandable were more likely to tie success or failure to their own efforts. Young adolescents' self-limiting beliefs are linked closely with the beliefs others hold about them. Consequently, if adults in the middle school view intelligence as fixed and innate rather than expandable and developed, not only will they reinforce students self-limiting beliefs, they will not hold the highest level of expectation for all of their students nor will they teach in ways that elevate capacity; make young people smart. Unfortunately, a considerable percentage of the middle school teaching community covet tacit assumptions about intelligence, which reduce their expectations for certain kinds of students (Goodwin, 2000). Only when teachers can embrace a belief in their capacity to make learning happen for every child, can middle school classrooms become equitable places for all learners.

Currently, most middle school classrooms are suited to serve students with strengths in the two most celebrated of the intelligences, linguistic and mathematical, (Gardner, 1993), the ability to sit still for six hours a day, and, who generally come from white, English-speaking, two-parent families (Gay, 1994). Students who fall outside the lines of these conventional boundaries are at far greater risk of school failure. They struggle to gain ground in classrooms characterized by perspectives and practices associated with what is referred to as "the pedagogy of poverty"; the kind of teaching which relies heavily on giving information, textbook content, worksheets, paper and pencil tests, seatwork, and homework (Haberman, 1991).

Authentic pedagogy demands that instruction and assessment shift from such narrow and limiting conceptions of students and learning to models of curriculum, instruction, and assessment that reflect an image of students as capable of significant learning. This kind of pedagogy helps students develop thinking skills for deeper understanding: posing questions, gathering information, reasoning, synthesizing different perspectives, communicating conclusions, and applying new learning, It engages students as contributing, socially conscious, democratic citizens, and, consequently, that insures our students can learn what they need to improve our world (Beane, 1997; Wheelock, 1998). Such pedagogy, as described here, was identified in research as responsible for marked student improvement across diverse student populations (Newman & Wehlage, 1995).

Moreover, assessment ought to be conceptualized to address its fundamental purpose: enhanced understanding, self-reflection, and further learning progress, rather than its more commonly applied purpose of comparing students in ways that more often reflect a student's home support and resources rather than their growth on important academic standards. Standardized testing and other traditional means of assessment have a long history of sorting and selecting certain students to receive inferior educational experiences, especially girls, students of poverty, and members of visible racial and ethnic groups (Garcia & Pearson, 1994), yet they prevail in most middle schools. If we honor diversity, it is unacceptable to continue to use singular measures of assessment that are inequitable.

While pedagogy matters in our drive to create equitable learning opportunities, the nature of the curriculum is fundamental to an equitable classroom. As Sonia Neito (1992) explains,

> Children who are not in the dominant group have a hard time finding themselves or their communities in the books they read or the curriculum to which they are exposed." (p. 76)

When content does not reflect all children's lives or in fact distorts it, young adolescents cannot connect school with their known world. Liberating pedagogy alone is not sufficient. Studying distorted views of Native Americans in cooperative learning groups would not constitute a socially equitable setting for young adolescents. An equitable middle school classroom must allow every child meaningful entry points into the learning process.

Entry points invariably entertain the curriculum issue, and with the current national focus on accountability via tested content, the curriculum question is even more pressing. The standards movement has articulated the 'what' of curriculum in such a way as to potentially endanger democratic schooling in many states. How is it possible to design a curriculum with entry points for all of our children if they are not all in that curriculum? The once defined mainstream in the United States is no longer the mainstream of today. Since 1993, when James Beane wrote the seminal middle school curriculum text, *From rhetoric to reality: A middle school curriculum*, the middle school community has been invited to rethink the curriculum. Beane (2003) states that the middle school curriculum should emphasize a general education for all young adolescents. Consequently, what is offered in the school program would be intended for all students and all students would be involved in it. He goes on to say that young adolescents are not ready, developmentally, to make decisions about their futures, even though they may express early preferences or inclinations.

A new pedagogy for our next generation of middle schools will emerge from altered beliefs about the nature of our young people, altered beliefs about the nature of intelligence, and learning, and altered views about the role of schooling in the lives of all Americans. The synthesis of National Curriculum Standards provided in *Best Practice* (1993) found below, offers a remarkably comprehensive list of recommendations on which to build an equitable middle school program of curriculum and instruction.

More

- More emphasis on active, hands-on learning;
- More acceptance of the noise and movement which accompanies students actively doing, talking, and collaborating;
- More reading of whole, original, real books and nonfiction materials;
- More deep study of a smaller number of carefully chosen topics;
- More emphasis on higher-order thinking; learning each content field's key concepts, principles, and ways of knowing;
- More responsibility and choice for students; e.g., picking their own books, writing topics, and team partners; setting goals, keeping classroom records, etc.;
- Honoring and modeling of the principles of democracy in school;
- More attention to the affective needs and the varying cognitive styles of individual students;
- More co-operative, collaborative activity; more sense of the classroom as an interdependent community;
- More heterogeneous classes where individual needs are met through inherently individualized activities rather than segregation of bodies;
- More delivery of special help to students in regular classrooms;
- More team-teaching by teachers;
- More trust in teachers' descriptive evaluation of student growth, including qualitative/anecdotal observations.

Less

- Less presentational, whole-class, teacher-directed instruction, e.g., lecturing;
- Less student passivity: sitting, listening, receiving, and absorbing information;
- Less prizing and rewarding of silence in the classroom;
- Less classroom time devoted to fill-in-the-blank worksheets, dittos, workbooks, and other "seatwork";
- Less student time spent reading textbooks and basal readers;
- Less attempts by teachers to thinly "cover" large amounts of material in every subject area;
- Less rote memorization of facts and details;
- Less stress on competition and grades;

- Less tracking or leveling students into "ability groups";
- Less use of pullout special programs which erode the sense of class-room community and stigmatize some students;
- Less use of and reliance on standardized tests. (Zemelamn, Daniels, & Hyde, 1993, p. 11)

INCLUSIVE, COLLABORATIVE CULTURES

Student's motivation to achieve in school depends on the school's capacity to insure that students feel they can belong in school and will benefit from it (Steele, 1997). It also depends upon the school's ability to create a sense of safety in the place of learning. For many students the norms of class-room life are unsafe in numerous ways. Instructional norms celebrate quick wit, fast answers and on the spot knowledge. Such norms celebrate a very limited vision of intellectual activity and exacerbate inequities among students whose learning styles and cultural orientations differ. Equitable classrooms have altered norms that emphasize steady effort and improve-ment over quick wit and speed, with attention to thinking, understanding, redoing work, polishing products and taking risks. Classroom norms that support success for all allow students to learn free of fear and anxiety from punitive outcomes (Caine & Caine, 1997). Instead, they encounter norms that encourage accountability to the group, the class, themselves, the com-munity, and to quality itself. In one highly equitable middle school setting where two teachers and forty-five students work in an integrated learning community, and where letter grades have been abandoned and replaced with authentic assessment: student self-assessment: portfolios, and, student-led parent conferences, an observing visitor asked a student to explain why every student in that team seemed to be working with such collaborative commitment to quality. One 8th grade student responded, "It may seem hard to believe this but we don't want to let each other down."

For a learning setting of this sort to take shape, middle schools will have to become deeply caring and collaborative cultures in which every child feels known, understood, included and valued. The single greatest com-plaint of students in middle and high schools is, "'They don't care' . . . they feel alienated from their school work, separated from adults who try to teach them, and adrift in a world perceived as baffling and hostile" (Nod-dings, 1992, p. 2). Students express concern about their peer relationships, noting that they too are the source of considerable stress. In middle schools where the culture and structure divide students in ways that accen-tuate class, gender and race differences, they contribute to the isolation of certain groups of students, the potential escalation of hostility and bully-ing, and the failure to provide students with the equal chance to be a welcomed member of the group. Dubois and Hirsch (1990) note that cross race friendships diminish in the middle school years, yet in middle schools that cultivate compassion and caring across diverse groups, inclusive relationships are more likely. Unequivocally, the quality of relationships in middle schools impact equitable student learning and success.

To the extent that accountability systems in middle schools become exclusively focused on cognitive achievement, schools will be further handicapped in their efforts to create the kind of trusting relationships needed to make our young people feel safe. It is unjust and disrespectful to tell our young people that we are trustworthy and then create competitive, fear-based schools. Moreover, such school cultures will sustain the gap between students who are doing well and those who are not. Disengaged students who are especially vulnerable need to lean heavily on affiliations with teachers and peers in order to succeed. When they encounter school environments that are hostile, competitive cultures, they retreat. This is true, however, of all young adolescents and many apparently successful students describe school conditions that undermine their sense of safety and well being in school (Gay, 1994; Pipher, 1996).

The current reform agenda for most middle schools, swayed by high-stakes testing, the standards movement, and accountability, is not one which supports caring, collaborative school cultures. In fact, these pressures wreak havoc with educators' commitment and, even capacity, to create to a people-centered, caring, democratic, collaborative schools and classrooms. Punitive, threatening policies not only fail to motivate students, they contribute to disengaging students from teachers and even peers with whom they are forced to compete (Wehlage & Rutter, 1986). Likewise, teachers under pressure of high-stakes rewards and sanctions may inadvertently sabotage the responsive relationships needed for meaningful learning (Jones & Whitford, 1997). When relationships are devalued, middle schools and classrooms become impersonal factories lacking the trust and intimacy needed to carry out powerful learning. Equitable middle schools must be places in which everyone learns together in supportive and caring relationships. As Jeannie Oakes notes, "Educative environments are guided by a vision of civic virtue" (Oakes, Quartz, Regan, & Lipton, 2000).

To create safe havens for learning has no doubt been a cornerstone goal of the middle school concept (Knowles & Brown, 2000). Exclusion is devastating for young adolescents. Collaborative classroom cultures, however, require attention to far more than a collection of new methods. Equity in classroom life depends upon students having adult help in learning the value of diversity in the human community. Differences are not to be invisible; rather students need our help in order to learn how to understand and respect and value those unlike themselves. This means that all students, through democratic means, in any given classroom, will have to play an active part in shaping the life of that room. It is nearly impossible to talk students into an affect of respect. Unless all students are heard and taken seriously, truly caring cultures will remain a lofty ideal. Students must see that their ideas, questions and concerns are valuable and worthy of use. Not only is this an act of supreme respect, but also it invites students to consider themselves as scholars, problem-solvers, and valued members of the community.

The implication here is that fair and equitable classrooms are vital learning communities where:

- Students are known well as individuals and members of the community;
- Students learn how to know and respect one another;
- Students have power, choice and voice in classroom life; and
- Risk taking is encouraged and supported.

For many middle schools that have created elaborate advisory programs intended to enhance the level of caring in the school, the results have been disappointing (Galassi, Gulledge, & Cox, 1998). This is often so because an advisory program's affective goals run counter to the essence of that school's culture. As one middle school student queried during a focus group I conducted, "Do they really want us to like each other and work together or not?"

There is abundant evidence that students suffer in middle schools that allow interpersonal hostilities to exist. If students face encounters with prejudice, from teachers or peers, they are increasingly vulnerable to emotional stress and school failure (Resnick et al., 1997). These hostile encounters are more likely to occur in middle schools that have sorted and separated students into academic subgroups that inadvertently develop notions about themselves as members of that school. It is difficult to create cliques and to dispel them simultaneously. Interdisciplinary teams that attempt to become caring communities find this goal blocked because the internal academic tracking disallows these subgroups to interact in ways that support an equitable team community culture. Moreover, with attention so tightly fixed on high-stakes achievement, many teams dare not devote any class or team time to challenging these interpersonal barriers for fear of falling behind.

It is well-established knowledge that effective and equitable middle grades schools are distinguished by a synergy of interconnected structures, programs and practices that evoke higher levels of caring and connectedness (Strahn, Smith, McElrath, & Toole, 2001) Certainly, practices like looping, multi-age grouping, team organization, flexible block scheduling, advisory-type programs, open enrollment athletics, and detracking all advance the equity agenda. It is clear, for example, that team planning and teaching arrangements provide teachers with the opportunity to view students through the diverse perspectives of several colleagues. This can create the cognitive dissonance needed to shift teachers' thinking about student capacity and potential (Doda, 1984). The aggressive use of this opportunity or other recommended middle school structures is what ultimately yields results.

MIDDLE SCHOOLS FOR SOCIAL EQUITY

Building a culture that supports social equity demands that middle schools cultivate collegial professional communities committed to creating more compelling and equitable learning environments. Middle schools aspiring to reach all learners can no longer afford to sustain isolated or balkanized cultures. A faculty's capacity to effect student learning is linked to its capacity to behave as a collective, collaborative learning community (Senge, 1994). This means that teachers in any middle school would acknowledge and accept their individual and collective responsibility to make learning happen for every child, and believe that every child can develop the knowledge and skills needed to be successful.

Cultivating this kind of culture is challenging as teachers have long labored in a professional culture that supports native ingenuity as the key to great teaching. Middle schools must redefine teaching as a collaborative profession and plan for teacher learning in ways that reflect this. Unless school cultures are dramatically collaborative, where teachers envision themselves as agents of learning and social justice, the equity agenda will be compromised. Many middle schools have large signs boasting their commitment to "success for all," yet it is often precisely these schools that violate their ambitious agenda in subtle ways. Take for example middle schools that tend to have disproportionate number of minorities in their In School Suspension programs, or schools that have awards allocated and dispersed to the same small group of students on a repeat basis. Consider the many schools that still continue to employ high-school-like athletic cut policies, which can endanger students' identity development and sense of inclusion (McEwin & Dickinson, 1996). Likewise, consider the inordinate number of middle schools that still place their least experienced teachers with their most needy students in classes commissioned for remediation.

Reculturing middle grades schools is a collective enterprise involving all educators, organizations, associations and agencies that work on behalf of middle grades education. As Oakes and others observed in their study of sixteen *Turning Points* schools:

As at most of the 16 schools we studied, many faculty members were solidly committed to the principles of racial equality and fairness, and they struggled with discrimination, inequality and injustice.... there were also schools that showed concern for gender fairness, and they questioned and challenged many of the commonly accepted "limits" that schools place on special education students. They tried to change the curricula and structure to expand access, provide extra support when needed, and improve relations among diverse groups of children. (Oakes et al., 2000, p. 571–572)

Although the Turning Points reform approach was in many ways a "best case" example, it provided little support for the most difficult reform challenges the schools confronted.... As is usually the case, little attention was paid to the profound cultural and political challenges that lay at the heart of reform. (p. 574)

In these middle schools, faculty engaged in discussing the often "undiscussables," struggling with fundamental moral issues at the heart of middle school reform. Reculturing, however, not only includes the internal workings of middle schools, but the internal workings of those seeking to support them. Never will America's middle school reform agenda be free from the venerable tensions in our society; between the concern for the common good and concern for the individual liberties and private interests of its citizens. This will always play out in schools. The challenge remains however, for middle grades schools to address the following questions:

- How can middle schools become places of stimulating learning for every child?
- How can middle schools actively support and enhance social justice?
- How can middle schools become places that are inclusive and socially just?
- How can middle schools become places of genuine collaboration and participation?
- How can middle schools educate all children equally well with the demands of those who wish for competitive advantage?
- How can middle schools educate communities and families about the nature of truly equitable middle schooling?

In the early years of middle school reform, the equity agenda focused almost exclusively on eliminating "star systems" which celebrated or recognized a narrow group of young people. The junior high school was notorious for competitive norms that sorted and selected students for many reasons. The modern middle school has made strides toward equity. Many middle schools have altered practices in profound ways to rid themselves of those remnants (Wheelock, 1992). What matters most, however, in our equity reform work ahead, is that we strive to become a socially conscious educational community which asserts that social equity is indeed one of our fundamental roles in our students' lives, in our schools, and in our society.

REFERENCES

Annie E. Casey Foundation. (1998). When teens have sex: Issues and trends-Kids COUNT special report. Baltimore, MD: Author.

Beane, J. (1993). *A middle school curriculum: From rhetoric to reality* (2nd ed.). Columbus, OH: National Middle School Association.

Beane, J. (1997). *Curriculum integration: Designing the core of democratic education.* New York: Teachers College Press.

Beane, J. (2001). Introduction: Reform and reinvention. In Dickinson, T. (Ed.). *Reinventing the middle school.* (p. xix). RoutledgeFalmer.

Beane, J. (in press). Creating quality in the middle school curriculum. In S.C. Thompson (Ed.), *Middle level education issues for policy makers.* Greenwich, CT: Information Age Publishing.

Braddock, J.H. II, & Slavin, R.E. (1992, September). *Why ability grouping must end: Achieving excellence and equity in American education.* Center for Research on Effective Schooling for Disadvantaged. Johns Hopkins University. Paper presented at the Common Destiny Conference, Washington, DC.

Caine, R.N., & Caine, G. (1997). *Education on the edge of possibility.* Alexandria, VA: Association for Supervision of Curriculum Development.

Carnegie Council on Adolescent Development. (1989). *Turning points: Preparing America's youth for the 21st century.* The Report of the Task Force on Education of Young Adolescents. New York: Carnegie Corporation of New York.

Clinchy, B.M. (1997). The standardization of the student. In E. Clinchy (Ed.). *Transforming public education: A new course for America's future.* New York: Teachers College Press.

Corbett, D., & Wilson, B. (1997). *Urban students' perspectives on middle school: The sixth grade year in five Philadelphia middle schools.* Philadelphia Education Fund.

Dickinson, T.S. (2001). Reinventing the middle school: A proposal to counter arrested development. In T.S. Dickinson (Ed.). *Reinventing the middle school* (pp. 3–20). New York: RoutedgeFalmer.

Doda, N.M. (1984). *Teachers' perspectives and practices in two organizationally different middle schools.* Unpublished doctoral dissertation, University of Florida, Gainesville.

Donahue, P.L., Voekl, K.E., Campbel, J.R., & Mazzeo, J. (1997). *The NEAP reading report card for the nation and the states* (NCES 1999-500). Washington, DC: U.S. Department of Education, Office of Education Research and Improvement. National Center for Education Statistics.

Dubois, D.L., & Hirsch, B.J. (1990). School of neighborhood friendships of Blacks and Whites in early adolescence. *Child Development, 61,* 524–536.

Dweck, D., Kamis, M., & Wood, D. (1995, April). Praise, criticism and motivational vulnerability. Symposium conducted on the biannual meeting of the Society for Research in Child Development, Washington, DC.

Einbender, L., & Wood, D. (1995). *An authentic journey: Teachers' emergent understanding about authentic assessment and practice.* New York: National Center for Restructuring Education, Schools and Teaching.

Farkus, S., & Johnson, J. (1997). *Kids these days: What Americans really think about the next generation.* New York: Public Agenda.

Felner, R.D., Jackson, A.W., Kasak, D., Mulhall, P., Brand, S., & Flowers, N. (1997). The impact of school reform for the middle years: Longitudinal study of a network engaged in *Turning Points*-based comprehensive school transformation. *Phi Delta Kappan, 78*(7), 528–550.

Fullan, M. (2001). *The new meaning of educational change.* New York: Teachers College Press.

Gallassi, J.P., Gulledge, S.A., & Cox, N.D. (1998). Middle school advisories: Retrospect and prospect. *Review of Educational Research. 67,* 301–338. Washington, DC: AERA.

Garcia, G.E., & Pearson, P.D. (1994). Assessment and diversity. In L. Darling-Hammond (Ed.). *Review of Educational Research, 20,* 337–392. Washington, DC: AERA.

Gardner, H. (1993). *Frames of mind: The theory of multiple intelligences.* New York: Basic Books.

Gay, G. (1994a). *At the essence of learning: Multicultural education.* West Lafayette, IN: Kappa Delta Pi.

Gay, G. (1994b). Coming of age ethnically: Teaching young adolescents of color. *Theory into practice, 33,* 149–155.

Goodlad, J. (1984). *A place called school* New York: McGraw Hill.

Goodwin, A.L. (2000). Honoring ways of knowing. *WEEA Digest,* March 2000, 1–9. Boston: Women's Educational Equity Act Resource Center.

Haberman, M. (1991). The pedagogy of poverty versus good teaching. *Phi Delta Kappan, 72*(4), 290–294.

Haberman, M. (1997). Unemployment training: The ideology of nonwork learned in urban schools. *Phi Delta Kappan, 78*(7), 499–503.

Henderson, V., & Dweck, C. (1990). Motivation and achievement. In S.S. Feldman & G.R. Elliott (Eds.). *At the threshold: The developing adolescent.* Cambridge, MA: Harvard University Press.

Huber, T., & Pewewardy, C. (1990). *Maximizing learning for all students: A review of literature on learning modalities, cognitive styles, and approaches to meeting the needs of diverse learners.* (ERIC Document Reproduction Service No. ED 346082)

Jackson, A.W., & Davis, G.A. (2000). *Turning points 2000: Educating adolescents in the 21st century.* New York: Teachers College Press.

Jones, K., & Whitford, B.L. (1997). Kentucky's conflicting reform principles: High stakes School accountability and student performance. *Phi Delta Kappan, 79*(4), 276–287.

Kohl, H. (1992). I won't learn from you! Thoughts on the role of assent in learning. *Rethinking schools, 7*(1), 16–17.

Kohn, A. (1986). *No contest: The case against competition: Why we lose in our race to win.* Boston: Houghton Mifflin.

Knowles, T., & Brown D.F. (2000). *What every middle school teacher should know.* Portsmouth, NH and Westerville, OH: Heinemann and National Middle School Association.

Ladson-Billings, G. (1994). *Dreamkeepers: Successful teachers of African American children*. San Francisco: Jossey-Bass.

Lipman, R. (1998). *Race, class and power in school restructuring*. Albany: State University of New York Press.

Lounsbury, J., & Clark, D. (1990). *Inside grade eight: From apathy to excitement*. Reston, VA: National Association of Secondary School Principals.

Loveless, T. (1999). *The tracking wars: State reform meets school policy*. Washington, DC: The Brooking Institution.

McDaniel, J.E., Necochea, J., Rios, F.A., Stowell, L.P., & Kritzer, C. (2001). The arc of equity in reinvented middle schools. In T. Dickinson (Ed.). *Reinventing the middle school* (pp. 56–78). New York: RoutledgeFalmer.

McDonnell, L.M., Burnstein, L., Ormeth, T., Catterall, J., & Moody, D. (1990). *Discovering what schools really teach: Designing improved coursework indicators*. Report for the Office of Educational Research and Improvement. US Department of Education, June 1990.

McEwin, C.K., & Dickinson, T.S. (1996). Placing young adolescents at risk in interscholastic sports programs. *Clearing House, 69*(4), 217–221.

Meier, D. (1995). *The power of their ideas: Lessons for America from a small school in Harlem*. Boston: Beacon Press.

National Center for Educational Statistics, National Educational Longitudinal Survey of 1988 (NELS:88), (NCES no. 91-460), Washington, DC: Office of Educational Research and Improvement, April 1999.

National Middle School Association. (1995). *This we believe: Developmentally responsive middle level schools*. Columbus, OH: Author.

National Middle School Association. (2001). *This we believe-and now we must act*. Westerville, OH: Author.

Neito, S. (1992). *Affirming diversity: The sociopolitical context of multicultural education*. White Plains, NY: Longman.

Newman, F.M., & Wehlage, G.G. (1995). *Successful school restructuring: A report to the public and educators by the Center on organization and restructuring of schools*. Madison, WI: Board of Regents of the University of Wisconsin System.

Noddings, N. (1992). *The challenge to care in schools*. New York: Teachers College Press.

Noguera, P. (2000). When race and class are not an excuse. In M. Klonsky & W. Ayers (Eds.), *A simple justice*. New York: Teachers College Press.

Oakes, J. (1990). *Multiplying inequalities: The effects of race, social class, and tracking on opportunities to learn*. Mathematics and Science Education, 1990. Report #R-3928-NSF. Santa Monica, CA: Rand.

Oakes, J., Quartz, K.H., Regan, S., & Lipton, M. (2000). Civic virtue and the reform mill: The struggle of schools that are as good as they are efficient. *Education Week, 19*(24), 571–572.

Oakes, J., Quartz, K.H., Ryan, S., & Lipton, M. (2000). *Becoming good American schools: The struggle for civic virtue in education reform*. San Francisco: Jossey-Bass.

O'Loughlin, M. (1995). Daring the imagination: Unlocking voices of dissent and possibility in teaching. *Theory into practice. 34*(2), 107–115.

Pipher, M. 1996). *The Shelton of each other: Rebuilding out families*. New York: G. P. Putnam.

Quintana, S. M. (1998). Children's developmental understanding of ethnicity and race. *Applied and Preventive Psychology, 7,* 27–45.

Reese, C.M., Miller, K.E., Mazzeo, J., & Dossey, J.A. (1997). *NAEP 1996 Mathematics report card for the nation and the states.* Washington, DC: U.S. Department of Education, Office of Educational Research and Improvement, National Center for Education Statistics.

Senge, P.M., Kleiner, A., Roberts, C., Ross, B.R., & Smith, B.J. (1994). *The fifth discipline fieldbook: Strategies and tools for building a learning organization.* New York: Doubleday.

Singham, M. (1998). The canary in the mine: The achievement gap between black and white students. *Phi Delta Kappan, 80*(1), 8–15.

Sizer, T.R. (1996). *Horace's hope: What works for the American high school.* Boston: Houghton-Mifflin.

Steele, C.M. (1997). A threat in the air: How stereotypes shape intellectual identify and performance. *American Psychologist, 52*(6), 8–15.

Strahan, D., Smith, T.W., McElrath, M., & Toole, C.M. (2001). Connecting caring and action: Teachers who create learning communities in their classrooms. In T.S. Dickinson (Ed.), *Reinventing the middle school.* New York:RoutledgeFalmer.

Wehlage, G., & Rutter, R. (1986). Dropping out: How much do schools contribute to the problem? *Teachers College Record, 87*(3).

Wheelock, A. (1992). *Crossing the tracks: How "untracking" can save America's schools.* New York: New Press.

Wheelock, A. (1998). *Safe to be smart: Building a culture for standards-based reform in the middle grades.* Columbus, OH: National Middle School Association.

Zemelman, S., Daniels, H., & Hyde, A. (1993). *Best practice: New standards for teaching and learning in America's schools.* Portmouth, NH: Heinemann.

CHAPTER 6

THE ROLE
OF ACCOUNTABILITY
IN MIDDLE LEVEL SCHOOLS

Dan French

INTRODUCTION

Three years ago, my youngest daughter, at the time an eighth grade student, wrote an essay for her school about the Massachusetts Comprehensive Assessment Test (MCAS), our state's high stakes test. She wrote:

> The test is supposed to be helping to improve kids' education, yet it is taking away about two weeks of our learning. During one of those weeks, the seventh graders go out to different jobs to experience the working life; it is called City Sites. Because of the MCAS, we, the eighth graders, can't get to experience that. Last year it was so fun for me to go out and work. It wasn't just a week of fun, though. I learned a lot. There are many other valuable activities I feel would be taken out of the curriculum if the teachers have to follow the test. These units and activities are the ones that mean the most; they are the ones that teach the life lessons. (French, unpublished essay, 2000)

This is one of the many reasons why Scott Thompson, assistant director of the Panasonic Foundation, wrote that the high stakes testing movement

Reforming Middle Level Education: Considerations for Policymakers, pages 85–107
Copyright © 2004 by Information Age Publishing
All rights of reproduction in any form reserved.

is the "evil twin of the standards-based movement, becoming its own worst enemy" (2001, pp. 358–362).

Thompson goes on to quote Sandra Feldman, president of the American Federation of Teachers, who observed, "When tests are allowed to become the be-all and end-all, they deform, not reform, education" (as cited in Thompson, 2001, p. 359).

Under the mantel of accountability, state and federal policies are increasingly mandating testing and more testing in uniform and limited ways. This high stakes standardized testing movement ignores the fundamental roots and meaning of "accountability," creating a punitive educational environment that effectively curtails educational innovation.

What is accountability? What is the impact of the high stakes, standardized testing movement on the middle grades? What local, state, and federal policies best promote true accountability for students, schools, and districts at the middle level?

THE REAL MEANING OF ACCOUNTABILITY

It is helpful to think about accountability in public schools, and in particular, the middle grades, by revisiting the definition of the word accountability. According to the Merriam-Webster Online Dictionary (2003), accountability means, "the quality or state of being accountable; *especially:* an obligation or willingness to accept responsibility or to account for one's actions." Accountable means, "subject to giving an account: answerable, and capable of being accounted for: explainable." And finally, account means, "a statement explaining one's conduct," or "a statement or exposition of reasons, causes, or motives."

Essentially, accountability, then, means an obligation and willingness to accept responsibility to explain and be answerable to one's actions, including the reasons, causes, and motives. Applied to the education arena, this definition implies distributing responsibility for student outcomes more equitably. Not only should we be measuring the outcomes of student learning in multiple ways, we should also be closely examining and assessing teacher, school, and district practices—practices which we know make a profound difference in how much students are engaged in learning, in the quality of what students learn, and, ultimately, on student performance. True accountability calls for a strong emphasis on the process of educating students, knowing that it is the quality of this process that will be the strongest determinant of what students learn and how they demonstrate their learning.

For students, this definition of accountability means creating assessment opportunities in which students must demonstrate their knowledge, skills, and understanding, and be able to explain the underlying principles and concepts of what they have learned, the process of their learning, and its application to the real world. This form of assessment must be rooted in and based upon students' curriculum experiences and provide opportunities for students to demonstrate, in multiple ways, what they have learned and its application.

This more comprehensive notion of accountability calls for teachers, schools, and districts to be intensely reflective of their practices, and their impact on student learning. Schools and faculties should be engaged in a continuous cycle of analysis, diagnosis, research, and improvement. The most successful schools—those able to improve and sustain student learning over time—are those in which teachers are most reflective about their craft and the art of teaching. In fact, one of Glickman's key findings is that teachers in the most successful schools are less satisfied with their instructional practice than teachers in less successful schools (Glickman, 1993). This finding indicates a continuous process of seeking to refine and improve one's teaching. Glickman (1993) has also found that faculty in successful schools are information consumers and producers, and engaged in collaborative practices and shared governance. Such a professional culture requires teachers to be able to justify and validate why they choose certain practices and how these choices shape each and every student's engagement in learning, leading to higher student performance in its multiplicity of forms.

This definition of accountability more equitably distributes the responsibility for student performance, instead of laying it solely at the feet of students. This definition also suggests that we will only reach the universal goal of successfully educating all students by creating adult cultures of reflection and inquiry at the state, district, and school levels, and holding those cultures responsible for explaining their educational practices and justifying how they enable all students to learn in meaningful ways. According to Richard Elmore, this definition of accountability is "internal accountability" where one is able to articulate and put into practice "a coherent, explicit set of norms and expectations about what a good school looks like" (2002, p. 37).

THE CURRENT STATE OF AFFAIRS: A MISUSE (ABUSE) OF ACCOUNTABILITY

Given this definition of accountability, how do our current state and national policies stack up? Do our accountability policies embrace this broad concept of a willingness and obligation to accept responsibility for and explain one's actions to peers, students, and communities? Do they nurture a culture of reflection and inquiry among adults at the classroom, school, and district level? Do they place the greatest responsibility for student achievement upon the adults' practices and policies, rather than holding students solely responsible?

The federal *No Child Left Behind Act of 2001 (NCLB)* has unleashed an unprecedented federal mandate of testing and more testing as the answer to educational accountability. As summarized by Elmore (2002), NCLB requires of all states a single test-based accountability system, annual testing at every grade level, including disaggregating students' test scores by race and income status, setting a single definition of adequate yearly progress (AYP) by which schools must increase their test scores, and establishing a single target date by which all students must exceed a state-defined proficiency level. Hovering over this entire testing system is a host of sanctions for students, schools, and districts that do not meet prescribed targets and benchmarks and rewards for those that do. As Elmore (2002) goes on to say, the federal government has interpreted accountability to mean "testing alone."

The federal mandate of NCLB has greatly influenced state accountability models. Massachusetts has followed a path that is common and familiar for many states. The 1993 Education Reform Act called for a broad assessment model, including employing "a variety of assessment instruments. . . . As much as is practical . . . such instruments shall include consideration of work samples, projects, and portfolios, and shall facilitate authentic and direct gauges of student performance. . . . The assessment instruments shall be designed to avoid gender, cultural, ethnic, or racial stereotypes and shall recognize sensitivity to different learning styles and impediments to learning" (1993, pp. 21–22).

However, in response to conservative forces within the state and the advent of NCLB, this comprehensive definition of accountability has been replaced by one single, paper and pencil, on-demand high stakes test. The test determines, as is true in an increasing number of states, whether or not a student graduates from high school, a critical factor in future education and employment. In many states, the results of these tests also determine whether a student is promoted from grade to grade, ignoring the avalanche of research confirming that grade retention retards academic achievement and is one of the most significant factors leading students to drop out of school (Smith & Shepard, 1989).

This type of external accountability has not been effective in improving the learning environment in schools for all students. For a host of reasons, "external accountability alone does not guarantee high performance if schools lack the internal capacity—that is, the requisite human, technical, and social resources—to improve" (Rallis & MacMullen, 2000, p. 769). As explained by Elmore, "Low-performing schools aren't coherent enough to respond to external demands for accountability" (2002, p. 37). Quite simply, state-administered high stakes, on-demand tests, in which students are punished if they do not pass, often with lifelong consequences, do not create the adult culture of reflection and inquiry that is necessary to fundamentally improve education for all students. NCLB and accompanying state high stakes testing initiatives have misinterpreted, misused, and even abused, the term "accountability" to focus solely on measuring a very narrow range of student output through a single test.

NO ONE MEASURE CAN ADEQUATELY ASSESS A STUDENT'S KNOWLEDGE

The late United States Senator Paul Wellstone related his own story about being affected by standardized tests. "I was one of those students who received consistently low scores on standardized tests, from my early school days to my graduate school entrance exams. Because of a learning disability, I did poorly on the tests and would have been held back. I was told repeatedly by some advisors that on the basis of my test scores I would fail academically. I'm convinced that I never would have received my doctorate [nor become a U.S. Senator], if I had taken the results of standardized tests too seriously or listened to those who put so much credence in what they measured" (Wellstone, 2000a, p. 17A).

Through his own personal story, Wellstone questions the validity of one test being able to accurately measure a student's abilities, proficiencies, skills, knowledge, and understanding. Indeed, many studies have documented the multiple factors other than a student's skills and knowledge that affect the outcome of test-taking. The amount of sleep, stress about test-taking, the time of day, one's emotional state, and distractions at the testing site have all been found to have significant influence on how students fare on standardized tests (Sacks, 2000). In states with high stakes tests, up to 50 to 80% of test score changes could be related to these temporary factors (Kane & Staiger, 2001). It is for these reasons that one Stanford University researcher, David Rogoso, concluded that two students with similar achievement levels on other indicators are more likely than not to have significantly varying standardized test scores (as cited in Viadero, 1999, p. 3).

Standardized tests are also poor predictors of how well students can apply knowledge. Amrein and Berliner (2002), in comparing students' scores on high stakes tests in 18 states as compared to the same cohort of students' scores on other standardized tests (such as NAEP and SAT tests), found that there was little transfer of knowledge as a result of higher performance on a high stakes test. They concluded that, "While a state's high stakes test may show increased scores, there is little support in these data that such increases are anything but the result of test preparation and/or the exclusion of students from the testing process" (p. 2).

Even more important, despite the fact that high stakes tests play an often highly detrimental role in limiting a student's future life opportunities, standardized test scores are far from an accurate predictor of how students will do in later life. In a study by former Harvard and Princeton presidents Derek Bok and William Bowen, out of 700 African American freshmen students who would not have been accepted into their respective universities based solely on their test scores, most became successful professionals and civic leaders. The researchers concluded that test scores predict only a small percent of the variance in academic performance among Black students (Bok & Bowen, 2000). By giving too much power to the test, we risk losing a host of such leaders and professionals.

Finally, racial bias and racism continue to play a damaging role in the stagnant gap in achievement between White students and Black and Latino students. Largely due to "stereotype threats," African-American students have been found to perform significantly below their potential on tests in which they know they are being assessed on their intellectual performance. This phenomenon stems from the historically rooted and substantiated fear that tests created by the dominant culture will inevitably result in poor performances by students of color (Steele, 1999).

THE UNRELIABILITY OF HIGH STAKES TESTS

Virtually every state, where high stakes testing is used, has experienced significant errors that have had deleterious effects on students and schools. For example, a Massachusetts senior detected a second answer to a question on the state's high stakes test, resulting in 449 students who had failed and would not have graduated to immediately become eligible to graduate (Kurtz & Vaishnav, 2002). In the same school year, a Massachusetts history teacher found an error in one multiple choice question on the state's 8th grade standardized test which resulted in 666 students failing the test who would have otherwise passed. Many of those 666 students would have been retained in 8th grade (Vaishnav, 2002).

In 2000, 47,000 Minnesotan students were marked wrong on a test question, with almost 8,000 eighth through twelve grade students incorrectly receiving failing grades and 54 high school seniors denied diplomas; all because the testing company, NCS Pearson, made a scoring error on the test (Henriques & Steinberg, 2001). McGraw-Hill has admitted that it has made scoring errors in New York, Indiana, Nevada, Tennessee, South Carolina, and Wisconsin (Henriques & Steinberg, 2001). Recently, in Texas, after a 10th grade math test question was published in the *Houston Chronicle*, the paper received a wave of phone calls complaining that the question was worded incorrectly so that there could be no right answer. When the state education agency then gave credit to all students for the question, it resulted in an additional 4,640 students passing the Texas Assessment of Knowledge and Skills (TAKS) test (Gibbons, 2003).

THE UNTOLD STORY: PUSHOUTS AND DROPOUTS

While advocates tout that high stakes testing has led to increased student achievement across race and income, other studies have concluded that students "lost" from the testing pool—through grade retention, dropping out, or being excluded from taking the test because of having special education or bilingual status—create the appearance of an improving school, when it fact the opposite may very well be true (FairTest, 2001). In Texas, a recent audit of 16 middle and high schools within the Houston Public Schools found that of the 5,500 students who had been recorded as having left the system, over half were dropouts when they had not been recorded as such (Schemo, 2003). In one Houston high school with an entering freshman class of 1,000 students that dwindled to 300 students by their senior year, not one dropout was reported. A school administrator, now considered a whistle-blower by the district, speaks of the untold district pressure to push students out of school while keeping the reports of dropouts down. As Robert Kimball, an assistant high school principal, explains, "You need to understand the atmosphere in Houston. People are afraid. The superintendent has frequent meetings with principals. Before they go in, the principals are really, really scared. Panicky. They have to make their numbers" (Winerip, 2003, p. B7). Until now, Houston has been ballyhooed as the district from which Rod Paige, U.S. Secretary of Education, rose to prominence because of the increase in test scores on the state high stakes test. Consequently, Houston won a Broad Foundation award for improved student achievement. Unfortunately, this renown came at the expense of thousands of students, disproportionately low-income, Black, and Hispanic students, who left the district without successfully completing their education (Haney, 1999; McNeil, 2000; Winerip, 2003).

This data mirrors that of the entire state of Texas. The dropout rate in Texas has dramatically increased as has the percent of students being exempted from taking the Texas Assessment of Academic Skills (TAAS, the precursor to the new TAKS) because of special education and bilingual placement, while the college enrollment rate remains among the lowest in the nation. Black and Latino students are disproportionately represented in dropouts and TAAS exemptions (Haney, 1999; McNeil, 2000; Orfield &

Ward, 2000), and twice as many Black and Latino students failed TAAS as did White students (McNeil, 2000; Orfield & Ward, 2000).

The same holds true in Massachusetts since the advent of its high stakes test, the Massachusetts Comprehensive Assessment System (MCAS). "In some districts, especially high-need districts, the total number of students lost from the class combined with the number failing the MCAS after three rounds of testing actually equals or exceeds the number of students passing" (Wheelock, 2002, p. 1). Disturbingly, researchers found that the achievement gap between White students and African American and Latino students has been found to be significantly larger on the MCAS than it is for students' classroom math grades (Brennan, Kim, Wenz-Gross, & Siperstein, 2001). The percent of middle grades dropouts has significantly increased and these dropouts are disproportionately African-American and Latino. It is no coincidence that in the ten states with the lowest dropout rates, only one had a high stakes test; while in the ten states with the highest dropout rates, nine of them have a high stakes test (Clarke, Haney, & Madaus, 2000).

THE STIFLING IMPACT ON TEACHING AND LEARNING

In many states with high stakes testing programs, we have observed a movement away from the successful middle grades teaching and learning practices that prepare students for high school and beyond. High stakes testing pressures teachers to focus on curriculum coverage rather than depth and understanding, encourages teacher-centered instruction such as lectures and textbooks rather than more engaging teaching, and lessens student choice, resulting in an inevitable decrease in motivation to learn (Sacks, 2000). In a North Carolina study of teacher practices, more than 70% of teachers reported that "students were spending more time practicing for end-of-grade tests than in the past" (Jones, Jones, Hardin, Chapman, Yarbrough, & Davis, 1999, p. 201). Eighty percent of teachers reported that students were spending more than 20% of their class time practicing test-taking and 28% of teachers reported that students spent more than 60% of instructional time practicing for tests (Jones et al., 1999).

In Texas, students in schools with high percentages of students of color spend substantial amounts of class time learning test-taking strategies, including how to "bubble" in answers and participate in test prep pep rallies (McNeil, 2000). Texas reading teachers reported that, due to the pressure of raising test scores, they had students engaged in test-taking drills 8–10 hours per week; as a result only 27% of teachers felt that rising TAAS scores reflected increased learning and higher-quality teaching (Weisman, 2000).

Across the nation, science, social studies, and the arts are increasingly being left out of the curriculum because they are not tested (Herszenhorn, 2003; Jones et al., 1999; McNeil, 2000; Orfield & Ward, 2000). In Massachusetts, one teacher in an urban high school reported over an email listserve, "Today my principal told us: There are two kinds of questions on the MCAS, multiple choice and open-ended. Our students did poorly on both. So we just have two things to do: teach them to answer multiple choice questions and to answer open-ended questions. We should do both in class from now on, and our students will get used to them, and everything should be fine" (Baker, 1998).

HIGH STAKES TESTS ENCOURAGE A CULTURE OF BLAME

Ultimately, high stakes tests do not create the culture of reflection and analysis among adult educators that is called for in a true accountability system. A 2001 Public Agenda poll found that only 27% of teachers stated that "students did poorly on high stakes tests because schools failed to adequately prepare them, with the other 73% of teachers blaming the design of the test, students' lack of ability to do well, and other external reasons." The report goes on to state that "other Public Agenda research has shown that teachers routinely say that many students arrive in their classrooms with terrible deficits—particularly those from unstable, unsupportive, or impoverished homes." As well, 81% of teachers feel that parents' lack of holding their children accountable is a primary cause for their resulting behavior or academic performance (Public Agenda, 2001).

High stakes testing, then, is reinforcing a school culture of blaming students and their parents for students' and schools' low performance—a culture that is the result of high pressure, punitive sanctions, and public embarrassment. This culture of blame is the antithesis of a culture of reflection and inquiry. Considering the damaging impact and questionable reliability of high stakes testing, the National Forum to Accelerate Middle Grades Reform, reflecting the stance of most national education and testing associations, has adopted the following language on high stakes testing:

The National Forum believes in standards and assessments that lead to high expectations, foster high quality instruction, and support higher levels of learning for every student. At the same time, the National Forum believes that no single test should ever be the sole determinant of a young adolescent's academic future, whether it be promotion to the next grade, special placement, or transition from the middle grades to high school. (National Forum to Accelerate Middle Grades Reform, 2002)

IS THIS WHAT THE PUBLIC WANTS?

Given the overwhelming data that questions the efficacy of an external, high stakes testing approach to accountability, we should ask the question, "Is this what the public really wants?" Much recent evidence suggests not. A 2001 Public Agenda poll found that 75% of parents and 90% of teachers feel that "it is wrong to use the results of just one test to decide whether a student gets promoted or graduates" and more than 80% of both parents and teachers stated that schools should use teacher evaluations along with standardized tests to make these decisions. In the same survey, 83% of teachers worry that, as a result of high stakes testing, "teachers will end up teaching to the tests instead of making sure real learning takes place," while 82% felt that "schools today place far too much emphasis on standardized tests" (Public Agenda, 2001).

Similarly, in a series of focus groups that included students, parents, educators, policy makers, and community members, the Mid-Continent Research for Education and Learning found that participants "expressed widespread reservations about judging schools or students based upon a single measure." In particular, employers noted that "standardized tests bear little resemblance to what they expect of their employees in the real world" (Goodwin, 2003, p. 3). Participants worried that high stakes tests had the potential of causing districts and schools to ignore other issues "that appear to be at the heart of the public's concerns about their schools," including character, values, safety, and discipline (Goodwin, 2003, p. 4).

CONSTRUCTING A SYSTEM TO REFLECT THE TRUE MEANING OF ACCOUNTABILITY

Is it possible to create a public accountability system that has as its foundation an understanding that the quality of what and how we teach students makes the most profound differences in student engagement and achievement? Can we construct an accountability system that embraces and engenders in districts, schools, and teachers an obligation and willingness to explain their educational practices and how they contribute to student engagement and performance? How do we create an accountability system in which students must demonstrate their understandings in ways that require the student to explain what she learned, how she learned, and how her new knowledge can be applied to real life situations?

Such an accountability system would look quite different than the current high stakes testing movement. Rather than holding students solely accountable via a single high stakes test, such a system would build school and district cultures that "examine their practices explicitly, publicly, and collectively" (Rallis & MacMullen, 2000, p. 770). Building an inquiry-based culture would require data collection from multiple sources on the process of educating students, reflective analysis and inquiry, and varied measures to assess both student engagement and achievement. In addition to standardized test scores, schools and districts would collect and analyze multiple data to give a richer picture of the school and its students, for example, authentic assessment measures (portfolios, exhibitions, projects); course enrollment patterns and grade distribution; graduation and college-going rates; attendance, suspension, and dropout rates; and documentation of instructional practices (curriculum documents, lesson plans).

Seymour Sarason (1982) argues that if we are to avoid "the predictable failure of education reform," we must understand that schools are comprehensive, complex, and integrated systems, and that reform must approach the improvement of student learning from this vantage point rather than focusing on single, additive programs. Indeed, in a longitudinal study of Illinois middle schools that were implementing a comprehensive set of reform principals articulated in the Carnegie Corporation's much-recognized *Turning Points* (1989) report on middle grades reform, Felner, Jackson, Kasak, Mulhall, Brand, and Flowers (1997) found that "perhaps the most important lesson about implementation we have learned is that successful [middle grades] reform must be comprehensive and integrative" (p. 63) in order to improvement and sustain student achievement. What these authors speak of is the need for a comprehensive focus on all aspects of a school that helps create quality teaching and learning—for example, governance, schedule, instruction, curriculum, assessment, and student support.

We can assume, then, that any accountability system must also be comprehensive and integrative. There is no single instrument that can measure the complexity of the inputs and processes of districts, schools, teachers, and the resulting engagement and academic performance of students. With this in mind, I outline five components of an effective statewide and nationally supported comprehensive accountability system:

- *A Vision of Learning.* The heart of any accountability system is a definition and vision of high quality instruction that leads to high student engagement and achievement for each student.
- *School Accountability.* The system provides ways for schools and the adults working in them to assess and reflect on their practices and the impact of these practices on instruction and student performance.
- *District Accountability.* The system provides ways for school districts and the adults working in them to assess and reflect on their practices and the impact of these practices in supporting schools to provide high quality instruction leading to high student performance.

- *Student Accountability and Diagnostic Testing.*   The system provides ways to assess the quality of student work and academic performance, as well as students' understanding of their work, in multiple and meaningful ways. The system also allows for some diagnostic, comparison testing in the basic skills of literacy and mathematics to ensure that students are literate.

- *Accounting to the Public.*   The system tracks student engagement and performance in multiple ways across time and reports this information, disaggregated by race, income, gender, and language, in meaningful and understandable ways to the public.

A Vision of Learning.   A vision of learning must be the basis of any sound education system and based on what we want students to learn. Carl Glickman (2002) argues that learning, and subsequently what we assess for student learning, should be about a broader concept of "how to prepare citizens on how to live one's life" (p. 5). Newmann, Bryk, and Nagaoka (2001) argue that the "contemporary demands of productive work, responsible citizenship, and successful management of personal affairs extend well beyond giving correct answers and following proper procedures for the work traditionally assigned in school (2001, p. 9).

These educators argue that any education, and therefore accountability system, must have as its foundation a conception of teaching and learning that is framed around students using their minds well in all aspects of living in a pluralistic, democratic, and multicultural society—contributing as citizens to a democracy, raising healthy families, being respectful and caring neighbors, leading a life of opportunity and fulfillment, and participating in the world of work in a meaningful and productive manner.

If we enter the accountability arena with these tenets in mind, then the principles of learning, and, subsequently what we would expect to be held accountable for, would look quite different from the endless standards to which educators, parents, and students are now subjected to in most states. Rather, as cited by Newmann, Bryk, and Nagaoka (2001), we would look to assess and hold accountable "authentic, intellectual work," work that is meaningful and significant, work in which adults engage in during the course of their daily personal, civic, and professional lives. They pose three characteristics of authentic intellectual work:

- Construction of knowledge that involves interpretation, evaluation, analysis, synthesis, and organization of prior knowledge or solving new problems or understandings.

- Disciplined inquiry, or using prior knowledge to gain in-depth understanding that enables one to communicate what they come to know and understand in multiple ways.

- Value beyond school in which knowledge has "utilitarian, aesthetic, or personal value." (p. 11)

Ironically, teaching to these principles of learning are also the best means of preparing students to perform well on traditional standardized tests. A Chicago study compared how students fared in classrooms in which they were engaged in authentic intellectual work as compared to classrooms in which students received low-level assignments. In classrooms emphasizing authentic intellectual work, students' learning gains on the Iowa Test of Basic Skills (ITBS) in reading and mathematics were 20% greater than the national average, while students' learning gains were 22–25% lower in classrooms in which there was greater emphasis on lower-level skills. Student gains in classrooms emphasizing authentic intellectual work were equal for students with prior high and low achievement levels, as they were for students across race, gender, and income groups at the elementary, middle, and high school levels (Newmann, Byrk, & Nagoka, 2001).

In an earlier study on the impact of authentic intellectual work on traditional indicators of student performance, researchers estimated that "regardless of race or gender, an average student would move from the 30th to the 60th percentile if he or she received high authentic pedagogy instead of low authentic pedagogy" (Newmann, Marks, & Gamoran, 1995, p. 7). Put simply, "results . . . show that the more frequently teachers used interactive instruction, the more their students learned in both reading and mathematics" (Smith, Lee, & Newmann, 2001, p. 21).

Similarly, in a study on middle school students' math performance, researchers found that "the greatest student gains on the mathematics performance assessment were related to the use of instructional tasks that engaged students in high levels of cognitive processing, especially those that encouraged [higher levels] of thinking. On the other hand, student performance gains were relatively small when instructional tasks were procedurally based and able to be solved with a single, easily accessible strategy, single representations, and little or no mathematical communication" (Stein & Lane, 1996, p. 74).

What would an articulated vision of teaching and learning, as the foundation of an accountability system, look like? Ideally, a concise three-to-five page document outlining: (1) a set of streamlined competencies of what students should know and be able to do—broad habits of mind, skills, and content knowledge—by the time they graduate from middle school, and (2) a definition of what constitutes authentic intellectual work for a graduating middle grade student. This document should be presented to students and families as they enter the middle grades, setting up clear, public guidelines of what is expected of a middle grades student as she moves into high school. This document should then frame teachers' work as they construct curricular and instructional experiences that immerse students in these competencies and the qualities of authentic intellectual work, as well as assessment experiences that require students to demonstrate what and how they have learned in multiple ways. Such a document would be constructed to allow flexibility for teachers and schools to root their curriculum in local contexts and students' backgrounds and cultures.

   School Accountability.   School accountability means holding students accountable for their learning and measuring what they have learned, as well as assessing and reflecting on a school's practices and the impact of these practices in leading to quality instruction and high student engagement and achievement. How do schools create professional learning communities of adults who are engaged in the discourse of their craft and practice of teaching? How are adults held accountable for their daily work with students? How can a school be structured to ensure that every student is engaged in demanding and challenging academic work? How do middle schools engage families in meaningful ways that enhance a student's performance? These are the questions that should drive school accountability practices and measures.

Middle schools in which teachers are actively engaged in collaboratively looking at student and teacher work, in peer observation, action research, and other significant collaborative work focused on teaching and learning, are holding themselves responsible and accountable to hone their instructional practices. Middle schools in which teaching teams share the same students, and in which every teacher has a student load of no more than 80 students, are accountable adult cultures. Schools in which the adults primarily discuss instruction and curriculum during team time are holding themselves, rather than students and parents, accountable for students' performance. Schools in which students are grouped into heterogeneous and flexibly grouped classes are holding themselves accountable for providing every student with access to a quality curriculum. Schools in which families are asked in meaningful ways to engage in their child's education and in the life of the school, rather than solely contacting families when their child has done something wrong, are holding themselves accountable for building the types of family involvement that have been proven to raise student performance. These are a few of the many factors that we know contribute to high student engagement and high quality instruction, and subsequently, high student achievement.

The critical question is what would a high quality school accountability component look like? Periodic school quality reviews are a promising model that has demonstrated the potential of thoughtful school examinations leading to improved practice and hence, higher student engagement and achievement. This process has been successfully used as an accountability tool in Rhode Island, as part of their state accountability system; in

Massachusetts, both with the state charter schools and with the Boston Pilot Schools, a group of 19 schools that are members of the Boston Public Schools, yet by teacher union contract have charter-like autonomy; and in *Turing Points,* a national model of middle school reform, to identify demonstration schools, or schools which best exemplify in practice and outcomes the *Turning Points* middle grades principles. School quality reviews generally include the following components:

- They are based on a set of public benchmarks of what constitutes the practices and policies of an effective school.
- They require a process of self-examination, reflection, and assessment on the part of the school, based on the benchmarks, and the synthesis of this self-assessment into a document for public review, which is often a school portfolio.
- They involve a team of external practitioners, usually teachers and administrators from other schools and districts; higher education, community, and business representatives; and parents, who spend several days to review data and collect other multiple forms of documentation (e.g., school portfolios, classroom and team observations, shadowing students, interviews) that provide evidence of a school's progress in meeting the benchmarks.
- The team reports findings and recommendations from the external review that is made public to the administration and faculty of the school, the larger public, and an accrediting body. The report articulates a set of strengths, concerns, and recommendations. These recommendations effectively become a roadmap for future school improvement efforts.
- A school's status with the district is directly tied to its performance on the school quality review. Based on the review the accrediting body may approve the school for continuation, continuation on probation or with explicit target goals, or closure.
- They are cyclical, occurring every four to five years, significantly reducing the chances of a school's performance markedly deteriorating and having a harmful effect on students (Center for Collaborative Education, 1998; Massachusetts Department of Education, 1999; Rhode Island Department of Education, 1998).

The school quality review process is a proactive accountability strategy ensuring that schools are engaged in quality educational practices that lead to high student engagement and achievement. Many schools that have undertaken school quality reviews have found that this process, while requiring an intense level of self-assessment and examination by the entire school community, has resulted in substantial improvements in teaching and learning—often prior to the external review team's visit.

District Accountability.   Too often, we forget that the primary purpose of school district offices and infrastructures is one of supporting schools to provide high quality instruction. While NCLB focuses primarily on district and school rewards and sanctions for "adequate yearly progress" on state high stakes tests, it provides little in the way of articulating a positive vision of the role of districts in assisting schools. The district results of this philosophical bent is far too often overly bureaucratic, with top-down mandates to schools emphasizing a one-size-fits-all model of reform.

In an analysis of the Edna McConnell Clark Foundation's work with six urban districts on standards-based middle grades reform over multiple years, a study found that "improving an entire district proved to be harder than improving individual schools. The school systems lacked the capacity... to formulate and implement real change," often operating "in near-total isolation" (Mackinnon, 2003, p. 6). District capacity was further compromised by its almost religious adherence to raising test scores on state high stakes standardized tests. The foundation's "ability to help districts reconcile competing demands—between high stakes state accountability systems and their own aspirations for meaningful reform—was crucially limited. In general, the districts took the position that they needed to satisfy the demands of their states first [by raising test scores], then tackle major reform" (p. 44).

If the most successful schools are those which are inquiry-minded, in which faculty are constantly seeking ways to improve their teaching, and are continually engaged in assessing and reflecting on multiple sources of data about instructional practice and student performance, then the district's role with schools must change. How can we hold districts accountable for creating the conditions that enable schools to become inquiry-minded and engage in instructional practices that result in authentic intellectual work for all students? What district practices help create these types of schools?

First and foremost, districts need to provide schools with maximum flexibility and autonomy to create the professional learning cultures and the instruction, curriculum, and assessment practices that best assist all students to learn at high levels. Such flexibility demands that districts grant schools charter-like autonomy over budget, staffing, curriculum, governance, and the school calendar, for example, having the ability to create staffing patterns to significantly reduce student-teacher loads, to set longer blocks of learning time, and to carve out substantial amounts of collaborative faculty planning time. The Edmonton, Canada Public Schools is one example of a district that grants its schools almost complete budget and staffing autonomy, with schools controlling 92 cents of every district dollar, in exchange for increased accountability provisions. As a result, student performance on provincial tests has steadily risen over the years (McBeath, 2001).

Placing accountability and decision making over instructional practices in the hands of those educators closest to students has implications for how districts are structured. Districts need to recast themselves to provide voluntary, not mandated, services to schools that assist them in creating accountable adult learning communities and high quality instructional practices. Such support would include offering, not mandating, resources for school-based professional development, hosting structured site visits to schools with exemplary practices, and providing facilitative assistance in adopting selected practices—all at the disposal of, rather than force-fed to, schools. Districts can play a significant role in creating collaborative professional networks for faculty and administrators to share practices, engage in joint study, problem solve, and exchange critical friends visits around selected instructional practices and dilemmas. Collaborative relationships between schools and their faculty and administrators represent some of the most powerful professional development in supporting and nurturing high quality practice in schools.

What would a district accountability system look like? Rather than solely judging districts based on the aggregate student scores on high stakes tests, a true district accountability process would measure and hold districts accountable to practices that support schools becoming high-performing middle schools. While there are not necessarily any good, positive models that currently exist, such a system would be similar to that of school quality reviews, except at a district level. A district quality review system would contain similar elements—public benchmarks of what constitutes sound district practice (e.g., levels of autonomy granted to schools, resources provided, network practices, and public engagement) and a process of district self-assessment followed by an external visiting team that collected and assessed evidence. There would be a culminating report of findings and recommendations leading to a roadmap for improvement.

Student Accountability and Diagnostic Testing. Assessment has its greatest impact on improving student learning and in accurately gauging a student's performance when it is embedded in curriculum and instruction in meaningful ways, and when it is the result and product of authentic intellectual work. It is virtually impossible for authentic intellectual work to be state-administered in a one-size-fits-all model to all students in all schools and districts. Such a system removes the assessment from the local context of learning, thus ensuring its lack of authenticity. The goals, then, are to create a system of locally developed and administered authentic assessment systems that measure whether students have mastered state competencies.

A locally administered assessment system, governed by state guidelines that provide consistency while also allowing flexibility and innovation, does not preclude the need for statewide assessment data that allows for diagnosis in literacy and math, as well as data that can be used for comparison purposes among districts enrolling similar demographics of students. Low-stakes standardized tests can provide one legitimate method of publicly tracking the progress of schools and students from year to year, both their overall progress and their progress in closing the achievement gap between low-income students and their more affluent peers, and between White students and African-American and Latino students.

What would a locally-based student assessment and diagnostic testing system look like? Under such a system, each school in the state would develop its own accountability and assessment plan, using state and district guidelines. The plan, developed by teachers, administrators, and parents and approved by the school governing body and the district, would outline how the school will ensure that students will demonstrate that they meet the state competencies. Plans would be encouraged to include authentic assessments, including portfolios, exhibitions, performance tasks, student products, and external reviews, as well as a description of how the school will use this information to improve itself. Such a plan would assist teachers to focus on high quality instruction and curriculum, rather than teaching to the test. These plans would be subject to review by the state department of education (MassCARE, 1998).

The Maine Department of Education has endorsed just such a local assessment model. While using a state standardized test, the Maine Educational Assessment (MEA), as a diagnostic assessment tool that allows district comparison of student performance, the beacon of its assessment program is a requirement for every district to develop a local assessment system to measure student performance. "It is important to recognize that districts and schools have a great deal of latitude in determining what to include in their assessment system. … Local assessments may include portfolios, performances, and demonstrations, in addition to other measures of achievement. Commercially produced assessment tools may be part of the local assessment system but may not carry a majority of the weight in determining student performance" (MDOE website, 2003).

Accounting to the Public. Finally, a true accountability system must track student engagement and performance in multiple ways across time; there must be meaningful ways in which we assess how our students are doing. Certainly, the results of school and district quality reviews and the engagement of parents and community members in the review of authentic student assessments, provide considerably more information to the public on how their schools are faring. In addition, we need to be able to report a range of data on student engagement and performance in understandable and easily accessible ways to the public.

What would a system of accounting to the public look like? Within a public reporting system, multiple indicators of student engagement and performance would be included, all disaggregated by race, income, gender, school, and language. Student engagement, which indicates a school's power of attracting and the ability to hold students' interests, includes such indicators as waiting lists and rates of attendance, suspension, expulsions, dropouts, and transfers. Student achievement includes such indicators as course failures, grade retentions, enrollment in high-level classes and special education, achievement on standardized tests and authentic assessments, and graduation and college-going rates (districts can track graduation and college-going rates back to the sending middle school).

This aggregated data should be provided annually in easy-to-read form for the general public, encouraging widespread discussion of the data. Presentations, focus groups, poster analysis, and newsletter syntheses are all good ways to get the data distributed and discussed. A school open to conversing about its data is usually a school that is likely to search for and adopt effective practices for meeting the needs of all its students.

CONCLUSION

Our nation has embraced the misguided notion that the use of one single high stakes test is the best measure of accountability in public education. Yet, such a notion defies the building of a culture of moral obligation and responsibility to reflect on and account for our actions in improving student learning. Ultimately, it is we, as parents, educators, policymakers, and community members, who are responsible for our children. Yet, we are creating accountability systems in which it is only our students who are being held accountable for their actions, using narrow and rigid definitions of learning that must be demonstrated in a narrow and rigid manner. This is one of the reasons why the late U.S. Senator Paul Wellstone stated, "Allowing the continued misuse of high stakes tests is, in itself, a gross failure of moral imagination, a failure of both educators and policymakers, who persistently refuse to provide the educational resources necessary to guarantee an equal opportunity to learn for all our children" (Wellstone, 2000b, p. 1).

In this chapter I have presented a different model of accountability, one that is framed around the responsibility and obligation to account for one's actions—at the district, school, teacher, and student levels. Such a system must be framed around a strong and vibrant vision of teaching and learning, school and district quality reviews, state diagnostic testing, multiple forms of locally developed and administered authentic assessments, and annual public reporting of multiple indicators of school and district practices as well as student engagement and performance. Such a system is far more complex and far messier than that of a single high stakes test. However, ultimately, it is work that will go much farther in creating personalized and humane schools that are more successful in educating the increasingly diverse student population that our public schools serve.

Dennie Palmer Wolf of the Annenberg Institute for School Reform writes, "...the purpose of accountability is to ensure that all those responsible play their part in securing [the right of a quality public education] for all children. The Emancipation Proclamation did not secure equal rights for African Americans. It has taken, and continues to take, entire communities of stakeholders ..., actively working over long periods, to detect inequities and shortcomings and change both large institutions and daily habits. The same kind of broadly based and long-term efforts is needed to secure the right to a high-quality public education [for all children.]" (2003, p. 11). Rather than rely on simple mandates with harsh consequences, such as NCLB, let's harness the moral will and courage, as well as the resources, to enable this inalienable right to be actualized for every middle grade student.

REFERENCES

Coalition for Authentic Reform in Education. (1997, December). *A call for an authentic state-wide assessment system.* Cambridge, MA.

Amrein, A., & Berliner, D. (2002). High-stakes testing, uncertainty, and student learning. *Educational Policy Analysis Archives, 10*(18). Retrieved March 27, 2002, from http://epaa.asu.asu.edu/epaa/v10n18.

Annenberg Institute for School Reform. *A framework for accountability.* Retrieved April 17, 2002, from http://www.aisr.brown.edu/accountability.

Baker, J. (1998, December 11). *Driving the curriculum.* Email posted on the Coalition for Authentic Reform in Education listserve.

Bok, D., & Bowen, W. (2000). *The shape of the river.* Princeton, NJ: Princeton University Press.

Brennan, R., Kim, J., Wenz-Gross, M., & Siperstein, G. (2001). The relative equitability of high-stakes testing versus teacher-assigned grades: An analysis of the Massachusetts comprehensive assessment system (MCAS). *Harvard Educational Review. 71*(2), 173–216.

Center for Collaborative Education. (1998). The Boston public schools' school self-study guide: As prepared for the Boston Pilot Schools' accountability process for use with the school quality review process. Boston, MA.

Clarke, M., Haney, W., & Madaus, G. (2000). High stakes testing and high school completion. *National Board of Educational Testing and Public Policy, 1*(3), 1–12.

Elmore, R. (2002). Testing trap. *Harvard Magazine, 105*(1), 35–40.

Feldman, S. (2000, July 12). Where we stand. *Education Week,* p. 17.

Felner, R., Jackson, A., Kasak, D., Mulhall, P., Brand, S., & Flowers, N. (1997). The impact of school reform for the middle grades: A longitudinal study of a network engaged in Turning Points-based comprehensive school transformation.

In R. Takanishi, & D. Hamburg (Eds.), *Preparing adolescents for the twenty-first century* (pp. 38–68). New York: Cambridge University Press.

French, Z.G. (2000). *MCAS.* Unpublished essay.

Gilbert, J. (2003). TAKS error doesn't add up, mathematicians say. *Houston Chronicle.* Retrieved August 13, 2003, from http://www.chron.com/cs/CDA/story.hts/front/2037303.

Glickman, C. (1993). *Renewing America's schools.* New York: Jossey-Bass.

Glickman, C. (2002, December 19). *The forthcoming battle over education standards and the future of American democracy* (abbreviated version). Unpublished paper. Southwest Texas State University.

Goodwin, B. (2003, July). Digging deeper: Where does the public stand on standards-based education? *Mid-continent Research for Education and Learning.* Issues Brief.

Haney, W. (1999). *Study of Texas education agency statistics on cohorts of Texas high school students, 1978–1998.* Unpublished manuscript. Boston College, Center for the Study of Testing, Evaluation, and Educational Policy, Newton, MA.

Henriques, D., & Steinberg. J. (2001, May 20). Right answer, wrong score: test flaws take toll. *New York Times.*

Herszenhorn, D. (2003, July 23). Basic skills forcing cuts in arts classes. *New York Times.* Retrieved August 3, 2003, from http://www.nytimes.com/2003/07/23/education/23SCHO.html.

Jackson, A., & Davis, G. (2000). *Turning points 2000: Educating early adolescents in the 21st century.* Columbus, OH: National Middle School Association.

Jones, G., Jones, B., Hardin, B., Chapman, L., Yarbrough, T., & David, M. (1999). The impact of high-stakes testing on teachers and students in North Carolina. *Phi Delta Kappan, 81*(3), 199–203.

Kane, T., & Staiger, D. (2001). Improving school accountability measures. *National Bureau of Economic Research, NBER Working Paper Series.* Working Paper 8156, retrieved on August 23, 2003 from http://www.nber.org/papers/w8156.

Kurtz, M., & Vaishnav, A. (2002, December 5). Student's MCAS answer means 449 others pass. *Boston Globe,* p. A1.

Mackinnon, A. (2003). *Standards-based middle grades reform in six urban districts, 1995–2001: A report on the program for student achievement of the Edna McConnell Clark Foundation.* New York: Edna McConnell Clark Foundation.

Maine Department of Education. (2003). *Local assessments.* Retrieved August 13, 2003, from http://www.state.me.us/education/Isalt/localassess.html.

Massachusetts Department of Education. (1999). Massachusetts charter school inspection handbook. Malden, MA.

Massachusetts State Legislature. (1993). *An act establishing the education reform act Of 1993.* M.G.L. Chapter 69, Section 29, section 1I. Boston, MA.

McBeath, A. (2001). Decentralized dollars and decisions: Reshaping Edmonton's central office to support principals and site-specific needs. *School Administrator. (81)*5, 12–16.

McNeil, L. (2000). Creating new inequalities: Contradictions of reform. *Phi Delta Kappan, (81)*10, 729–734.

Merriam-Webster On-Line Dictionary. Retrieved on August 8, 2003, from http://www.com/home.html.

National Forum to Accelerate Middle Grades Reform. (2002). *High-stakes testing policy Statement*. Retrieved August 8, 2003, from http://www.mgforum.org

Neill, M. (2001). Test scores unreliable means of assessing school quality. *FairTest*. Cambridge, MA, retrieved June 1, 2001 from http://www.fairtest.org

Newmann, F., Bryk, N., & Nagoaka, J. (2001). *Improving Chicago's schools: Authentic intellectual work and standardized tests*. Chicago Annenberg Research Project, Consortium on Chicago School Research, Chicago, IL.

Newmann, F., Marks, H., & Gamaran, A. (1995). Authentic pedagogy: Standards that boost student performance. *Issues in restructuring schools,* Center on Organization and Restructuring of Schools. Issue Report No. 8.

No child left behind act of 2001. Public Law 107-110. Retrieved August 8, 2003, from http://nochildleftbehind.gov/next/overview/index

Olson, L. (2001, May 23). Study questions reliability of single-year test-score gains. *Education Week.* p. 9.

Orfield. G., & Ward, J. (2000). Testing, testing. *The Nation*, 38–40.

Public Agenda: Reality check 2001. (2001, February 21). *Education Week*, p. S4.

Rallis, S., & MacMulllen, M. (2000). Inquiry-minded schools: Opening doors for accountability. *Phi Delta Kappan*, 766–773.

Rhode Island Department of Education. (1998). SALT pilot visit documents. Providence, RI.

Sacks, P. (2000). *Standardized minds: The high price of America's testing culture and what we can do to change it*. Cambridge, MA: Perseus Publishing.

Sarason, S. (1982). *The culture of the school and the problem of change*. Boston, MA: Allyn and Bacon.

Schemo, D.J. (2003, July 11). Questions on data cloud luster of Houston schools. *New York Times*, Section A., p. 1.

Smith, J., Lee, V., & Newmann, F. (2001). *Improving Chicago's schools: Instruction and achievement in Chicago elementary schools*. Chicago Annenberg Research Project, Consortium on Chicago School Research, Chicago, IL.

Smith, M., & Shepard, L. (1989). Flunking grades: A recapitulation. In M. Smith & L. Shepard (Eds.), *Flunking grades: Research and policies on retention* (pp. 214–236. New York: Falmer Press.

Steele, C. (1999). Thin ice: "Stereotype threat" and black college students. *The Atlantic Monthly, 284*(2), 44–54.

Stein, M., & Lane, S. (1996). Instructional tasks and the development of student capacity to think and reason: An analysis of the relationships between teaching and learning in a reform mathematics project. *Educational Research and Evaluation, 2*(1), 50–80.

Thompson, S. (2001). The authentic standards movement and its evil twin. *Phi Delta Kappan, (82)*5, 358–362.

Vaishnav, A. (2002, September 27). Teacher finds MCAS goof: 666 more students pass. *Boston Globe*, pp. B1&3.

Viadero, D. (1999, October 6). Stanford report questions accuracy of tests. *Education Week*, p. 3.

Viadero, D., & Blair, Julie (1999, September 29) Error affects test results in six states. (1999, September 29). *Education Week*, pp. 13–15.

Weisman, J. (2000, March 30). The Texas education myth: Only a test. *New Republic Online*. Retrieved April 3, 2000, from http://www.tnr.com

Wellstone, P. (2000a, January 13). Even a senator could fail this school test. *USA Today*, p. 17A.

Wellstone, P. (2000b, March 31). Text of remarks of a talk given at Teachers College, Columbia University.

Wheelock, A. (2002, September 12). Message posted to Coalition for Authentic Reform in Education listserve from the Progress through the Education Pipeline Project, Boston College, Boston.

Winerip. M. (2003, August 13). The zero dropout miracle: Alas! Alack! A Texas tall tale. *New York Times*, Section B, p. 7.

Wolf, D.P. (2003, Spring). Accountability: Everyone's concern, everyone's job. In *Rethinking accountability, voices in urban education* (Vol. 1). Annenberg Institute for School Reform at Brown University, RI.

CHAPTER 7

THE ROLE OF TEACHER PREPARATION, LICENSURE, AND RETENTION IN CREATING HIGH-PERFORMING MIDDLE SCHOOLS

C. Kenneth McEwin, Thomas S. Dickinson, and Tracy W. Smith

HIGH-PERFORMING MIDDLE SCHOOLS

In this current environment of accountability and high stakes testing, high-performing middle schools are a target of contemporary school reform. However, high-performing middle schools are but a means to an end. The end result of all middle school work—in organization, in curriculum, in instruction, and even in high stakes testing—is and should be the development of young adolescents who are capable, competent and well-grounded individuals. This has always been, and should remain, the ultimate purpose of the middle school.

Given this established end result of middle school education and the component parts which contribute to that end (National Middle School

Reforming Middle Level Education: Considerations for Policymakers, pages 109–129
Copyright © 2004 by Information Age Publishing
All rights of reproduction in any form reserved.

Association, 1995), what is a high performing middle school and how should it operate in today's educational climate? A high performing middle school is a school that provides for and achieves tangible and significant educational results for young adolescents in two major areas—the development of individual adolescents' intellectual ability at a high level and the development of a well-integrated individual identity.

This definition and purpose of high performing middle schools is not new. From its origins, the middle school has aimed at high performance—in the academic and intellectual areas that are a prime domain of this school organization and in the development of the young adolescent at a critical stage of development. The original conception and definition of the middle school, as articulated by Alexander and George, was for a school that performed at a high level:

> . . . a middle school is a school of some three to five years between the elementary and high school focused on the educational needs of students in these in-between years and designed to promote continuous educational progress for all concerned. (Alexander & George, 1981, p. 3)

Alexander and George further elaborated and operationalized this definition of a middle school by articulating twelve essential characteristics or elements of what they called "an exemplary middle school":

1. A statement of philosophy and school goals that is based on knowledge of the educational needs of boys and girls of middle school age and is used in school program planning and evaluation.

2. A system for school planning and evaluation which is specifically designed for the middle school level and which involves all concerned in the school community.

3. A curriculum plan for the middle school population that provides for their continuous progress, basic learning skills, use of organized knowledge, personal development activities, and other curriculum goals as locally determined.

4. A program of guidance which assures the availability of help for each student from a faculty member well known to the student.

5. An interdisciplinary teacher organization which provides for team planning, teaching, and evaluation, and for appropriate interdisciplinary units.

6. Use of methods of student grouping for instruction which facilitate multiage and other instructional arrangements to maximize continuous progress.

7. Block scheduling and other time arrangements to facilitate flexible and efficient use of time.

8. Planning and use of physical facilities to provide the flexible and varied program required for middle schoolers.

9. Instruction which utilizes a balanced variety of effective strategies and techniques to achieve continuous progress of each learner toward appropriate instructional objectives.

10. Appropriate roles for the various individuals and groups required for continued and dynamic leadership in the middle school, with a continuing program of staff development and renewal focused on the unique problems of middle school personnel.

11. A plan for evaluation of student progress and of the school itself to assure the achievement of the goals of the school.

12. Participation with other schools and with community groups in the continuing study of the middle school population and of society as a whole, to be responsive to changing needs and conditions of the future (Alexander & George, 1981, p. 18–19).

Given that the original articulation of the middle school as a concept and organization was formulated more than thirty years ago (Alexander & George, 1965, 1995), what evidence exists to indicate that the middle school can actually attain the two goals of intellectual and individual development? For without such evidence, the middle school as it existed in the minds of its founders is merely a dream.

Research on High Performing Middle Schools

Recent evidence, much of it high quality and rigorous research, confirms that the original definition and intent of a school for young adolescents can attain the two goals of intellectual and individual development. Foremost among the research evidence is the work of Mertens, Flowers, and Mulhall at the Center for Prevention Research and Development at the University of Illinois, Champaign (Flowers, Mertens, & Mulhall, 1999, 2000a, 2000b, 2002; Mertens, Flowers, & Mulhall, 1998a, 1998b, 2001, 2003; Mulhall, Flowers, & Mertens, 2002). Additionally, the work of MacIver and his colleagues from the Center for Research on the Education of Students Placed at Risk at Johns Hopkins University in Baltimore, Maryland indicates that through comprehensive whole school reform, in this case the Talent Development Middle School, even high poverty middle schools can achieve the twin ends of intellectual and individual development (Balfanz & Byrnes, 2003; Balfanz, & MacIver, 2000; Corbett, & Wilson, 2003; Herlihy, & Kemple, 2003; MacIver, & Epstein, 1991; MacIver, 2003; MacIver, MacIver, Balfanz, Plank, & Ruby, 2000; MacIver, & Prioleau,

1999; MacIver, Young, Balfanz, Shaw, Garriott, & Cohen, 2001; Plank, & Young, 1999; Ruby, 1999, 2003; Useem, 1998).

Additional evidence is also available from researchers such as Trimble (Trimble, 1995, 2002; Trimble, & Peterson, 2000) and others (Felner, Jackson, Kasak, Mulhall, Brand, & Flowers, 1997; Jackson, & Davis, 2000; Lipsitz, Jackson, & Austin, 1997). To summarize the thrust of their findings is a straightforward matter, middle schools that implement the entire range of the middle school concept (i.e., the range of elements articulated by Alexander and George that lead to exemplary middle schools) enable students to perform well on academic achievement tests and also demonstrate healthy development as individuals. Indeed, if schools in the middle want to emerge as high performing exemplary middle schools they already have a complete template, thirty-plus years of hard-won school- and classroom-based experience, and an emerging research base to provide direction. But as one of the authors of this chapter has indicated elsewhere (Dickinson, 2001), failure to implement the entire range of the middle school concept leaves a school in a state of arrested development and far short of the ends of intellectual and personal development.

PREPARING TEACHERS FOR THE MIDDLE SCHOOL

Evidence indicates that the quality of a teacher is the most salient school-related factor influencing student achievement (Rice, 2003). Additionally, broad and strong consensus exists for one key element for developing and sustaining high performing middle schools, schools that are exemplary in their intellectual and individual development of young adolescents—a high quality teaching staff characterized by appropriate licensure and professional preparation to teach, direct and support young adolescents (Cooney, 2000; Flowers et al., 2002; Gaskill, 2002; Hawk, Coble, & Swanson, 1985; Laczko-Kerr, & Berliner, 2003; McEwin, & Dickinson, 1995, 1996, 1997; McEwin, Dickinson, Erb, & Scales, 1995; McEwin, Dickinson, & Smith, 2003; National Forum to Accelerate Middle Grades Reform, 2002; National Middle School Association, n.d.; National Middle School Association/National Council for Accreditation of Teacher Educational-Approved middle level teacher preparation standards, 2001).

Essential Teacher Preparation Program Components

The prevailing rationale of licensure policies that require the specialized professional preparation of middle level teachers is the assurance that those licensed to teach young adolescents have demonstrated their abilities to be highly effective. Professional preparation programs designed to provide prospective middle level teachers with the specialized knowledge, skills, and dispositions needed to be highly effective include several essential components that are briefly presented here and more extensively described in the literature (Jackson & Davis, 2000; National Middle School Association, 2001; McEwin, Dickinson, & Smith, in press). Readers are encouraged to explore the nature of these components and to help other stakeholders better understand their importance. The following abbreviated descriptions are limited to elements unique to middle level preparation programs and do not include others, such as diversity and technology, that are essential to all quality teacher preparation programs.

Young Adolescent Development

Middle level teacher preparation programs include a strong emphasis on providing teachers opportunities to obtain a comprehensive understanding of the development of young adolescents, and the implications of that knowledge. Understanding the developmental realities of early adolescence provides a substantial basis upon which middle level teachers can build curriculum, assessment, and teaching skills (Elkind, 1998). This knowledge can only be gained through the formal study of young adolescent development and by working directly with young adolescents. Without a comprehensive understanding of the characteristics of young adolescents, and meaningful opportunities to transform that understanding into practice, the success of middle level teachers is limited. To continue allowing teachers without a comprehensive knowledge of the students they teach to practice hinders the success of many teachers, and therefore serves as a deterrent to student learning. To continue on this course is self-defeating and contributes to the failure of many middle level schools to be highly successful.

Middle School Philosophy and Organization

Middle level teacher preparation programs also include a focus on middle level philosophy and organization. Study of middle level philosophy and organization typically includes, but is not limited to (a) the origins and development of middle level schools, (b) effective middle level school organizational features and practices, (c) middle level philosophy, (d) middle level trends and issues, and (e) other information that helps middle level teachers understand the rationale for and context of middle level schooling (McEwin, Dickinson & Smith, in press). In effective middle level teacher preparation programs, prospective middle level teachers are provided opportunities to learn about the philosophical foundations of middle level education in order to develop a substantial understanding of the organizational structures that grow from and support middle level schooling and student learning.

Middle School Curriculum

Middle level curriculum is considered a high priority and an essential program component in middle level teacher preparation programs. Study in this area typically includes an emphasis on curriculum that is discipline specific, integrative and interdisciplinary (National Middle School Association, 1995, 2001, n.d.). Prospective middle level teachers learn about middle level curriculum through formal study and by working directly with the curriculum. Typical topics of study in middle level teacher preparation programs include past and present theorists of middle school curriculum and various curriculum designs, formats, and propositions important to the development of a deep understanding of that curriculum. Emphasis is also placed on how middle level curriculum can be designed to support and extend young adolescent learning (McEwin & Dickinson, 1996).

Middle School Planning, Teaching, and Assessment

Study of middle level planning, teaching, and assessment is an additional essential component of middle level teacher preparation programs. Prospective middle level teachers learn to plan, teach, and assess student work based on content knowledge and a comprehensive understanding of young adolescent development. Major emphasis is placed on learning a wide variety of teaching strategies and demonstration of the ability to apply these strategies effectively in classroom settings during internships and student teaching. Emphasis is also placed on constructing and employing assessment techniques ranging from traditional testing to authentic assessments, portfolios, exhibitions, and open-ended problems (McEwin, Dickinson & Smith, in press).

Subject Matter Knowledge

Middle level teacher preparation programs emphasize study in two content areas, for example mathematics and science or language arts and social studies. Knowledge in two content areas, rather than a single area, provides a solid academic foundation for effective middle level teaching and promotes an understanding of the connections and interrelationships among the various subject areas. As noted by the authors in an earlier publication, "The rationale for having two teaching fields includes, but is not limited to (a) teachers that teach on teams are knowledgeable in two disciplines, making it easier to integrate subject areas; (b) teachers are licensed to teach in two content areas which provides flexibility in employment whether or not the teachers teach on teams; and (c) content knowledge in two broad teaching fields more accurately reflects the nature of middle level curriculum (e.g., science rather than just biology or physics)" (McEwin et al., 2003, in press).

Middle School Field Experiences

An additional high priority component of middle level teacher preparation programs is that of providing and requiring early and continuing middle level field experiences. The priority given these clinical experiences reflects the views of practicing teachers about the essential components of professional preparation programs (Wilson, Floden, & Ferrini-Mundy, 2001). Middle level field experiences provide a context for learning about young adolescents, middle level instruction, middle level organizational features, and other key elements of successful teaching and schooling.

SPECIALIZED MIDDLE LEVEL TEACHER LICENSURE

The primary role of teacher licensure/certification agencies and professional practice boards is the protection of the public, including young adolescents enrolled in grades five through eight (i.e., grades K–8, 7–12). This protection includes assuring that all young adolescents are taught by highly qualified teachers who have the specialized knowledge, skills, and dispositions needed to be effective. On the surface, the assumption of the right of all young adolescents to be taught by highly qualified teachers does not seem to be unreasonable or controversial. However, there is considerable apathy and disagreement regarding the issue of whether middle level teachers need specialized professional preparation for the important and complex task of teaching young adolescents. This disagreement, in combination with the neglect of the welfare of this sometimes unpopular age group, has resulted in malpractice on the part of many policymakers, educators, and other stakeholders. Currently, in many states, virtually anyone with any kind of degree or licensure, or even no license at all, is permitted to teach young adolescents enrolled in the middle grades.

The Role of Policymakers

Historically, policymakers in many states have failed to create and maintain rigorous middle level teacher licensure regulations that require specialized middle level teacher preparation. Instead, licensure regulations have lumped middle level teacher licensure with those required to teach young children in elementary schools (i.e., grades K–8) and/or older adolescents in high schools (i.e., grades 6–12). Within the time limits of a single degree program, it is not possible to prepare prospective teachers to teach multiple developmental age groups.

The unwillingness of policymakers in many states to enact distinct middle level teacher licensure regulations has led to this *amalgamation* of elementary and middle grades, and middle and high school grades. The failure to create mandatory middle level teacher licensure—with inaction usually being couched in the name of flexibility of hiring the best teachers no matter what their backgrounds or professional preparations—has resulted in the majority middle level teachers being inadequately prepared to teach young adolescents when they begin their careers.

The willingness on the part of policymakers, educators, and other stakeholders to allow virtually anyone, including those who have entered the profession through alternative routes, to teach young adolescents has resulted in many thousands of students enrolled in grades five through eight being taught by teachers who, at least initially, do not have the specialized knowledge and skills needed to be highly successful (Gaskill, 2002; McEwin & Dickinson, 1997; McEwin et al., in press). One of the best ways of avoiding this malpractice, and moving toward the goal of having all middle schools become high achieving, is for all states to adopt mandatory middle level licensure regulations that focus directly and exclusively on middle level teaching (National Forum to Accelerate Middle Grades Reform, 2002; National Middle School Association, n.d.). Furthermore, dates should be set in each state for when all middle level teachers must meet these licensure requirements (Cooney, 2000).

Responsibility for the lack of distinct middle level teacher licensure does not rest solely on the shoulders of policymakers. In many circumstances policymakers have been misled by interest groups and influential individuals. Efforts of advocates for the specialized professional preparation of middle level teachers are often blocked by other educators, including members of teacher unions and administrators seeking flexibility in hiring teachers. Teacher unions frequently fight any regulation that narrows the range of grades in which teachers can be hired, for example changing licensure from grades 6–12 to 5–8 for middle level and 9–12 for high school. This self-serving motive places the ease of obtaining teaching positions ahead of what is best for the education of young adolescents. Additionally, superintendents and personnel directors in some districts fight attempts to establish separate mandatory middle level teacher licensure because it makes filling middle level teaching positions more difficult. In other words, administrative convenience is given a higher priority than the quality of education provided for young adolescents. Both of these scenarios have occurred over a period of several decades in numerous states with the results being weak licensure regulations for middle level teachers in many states, and in some states, no distinct middle level requirements at all.

The news is not all bad regarding the progress by states in moving toward distinct middle level teacher licensure regulations. Forty-four states now have some form of middle level teacher license or endorsement. However, only 21 of these states require the middle level teacher license to teach at the middle level (Gaskill, 2002). Some states, like Ohio and North Carolina, have successful middle level teacher licensure systems which have resulted in near universal offering of middle level teacher preparation programs at both public and private teacher preparation institutions (McEwin et al., in press).

A more recent development that serves as a potential deterrent to gaining implementation of distinct middle level teacher licensure in all states is the emergence of recommendations by some individuals to eliminate teacher licensure, and in some cases teacher preparation, altogether (Fraser, 2001; Rotherham & Mead, 2003; Walsh, 2001). These unwarranted and dangerous recommendations are ill-conceived and not based on what is known from successful practice or the research on teacher preparation and licensure (Darling-Hammond, 2000b, 2001, 2003; Fetler, 1999; Hawk et al., 1985; Laczko-Kerr & Berliner, 2002; National Reading Panel, 2000; Wilson, Floden, & Ferrini-Mundy, 2001; Wise, 2003).

Space limitations do not allow for a full discussion of the merits of the teacher preparation and licensure issue here. However, policymakers should carefully examine claims made regarding the rationale for elimination or weakening of teacher licensure regulations as well as be aware of the dangers inherent in some alternative certification systems. For example, the American Board for Certification of Teacher Excellence (ABCTE) is planning to identify and certify teachers who have not gone through traditional teacher preparation institutions and facilitate their entry into the teaching profession. This goal, along with the misleading name of this organization, does not seem illogical until it is discovered that their plan for certifying teachers is to have them take a test on a computer. As noted by Wise, "ABCTE will face quite a challenge in assessing the personal and interpersonal skills and dispositions required of teachers in today's classrooms. If the individuals pass the test, as well as a background check, they are then 'certified'" (Wise, 2003, p.1). This kind of alternate licensure/certification process is ludicrous and ignores the fact that "common sense and empirical data agree: Those who have trained longer and harder to do the complex work of teaching do it better" and that "the hiring of undercertified teachers results in the hiring of unqualified teachers" (Laczko-Kerr & Berliner, 2003, p. 38).

No Child Left Behind Legislation

The No Child Left Behind (NCLB) legislation, and related initiatives from the United States Department of Education, have also emerged as deterrents to efforts to establish distinctive middle level teacher licensure. For example, at the time of this writing, the Colorado Department of Education is phasing out middle level teacher licensure, and therefore, middle level teacher preparation programs. The rationale offered for this action is to provide flexibility for school districts, to comply with the No Child Left Behind legislation, and to provide "highly qualified" teachers for the middle level (O'Drobinak & Gottlieb, 2003). As described in the section addressing crucial components of specialized middle level teacher preparation programs, the term "highly qualified" used in this chapter is not in sync with that found in the No Child Left Behind legislation (Paige, 2002; *No Child Left Behind*, 2002).

As readers are likely aware, the definition used in the NCLB legislation carries with it the illusion of providing every child with a highly qualified teacher when, in reality, NCLB allows virtually anyone with a college degree, the ability to pass a state-approved content test, and no criminal record to be deemed a "highly qualified teacher." Young adolescents, as well as other youth attending our nation's public schools, need and deserve teachers who have received the professional preparation needed to be effective, not just those who can pass a test (Wise, 2003).

The term "highly qualified," as defined in NCLB legislation, is profoundly illogical and disguises the tragedy of assuming virtually anyone will do when it comes to teaching the youth of our nation. As noted by Troen and Boles (2003), current opinion among some of the public and among too many policymakers is that "we should recruit teachers from among the brightest of the population who have no teacher training, and should bypass education schools as a source of future teachers. This is a short-sighted and wrong-headed approach, which overlooks the fact that teaching is a skill that must be learned in order to be practiced successfully" (p. 149). What is really needed, especially at the middle level, is a large cadre of highly capable, well-prepared teachers who know their content, are expert at teaching that knowledge effectively, and understand the developmental realities of the age group they are teaching.

Middle Level Teacher Licensure and Political Compromise

A political compromise that frequently results from the conflicting agenda of those advocating for the establishment of specialized mandatory licensure of middle level teachers and those not supporting this licensure in the name of needed *flexibility* is that of overlapping, non-mandatory middle level teacher licensure. As discussed by the authors in more detail in a previous publication (McEwin et al., 2003), this situation rarely leads to increasing numbers of prospective middle level teachers receiving the professional preparation they need to become highly successful. When prospective teachers are making decisions about the preparation program they will enter, a major factor in their decision is employability. For example, if a prospective teacher can major in elementary education and be licensed by the state to teach grades K–8, select a middle level major and teach grades 6–8, or choose a secondary major and receive a license that includes grades 6–12, frequently that teacher candidate will select elementary or secondary education rather than middle level education because of the greater range of grade levels included in those options. This means that teacher candidates learn to be generalists in elementary education programs or enroll in secondary programs that focus on one or two content areas with little or no attention placed on the specialized knowledge, skills, and dispositions needed to become successful middle level teachers.

An additional result of this overlap situation is that specialized middle level teacher preparation programs are never developed by many institutions with other teacher preparation programs. Why would distinct middle level teacher preparation programs be established at institutions when programs in elementary and secondary education already result in licensure that covers all grades included in public schools? The results of these decisions on the part of institutions not to establish middle level teacher preparation programs leave prospective middle level teachers with no option but to enroll in programs designed to learn how to teach young children or high school students. The only way to solve this situation is for states to establish distinct middle level teacher license regulation that does not overlap with elementary and high school education (i.e., grades K–4, 5–8, 9–12).

The message of overlapping, non-mandatory licensure options are that specialized middle level teacher preparation programs are "nice to have, but not really necessary." In many states, this scenario is an accurate description of the current situation in teacher licensure. A major result of this situation is that the majority of current teacher preparation programs focus either on the elementary or high school level with the assumption that graduates of either group are, in some magical way, also well prepared to teach young adolescents (McEwin & Dickinson, 1996; McEwin et al., 2003).

An additional problem that arises as a result of political compromise is that of establishing an "add-on" middle level license/endorsement that is available, but not required, to teach at the middle level. The message delivered by such a license is that preparing teachers of young adolescents is not a worthy goal within itself. Typically, in these add-on endorsement plans, prospective teachers must first earn a degree and license in elementary education or a high school subject area before being able to *extend* their preparation to receive the add-on middle level license. Experience in numerous states has shown that this is one of the least effective ways to move toward the goal of having specially prepared teachers for young adolescents.

Among the negative implications of this plan is the clear message to prospective teachers that preparing to teach at the middle level is of secondary importance and that obtaining a middle level license is possible only after obtaining a *legitimate* preparation to teach at the elementary or high school level. Given these circumstances, it is not surprising that relatively few prospective teachers complete the extra work needed to qualify for the add-on middle level endorsement since it is not required for middle level teaching. In summary, the reasons for the lack of success of add-on endorsements and overlapping licensure patterns are many, with the end result being few prospective teachers selecting middle level teaching in those states with such licensure plans (McEwin et al., in press).

The implication of the lack of specialized middle level preparation and licensure is not that all middle level teachers are ineffective. Without a doubt, there are many successful middle level teachers who have not received specialized middle level teacher preparation and licensure. However, many of these teachers have learned to be effective middle level teachers through a "trial and error" experience while transforming themselves from teachers of young children or high school students to middle level teachers. As noted by the authors in an earlier publication "The trial and error approach leaves too much to chance and penalizes young adolescents who happen to be taught by teachers who are still in the interim 'learning period'" (McEwin et al., in press). This is not a model of teacher preparation that should continue in this new century if the goal of having high achieving middle schools for all young adolescents is to be attained.

The overall objective of middle level teacher licensure should be that all middle level teachers, novice and experienced, are prepared in programs that reflect the program components briefly described in this chapter and discussed more comprehensively in the literature (see, e.g., National Forum to Accelerate Middle Grades Reform, 2002; National Middle School Association, n.d., 2001; McEwin & Dickinson, 1995, 1997; McEwin, Dickinson & Erb, 1995; McEwin et al., in press). The responsibility of policymakers, especially those at professional licensure agencies and professional practice boards, is to create policies that ensure that all young adolescents are taught by teachers who, even in their first years of teaching, have received the specialized professional preparation to be highly successful.

Policymakers must stand ready to defy those who dismiss the uniqueness of young adolescents and the professional preparation needed by those who teach them. For without this stance, the needs of young adolescents will continue to be subservient to administrative convenience and other factors that often surface as higher priorities than middle level teacher preparation and licensure. It is time for policymakers to make courageous decisions that protect young adolescents from underprepared teachers who are routinely assigned to teach them in many states. The most effective way to change the traditional course of ignoring the needs of young adolescents by permitting underprepared, and even inappropriately prepared, teachers to teach them, is to strengthen the licensure regulations that determine the nature of teacher preparation programs. If this task is to be achieved in the current political climate, policymakers, educators, politicians, and other stakeholders must advocate for middle level teacher preparation and licensure as never before.

An additional way to ensure quality teachers for young adolescents is for policymakers to refuse to support alternate licensure plans that place teachers in middle level classrooms without the knowledge and skills needed to teach young adolescents. When alternate routes to licensure are provided, recipients of those licenses should be required to continue their professional preparation until they have demonstrated that they have the specialized knowledge, skills, and dispositions needed to be successful middle level teachers. America's middle schools must have specially prepared teachers who wish to teach young adolescents and have the proper professional preparation to do so effectively if all middle schools are to be *high achieving*.

RETAINING TEACHERS FOR HIGH-PERFORMING MIDDLE SCHOOLS

Although substantial evidence suggests that well prepared, capable teachers have the greatest impact on student learning (see Darling-Hammond, 2000a; Wilson et al., 2001), *preparing* teachers to do their important work with students is not sufficient. More must be done to provide ongoing support to novice teachers as they move into communities of teaching practice. Since the early 1990s, the number of people leaving teaching each year has exceeded the number entering the profession by an increasing amount (Darling-Hammond, 2003). Less than 20% of this attrition is due to retirement (Henke, Chen, & Geis, 2000; Ingersoll, 2001). Existing research has sought to explain teacher turnover as a function of individual characteristics of teachers. More recently, Ingersoll (1999, 2001) has examined the teacher turnover phenomenon from an organizational perspective. An organizational perspective is particularly informative and promising because if the causes of teacher turnover can be linked to organizations, so too, can the remedies. Therefore, the possibility of affecting change is within reach for school administrators and policymakers.

While it may not be possible to change the decision of a single teacher who has decided to leave the teaching profession, it is possible to make policy and organizational changes to address the sources of low retention. From his analysis, Ingersoll (2001) concluded, "Unless we develop policies to stem such attrition through better preparation, assignment, working conditions, and mentor support, we cannot meet the goal of ensuring that all students have qualified teachers" (p. 9). He emphasized the critical nature of the continuum of support teachers need as they move from their novice status into the professional culture of their schools, departments, or teams.

Conceivably, many teachers leave the middle school organization because they are inadequately prepared to teach the age group or to understand the organizational structure of the middle school. Compounding the problem, licensure regulations and legislation are allowing increasing numbers of inadequately prepared teachers to experience failure in middle level classrooms. Such licensure and legislative decisions are seldom made for the sake of increasing student learning. Rather, they are made to provide short-sighted solutions to complex staffing problems. Frequently, individuals coming into a middle level teaching experience without adequate knowledge about the age group or appropriate strategies and methods for teaching them can quickly become frustrated. Student discipline may become a problem because the teacher is unfamiliar with the characteristics of the students or how to respond to them appropriately. These factors contribute to the "revolving door" phenomenon in many of the nation's schools. Although total teacher turnover is fairly evenly split between teacher *attrition* (those who leave teaching altogether) and teacher *migration* (those who move to teaching jobs in other schools), the effects of either type of turnover can cause turmoil in individual schools and districts. High teacher turnover not only causes staffing problems but also leads to a lack of continuity and cohesion among teachers that may upset the school environment and impede student performance (Darling-Hammond, 2003; Ingersoll & Smith, 2003).

Not only is high teacher turnover potentially devastating to schools and students from an organizational perspective but also early attrition bears enormous costs to school districts. A recent study in Texas indicated that the state "is losing between $329 million and $2.1 billion per year, depending on the industry cost model that is used" (Texas Center for Educational Research, 2000, p. 2). The beginning teacher turnover rate is higher than the average rate for other teachers. Approximately 19 percent leave at the end of their first year of teaching. Given that teacher effectiveness increases sharply after the first years of teaching (Kain & Singleton, 1996), this kind of churning in the beginning teaching force is even more costly because the education system never receives the long-term payoff from its investment in novices who leave the profession.

Teacher Retention and School Culture

For many teachers, the decision whether or not to stay in teaching may be affected by the professional culture of the schools where they begin their careers. A study of 50 first- and second-year teachers at the Harvard Graduate School of Education revealed three types of professional culture (Kardos, Johnson, Peske, Kauffman, & Liu, 2001). The researchers labeled these professional cultures based on the new teachers' descriptions of their school work environments, especially their descriptions of their interactions with colleagues in their schools, departments, and/or teams.

Some of the teachers described a **veteran-oriented professional culture**. In veteran-oriented professional cultures, the norms of professional practice are determined by and designed to serve veteran teachers. These new teachers often reported working in schools with high proportions of veteran teachers with "well-established, independent patterns of work." In this type of environment, new teachers often reported feeling isolated due to their lack of experience and expertise. Little to no formal induction was provided to help new teachers as they established their professional life and identity in the school.

In contrast to veteran-oriented professional cultures, some participants in the same study described a **novice-oriented professional culture**. In novice-oriented professional cultures, youth, inexperience, and idealism prevailed. Novice-oriented professional cultures were often found in two types of schools: start up charter schools that were often staffed with new recruits, many without formal preparation as teachers, or urban schools that were often struggling with organizational problems and high teacher turnover rates. Schools with novice-oriented professional cultures were often characterized by high energy and vigorous commitment, but the staff often did not have sufficient professional guidance about how to teach.

Finally, some of these new teachers described the start of their careers in an **integrated professional culture**. In these schools professional exchange and collaboration was encouraged across all experience levels, and sustained support and professional development was provided for all teachers. In an integrated professional culture, novice and expert teachers were not placed in separate groups for support or professional development. Rather, novice teachers in integrated professional cultures not only believed that their expert colleagues understood the importance of mentoring them but that the experienced teachers also benefitted from the mentoring relationship.

Of the three types of professional culture (veteran-oriented, novice-oriented, and integrated), not only did respondents report greater satisfaction working in integrated professional cultures but also after their first year of teaching, a higher proportion of those who worked in integrated cultures remained in public schools (89% versus 83% for novice oriented, and 75% for veteran-oriented cultures). Perhaps more significant, 83% of the respondents who had worked in integrated professional cultures during their first year were still teaching in the same school during the second year, compared with only 55% of those who began work in veteran-oriented cultures and 67% who worked in novice-oriented cultures in their first year.

For teachers who receive specialized professional preparation to work with young adolescents in middle level schools, work in an integrated professional culture is an especially good fit. A critical element of specialized preparation at the middle level includes learning to work with an interdisciplinary team of teachers to organize and maximize relationships for student learning (Jackson & Davis, 2000, McEwin et al., in press; Mertens, Flowers, & Mulhall, 2002). In this context, teachers work together to create lesson plans, share and discuss student progress, problems and issues, and integrate subjects around a central theme or issue. Research has demonstrated that in order for interdisciplinary teams to be effective, teachers on these teams need regular common planning time to work together as a group to integrate and coordinate curriculum, to develop student assignments and assessments, and to contact and involve parents (Erb & Doda, 1989; Flowers et al., 1999, 2000; George & Alexander, 1993; Howe & Bell, 1998; Warren & Muth, 1995).

Historically, schools have not been set up to support the learning needs of teachers. However, as new teachers continue leaving the profession, researchers and other stakeholders have begun to consider their needs more carefully (Feiman-Nemser, 2003). Typical school organizations keep teachers separated from one another, creating or reinforcing a sense of isolation and autonomy, and without easy access to one another, teachers may feel reluctant to share problems or ask for help, believing that good teachers figure things out on their own (Feiman-Nemser, 2003). Common planning time and deliberate teaming approaches provide teachers easy access to each other, and interdisciplinary approaches provide a student- and curriculum-focus consistent with the purpose of the middle school—promoting individual intellectual ability and integrated identity.

The evidence about teacher retention is clear. Teachers who are adequately prepared and supported to do their important work with students are more likely to remain in teaching. In deciding whether to stay in their schools, transfer to new schools, or leave public school teaching, new "teachers weighed, more than anything else, whether they could be effective with their students" (Johnson & Birkeland, 2002, p. 3). If young adolescents in America's middle level schools are to be successful, then the teachers who work with them must be not only highly qualified but also effective in their work with students.

CONCLUSION

Policymakers can contribute to the success of high performing middle schools by creating and supporting policies that promote (a) high quality specialized middle level teacher preparation programs, (b) middle level licensure that supports specialized middle level teacher preparation, and (c) a continuum of support for middle level teachers (i.e., induction and mentoring programs). If these actions are taken in a timely manner, increasing numbers of young adolescents will be taught by teachers who have the specialized knowledge, skills, and dispositions to help their students become capable, competent, and well-grounded learners.

REFERENCES

Alexander, W.M. (1965). The junior high school: A changing view. In G. Hass & K. Wiles (Eds.). *Readings in curriculum.* Boston, MA: Allyn & Bacon. [Reprinted as Alexander, W. M. (1995). The junior high school: A changing view. *Middle School Journal, 27*(3), 20–24.]

Alexander, W.M., & George, P.S. (1981). *The exemplary middle school.* New York: Holt, Rinehart and Winston.

Balfanz, R., & Byrnes, V. (2003, April). *Closing the mathematics achievement gap in high poverty middle schools: Enablers and constraints.* Paper presented at the annual meeting of the American Educational Research Association, Chicago.

Balfanz, R., & MacIver, D.J., (2000). Transforming high-poverty urban middle schools into strong learning institutions: Lessons from the first five years of the Talent Development Middle School. *Journal of Education for Students Placed at Risk, 5*(1 & 2), 137–158.

Cooney, S. (2000). *A middle grades message: A well-qualified teacher in every classroom matters.* Atlanta, GA: Southern Regional Education Board. Retrieved August 9, 2003 from http://www.sreb.org

Corbett, D., & Wilson, B. (2003, April). *Instructional coaches as reform lynchpins.* Paper presented at the annual meeting of the American Educational Research Association, Chicago.

Darling-Hammond, L. (2000a). Teacher quality and student achievement: A review of state policy evidence. *Educational Policy Analysis Archives, (8)*1. Retrieved August 9, 2003 from http://epaa.asu.edu/epaa/v8n1

Darling-Hammond, L. (2000b). Reforming teacher preparation and licensing: Debating the evidence. *Teachers College Record, 102*(1), 5–27.

Darling-Hammond, L. (2001). *The research and rhetoric on teacher certification: A response to "Teacher certification reconsidered."* Washington, DC: National Commission on Teaching and America's Future. Retrieved August 9, 2003 from http://www.nctaf.org/publications/index.html

Darling-Hammond, L. (2003). Keeping good teachers: Why it matters, what leaders can do. *Educational Leadership, 60*(8), 6–13.

Dickinson, T.S. (Ed.). (2001). *Reinventing the middle school.* New York: Routledge-Falmer.

Elkind, D. (1998). *All grown up and no place to go: Teenagers in crisis.* Reading, MA: Addison-Wesley.

Erb, T.O., & Doda, N.M. (1989). *Team Organization: Promise-Practices and Possibilities.* Washington, DC: National Education Association.

Feiman-Nemser, S. (2003). What new teachers need to learn. *Educational Leadership, 60*(8), 25–29.

Felner, R.D., Jackson, A.W., Kasak, D., Mulhall, P., Brand, S., & Flowers, N. (1997). The impact of school reform for the middle years: Longitudinal study of a network engaged in Turning Points-based comprehensive school transformation. *Phi Delta Kappan, 78,* 528–532, 541–550.

Fetler, M. (1999). High school staff characteristics and mathematics test results. *Education Policy Analysis Archives, 7(9).* Retrieved August 9, 2003 from http://epaa.asu.edu/epaa/v7n9.html

Flowers, N., Mertens, S.B., & Mulhall, P.F. (1999). The impact of teaming: Five research-based outcomes of teaming. *Middle School Journal, 31*(2), 57–60.

Flowers, N., Mertens, S.B., & Mulhall, P.F. (2000a). What makes interdisciplinary teams effective? *Middle School Journal, 31*(4), 53–56.

Flowers, N., Mertens, S., & Mulhall, P. (2000b). How teaming influences classroom practices. *Middle School Journal, 32*(2), 52–59.

Flowers, N., Mertens, S., Mulhall, P. (2002a). Four important lessons about teacher professional development. *Middle School Journal, 33*(5), 57–61.

Flowers, N., Mertens, S., Mulhall, P. (2002b). The relationship between middle-grades teacher certification and teaching practices. In V.A. Anfara, Jr., & S.L. Stacki (Eds.), *Middle school curriculum, instruction, and assessment.* Greenwich, CT: Information Age Publishing.

Fraser, J.W. (January 31, 2001). Time to cut the link between teacher preparation and certification? *Education Week.* Retrieved August 9, 2003 from http://www.edweek.org/ew/ewstory.cfm?slug=20fraser.h20

Gaskill, P.E. (2002). Progress in the certification of middle-level personnel. *Middle School Journal, 33*(5), 33–40.

George, P.S., & Alexander, W.M. (1993). The *exemplary middle school* (2nd ed.). Fort Worth, TX: Harcourt Brace Javanovich College Publishers.

Hawk, P., Coble, C.R., & Swanson, M. (1985). Certification: It does matter. *Journal of Teacher Education, 36*(3), 13–15.

Henke, R.R., Chen, X., & Geis, S. (2000). *Progress through the teacher pipeline: 1992–93 college graduates and elementary/secondary school teaching as of 1997.* Washington, DC: National Center for Educational Statistics.

Herlihy, C., & Kemple, J. (2003, April). *Impacts of the Talent Development Middle School model on achievement, attendance, and promotion: A third-party evaluation.* Paper presented at the annual meeting of the American Educational Research Association, Chicago.

Howe, A.C., & Bell, J. (1998). Factors associated with successful implementation of interdisciplinary curriculum units. *Research in Middle Level Education Quarterly, 21*(2), 39–52.

Ingersoll, R.M. (1999). The problem of underqualified teachers in American secondary schools. *Educational Researcher, 28*(2), 26–37.

Ingersoll, R.M. (2001). *A different approach to solving the teacher shortage problem* (Teaching Quality Policy Brief Number 3). Seattle, WA: Center for the Study of Teaching and Policy, University of Washington.

Ingersoll, R.M., & Smith, T.M. (2003). The wrong solution to the teacher shortage. *Educational Leadership, 60*(8), 30–33.

Jackson, A.W., & Davis, G.A. (2000). *Turning points 2000: Educating adolescents in the 21st century.* New York: Teachers College Press.

Johnson, S.M., & Birkeland, S.E. ((2002, April). *Pursuing "sense of success": New teachers explain their career decisions.* Paper presented at the annual meeting of the American Educational Research Association. New Orleans, LA.

Kain, J.F., & Singleton, K. (1996, May/June). Equality of educational opportunity revisited. *New England Economic Review, 87*–111.

Kardos, S.M., Johnson, S.M., Peske, H.G., Kauffman, D., & Liu, E. (2001). Counting on colleagues: New teachers encounter the professional cultures of their schools. *Educational Administration Quarterly, 37*(2), 250–290.

Laczko-Kerr, I., & Berliner, D.C. (2003). How undercertified teachers hurt their students. *Educational Leadership, 60*(8), 34–39.

Lipsitz, J., Jackson, A.W., & Austin, L.M. (1997). What works in middle-grades school reform. *Phi Delta Kappan, 78*(7), 517–519.

MacIver, D.J., & Epstein, J. (1991). Responsive practices in the middle grades: Teacher teams, advisory groups, remedial instruction, and school transition programs. *American Journal of Education, 99*, 587–622.

MacIver, D.J., MacIver, M.A., Balfanz, R., Plank, S., & Ruby, A. (2000). Talent Development Middle Schools: Blueprint and results for a comprehensive whole school reform model. In M.G. Sanders (Ed.), *Schooling at risk: Research, policy, and practice in the education of poor and minority adolescents* (pp. 292–319). Mahwah, NJ: Erlbaum Associates.

MacIver, D.J., & Prioleau, A.D. (1999, April). *Looping: Helping middle school teachers to be caring, daring, and effective.* Paper presented at the annual meeting of the American Educational Research Association, Montreal, Canada.

MacIver, D.J., Young, E., Balfanz, R., Shaw, A., Garriott, M., & Cohen, A. (2001). High quality learning opportunities in high poverty middle schools: Moving from rhetoric to reality. In T. Dickinson (Ed.), *Reinventing the middle school* (pp. 155–175). New York: RoutledgeFalmer.

MacIver, D.J. (2003, April). *"Removed from the list": A comparative longitudinal case study of a reconstitution-eligible school.* Paper presented at the annual meeting of the American Educational Research Association, Chicago.

McEwin, C.K., & Dickinson, T.S. (1995). *The professional preparation of middle level teachers.* Westerville, OH: National Middle School Association.

McEwin, C.K., & Dickinson, T.S. (1996). *Forgotten youth, forgotten teachers: Transformation of the professional preparation of teachers of young adolescents.* Background paper prepared for the Middle Grade School State Policy Initiative. Carnegie Corporation of New York.

McEwin, C.K., & Dickinson, T.S. (1997). Middle-level teacher preparation and licensure. In J.L. Irvin (Ed.). *What research says to the practitioner.* (pp. 223–229). Columbus, OH: National Middle School Association.

McEwin, C.K., Dickinson, T.S., Erb, T.O., & Scales, P.C. (1995). *A vision of excellence: Organizing principles for middle grades teacher preparation.* Westerville, OH: National Middle School Association.

McEwin, C.K., Dickinson, T.S., & Smith, T.W. (in press). Middle level teacher preparation: Status, progress, and challenges. In A.W. Jackson & G. Andrews (Eds.). *Leaders for a movement: The Professional preparation and development of middle level teachers and administrators.* Greenwich, CT: Information Age Publishing.

Mertens, S.B., Flowers, N., & Mulhall, P.F. (1998a). *The middle start initiative, phase I: A longitudinal analysis of Michigan middle-level schools.* Champaign-Urbana: University of Illinois, Center for Prevention Research & Development.

Mertens, S.B., Flowers, N., & Mulhall, P.F. (1998b). *The middle start initiative, phase K: A longitudinal analysis of Michigan middle-level schools.* Champaign-Urbana: University of Illinois, Center for Prevention Research & Development.

Mertens, S.B., Flowers, N., & Mulhall, P.F. (2001). School size matters in interesting ways. *Middle School Journal, 32*(5), 51–55.

Mertens, S.B., Flowers, N., & Mulhall, P.F. (2003). Should middle grades students be left alone after school. *Middle School Journal, 34*(5), 57–61.

Mulhall, P.F. Flowers, N., & Mertens, S.B. (2002). Understanding indicators related to academic performance. *Middle School Journal, 34*(2), 56–61

National Forum to Accelerate Middle Grades Reform. (2002). *Policy statement: Teacher preparation, licensure, and recruitment.* Newton, MA: Education Development Center. Retrieved August 9, 2003 from http://www.mgforum.org

National Middle School Association. (n.d.). *National Middle School Association's position statement on professional preparation of middle level teachers.* Westerville, OH: Author. Retrieved August 9, 2003 from http://www.nmsa.org/

National Middle School Association. (n.d.). *Position paper on curriculum integration.* Retrieved March 26, 2003, from http://www.nmsa.org/news/positionpapers/integrativecurriculum.htm

National Middle School Association/National Council for Accreditation of Teacher Educational-Approved middle level teacher preparation standards (2001). Westerville, OH: Author. Retrieved August 24, 2003 from http://www.nmsa.org

National Middle School Association. (1995). *This we believe: Developmentally responsive middle level schools.* Columbus, OH: Author.

National Reading Panel. (2000). *Teaching children to read: An evidence-based assessment of the scientific research literature on reading and its implications for reading instruction.* Washington, DC: National Institute of Child Health and Human Development.

No Child Left Behind. (2002). *NCLB legislation.* Retrieved August 9, 2003 from http://www.ed.gov/offices/OESE/asst.html

O'Drobinak, B., & Gottlieb, A. (2003). Middle grades reform lagging in Colorado. Denver, CO: The Piton Foundation. Retrieved August 9, 2003 from http://www.piton.org/Admin/Article/TermPaper.May2003.qrk.pdf

Paige, R. (2002). *Meeting the highly qualified teachers challenge: The secretary's annual report on teacher quality. Washington,* DC: U. S. Department of Education.

Plank, S., & Young, E. (1999, April). *In the long run: Longitudinal assessments of the Student Team Literature Program.* Paper presented at the annual meeting of the American Educational Research Association, Montreal, Canada.

Rice, J.K. (2003). *Teacher quality: Understanding the effectiveness of teacher attributes.* Washington, DC: Economic Policy Institute.

Rotherham, A.J., & Mead, S. (2003). Teacher quality: Beyond No Child Left Behind, A response to Kaplan and Owings. *NASSP Bulletin, 87*(635), 65–76.

Ruby, A. (1999, April). *An implementable curriculum approach to improving science instruction in urban middle schools.* Paper presented at the annual meeting of the American Educational Research Association, Montreal, Canada.

Ruby, A. (2003, April). *Science reform within whole school reform: Results from the Talent Development Middle School model.* Paper presented at the annual meeting of the American Educational Research Association, Chicago.

Texas Center for Educational Research. (2000). *The cost of teacher turnover.* Austin, TX: Texas State Board for Teacher Certification.

Trimble, S.B. (1995). *A theoretical framework for the analysis of high performing interdisciplinary team functioning in selected middle schools.* Unpublished doctoral dissertation, Florida State University, Tallahassee.

Trimble, S. (2002). Common elements of high performing, high poverty middle schools. *Middle School Journal, 33*(4), 7–16.

Trimble, S.B., & Peterson, G.W. (2000, April). *Multiple team structures and student learning in a high risk middle school.* Paper presented at the annual meeting of the American Educational Research Association, New Orleans.

Troen, V., & Boles, K.C. (2003). *Who's teaching your children? Why the teacher crisis is worse than you think and what can be done about it.* New Haven, CT: Yale University Press.

Useem, E.L. (1998). *Teachers' appraisals of Talent Development Middle School training, materials, and student progress: Results from six focus groups at Central East Middle School and Cooke Middle School.* Baltimore, MD: Johns Hopkins University, Center for Research on the Education of Students Placed at Risk.

Walsh, K. (2001). *Teacher certification reconsidered: Stumbling for quality.* Baltimore, MD: The Abel Foundation. Retrieved August 9, 2003 from http://www.abell.org

Warren, L.L., & Muth, K.D. (1995). The impact of common planning time on middle grade students and teachers. *Research in Middle Level Education, 18*(3), 41–58.

Wilson, S.M., Floden, R.E., & Ferrini-Mundy, J. (2001). *Teacher preparation research: Current knowledge, gaps, and recommendations* (Document R-01-3). University of Washington: Center for the Study of Teaching and Policy.

Wise, A.E. (2003). Testing does not equal teaching: One test does not make a highly qualified teacher. *NCATE News.* Retrieved August 9, 2003 from http://www.ncate.org/newsbrfs/testing_teach.pd

CHAPTER 8

LESSONS LEARNED FROM COMPREHENSIVE SCHOOL REFORM MODELS

Nancy Ames

BACKGROUND AND HISTORY OF CSR

For many years, the federal government funneled money into public schools with high concentrations of poverty, hoping that low-performing students would receive the extra help needed to catch up with their peers in reading and mathematics. In most cases, the funds were earmarked for certain students—those who were low-achieving or designated at risk of educational failure. This often resulted in students being pulled out of class for remedial instruction in reading and mathematics. Despite intensive intervention, few of these students ever caught up with their peers. When this approach failed, schools tried a variety of piecemeal approaches, sometimes piling one on top of the other.

In the last decade, due to the failure of these limited or piecemeal interventions, attention has increasingly turned to "comprehensive school reform" (CSR) as the key to real and lasting school improvement. CSR is a strategy for improving all aspects of school life, while giving schools ownership of the change process. By using a unified approach to school improve-

Reforming Middle Level Education: Considerations for Policymakers, pages 131–154
Copyright © 2004 by Information Age Publishing
All rights of reproduction in any form reserved.

ment, schools engaged in comprehensive school reform can leverage scarce state and local resources to accelerate the pace of reform. The ultimate goal of CSR is to increase academic achievement among all students, particularly those who are low-achieving, so that they can meet rigorous academic standards.

The seeds of comprehensive school reform were planted in the 1980s with the creation of several comprehensive approaches to whole school change. These included Larry Lezotte's *Effective Schools Model*, which grew out of research by Ron Edmonds and others; Theodore Sizer's *Coalition of Essential Schools*; James P. Comer's *School Development Program*; and Henry Levin's *Accelerated Schools.*,

With the 1991 creation of the New American Schools Development Corporation (NASDC), now known as NAS, the CSR movement accelerated. NASDC was a public/private venture that grew out of growing corporate concern over the poor performance of America's public schools. NASDC issued a request for proposals (RFP) for "Break-the-Mold" designs for whole-school transformation. It was looking for school reform models that would change all the components of the school at once, rather than tinkering around the edges. While hundreds of proposals were submitted, only 30 were genuinely responsive to the RFP. Of these, NASDC chose eleven proposals for initial funding, and seven of these eventually went on to develop, test, refine, disseminate, and scale-up new models. The final set included: ATLAS Communities; Audrey Cohen College (now called Purpose-Centered Education); Co-NECT; Expeditionary Learning Outward Bound; Modern Red Schoolhouse; National Alliance for Restructuring Education (now America's Choice); and Roots and Wings (now Success for All).

In November 1997, CSR gained even greater attention when the U.S. Congress approved $150 million to support its implementation in school districts across the nation. Four years later, CSR was written in as a core component of the No Child Left Behind (NCLB) Act. The goal of the CSR component is "to raise student achievement by assisting public schools across the country to implement effective, comprehensive school reforms that are based upon scientifically-based research and effective practices" (*No Child Left Behind Act*, 2001). Under the federal legislation, states provide competitive grants to school districts on behalf of specific schools that are ready to adopt comprehensive reforms to help students reach high standards. Each participating school receives at least $50,000 of CSR funds per year, renewable for up to three years.

In 2003, the federal government awarded another $308 million in funding. Approximately three-quarters of these funds are earmarked for Title I schools with high concentrations of poor students and/or schools in need of improvement. Research suggests that the monies are reaching their target. The average poverty rate of CSR schools is 70%. In addition, 40% of the CSR schools have been identified for Title I school improvement, and another 25% have been identified as low-performers by state or local policies (Borman, Hewes, Overman, & Brown, 2002).

A key feature of the federal CSR program that sets it apart from other reform initiatives is that it requires schools to adopt a proven, research-based model to accelerate their efforts to improve student achievement. (In rare instances, schools design their own home-grown models.) These "models" or "designs" provide road maps for schools that desire comprehensive change. Schools choose a model that matches their needs, and school personnel collaborate with the model designers to develop a school improvement plan using the particular model's framework. The model developers work closely with school personnel to reach a point where the school is coordinating and implementing different components of the improvement plan.

Thousands of schools have received funding so far, and more will be funded in subsequent rounds. Thousands more schools not funded by the federal CSR initiative are also implementing these models through the allocation of Title I funds or reallocation of state and local resources. These models represent a wide variety of ideas about the nature of the problems in U.S. education, possible solutions, and the best ways to bring about change. Some concentrate heavily on school organization and climate, while others focus more on curriculum and instruction. Several tackle all aspects of school life at once, while others are more targeted. Some are quite prescriptive, mandating a specific curriculum and carefully defined instructional strategies, whereas others provide a broad framework along with the structures, tools, and processes for change. Whatever their scope and focus, the basic goal of every model is the same: to provide the structure and strategies schools need to significantly improve achievement for all students.

Whether they use a nationally available model or develop their program locally, a school seeking funding for CSR under NCLB must coherently integrate the following eleven components. Schools are required to implement a comprehensive school reform program that:

- employs proven methods and strategies based on scientifically-based research (in most cases, this involves an externally-developed model);
- integrates a comprehensive design with aligned components;
- provides ongoing, high-quality professional development for teachers and staff;
- includes measurable goals and benchmarks for student achievement;
- is supported within the school by teachers, administrators, and staff;
- provides support for teachers, administrators, and staff;

- provides for meaningful parent and community involvement in planning, implementing, and evaluating school improvement activities;
- uses high-quality external technical support and assistance from an external partner with experience and expertise in school-wide reform and improvement;
- plans for the evaluation of strategies for the implementation of school reforms and for student results achieved annually; and
- identifies resources to support and sustain the school's comprehensive reform effort.

A few of these components are worthy of special note. First, the legislation requires CSR schools to access high-quality technical assistance from outside partners experienced in school-wide reform. Second, the CSR program provides incentives for schools to develop comprehensive reform programs based upon scientifically-based research and effective practices. These two components motivate many schools to select an externally designed, research-based model to support the change process. Third, CSR funds are not intended to support separate projects that are "added on" to existing programs or projects in a school. Rather, CSR grants are designed to help schools improve their entire educational program through changes in school organization and climate, improvements in curriculum and instruction, sustained professional development, enhanced involvement of parents, and the like. Finally, CSR funds help finance comprehensive reforms that take advantage of all the resources available to the school, including federal, state, local, and private resources. These resources support integrated strategies that enable all children, including children from low-income families, children with limited English proficiency, and children with disabilities, to reach challenging academic standards.

PROGRAM IMPACT

A number of researchers have studied the impact of these models on schools, teachers, and student outcomes. Overall, the impact of these CSR models has been highly variable across models, settings, and research conditions. While some researchers have found significant and educationally meaningful achievement gains, others have not.

In 1998, Ross and his colleagues at the Center for Research in Education Policy at the University of Memphis examined the influence of eight models on student performance, as measured by the Tennessee Comprehensive Assessment Program, the state-mandated standardized achievement test. Using the Tennessee Value-Added Assessment System, the study compared student gains in five subjects (reading, mathematics, language, science, and social studies) in 25 CSR schools with gains in matched control schools, other elementary schools in the district, and national norms. The study found that after two years, students in schools implementing CSR models showed significantly greater gains in performance than students in other schools. Furthermore, across all grades and subjects, these students were improving at a faster rate than the national average (Ross, Sanders, Wright, & Stringfield, 1998). In a subsequent study published a year later, Ross and his colleagues found that the effects varied by model, with Accelerated Schools, Roots and Wings, and Co-NECT having the strongest impact on student achievement. Moreover, high poverty schools seemed to derive the greatest benefits from comprehensive school reform compared to demographically similar schools that had not implemented a CSR program (Ross et al., 1999).

Based on an examination of performance trends across several sets of NAS schools three years into scale-up, Rand researchers found a great deal of variability in program implementation and impact across both settings and models (Bodilly, 1998). Among the four jurisdictions with ten or more NAS schools, Memphis and Kentucky schools appeared to be most successful in improving student achievement in mathematics, while Cincinnati and state of Washington did better in reading. Of the 163 schools for which there was comparative district- or state-level data, 81 schools (50%) made gains relative to the district in mathematics, and 76 schools (47%) made gains in reading.

More recently, researchers at the Center for Research on the Education of Students Placed at Risk (CRESPAR) completed a meta-analysis of 29 of the most widely implemented CSR models (Borman et al., 2002). The researchers identified more than 800 studies that appeared to link CSR with student achievement, of which 231 had sufficient achievement data to compute effect sizes as well as comparison groups. These studies showed that after an average of three years of implementation, the CSR schools significantly outperformed their matched comparisons. The overall effect size for the CSR models was 0.15, a small, but statistically significant effect. Put another way, the results of the meta-analysis revealed that the average student who participated in a CSR program outperformed approximately 56 percent of similar students who did not attend a CSR school. This number compares favorably to a meta-analysis of the achievement effects of Title I programs that typically use pullout approaches, where the effect size was 0.11. The researchers conclude that the overall effects of CSR are meaningful and greater in magnitude than those of other interventions designed to serve similar purposes and student populations (Borman et al., 2002).

The meta-analysis also revealed wide variability within and across program models and across study design features. For example, 34% required a specific curriculum, 41% required specific instructional strategies, and

45% required a parent outreach program. Nearly half (45%) required a faculty vote of 75% or more for adoption. Surprisingly, in light of the federal requirements, only 38% required student assessments and benchmarks, and only 33% required ongoing professional development (Borman et al., 2002).

THE DEVELOPMENT OF MIDDLE-GRADES MODELS

As more and more schools applied for CSR funding, it soon became apparent that few models were specifically geared toward middle-grades or high schools. Even those that claimed to serve students in grades K–8 or K–12 made few, if any, distinctions in program design or service delivery among the various grade levels. In addition, nearly two-thirds of the CSR funds were allocated to elementary schools, which had far higher levels of implementation than did middle-grades or high schools (Bodilly, 1998). The U.S. Department of Education, consequently, decided to boost the supply of effective secondary school models.

In 1999, the Office of Educational Research and Improvement issued a major Request for Proposals asking existing design teams to design, test, refine, and scale up models specifically earmarked for middle-grades or high schools. Following a heavy round of competition, the Department awarded seven five-year contracts to a diverse group of model developers. These included AIM at Middle-Grades Results (EDC); Different Ways of Knowing (Gale Institute); Making Middle-Grades Work (Southern Regional Education Board); Success for All (SFA Foundation); and Talent Development Middle School Model (Johns Hopkins University, Center for the Social Organization of Schools).

In addition to these federally-funded models, a few national foundations also sponsored the design, testing, and implementation of comprehensive school reform models at the middle level during the 1990s. For example, W.K. Kellogg Foundation launched Michigan Middle Start in 1994. While not originally designed as a CSR model, Middle Start (AED) has evolved into a major whole-school change program with a national focus and a strong presence in both Michigan and the Mid-South. Another CSR model, Turning Points (Center for Collaborative Education), grew out of more than a decade of research and development on middle-level education sponsored by the Carnegie Corporation.

Leaders from all seven of these middle-grades CSR models are members of the National Forum to Accelerate Middle-Grades Reform, a nationally recognized group of organizations and individuals dedicated to accelerating the pace of middle-grades school improvement. Each of the middle-grades models is different in scope, focus, and services offered. Yet, all are committed to the Forum's vision of high-performing middle-grades schools that are academically excellent, developmentally responsive, and socially equitable. In addition, each model emphasizes the following:

1. *Rigorous curriculum, instruction, and assessment aligned with content and performance standards.* All students are expected to meet high academic standards.

2. *Small learning communities.* The school has interdisciplinary teams at each grade level where every student has an adult advocate. Team teachers are given common time to set instructional priorities for their team, look at student work, and communicate with parents.

3. *Families and community as valued partners.* Families and community members are aware of and support the need for school improvement. Schools make ongoing efforts to forge strong partnerships with the community. Parents are involved in the life of the school as decision-makers, evaluators, mentors, teachers, and learners.

4. *Building school and district capacity to sustain reform.* The models use a variety of strategies to help stakeholders build the knowledge, skills, and dispositions to continue their improvement efforts. These strategies may include technical assistance, leadership institutes, and other professional development opportunities.

5. *Shared and effective leadership.* Leadership is shared and distributed throughout the school and through all levels of the school community. Principals encourage teachers to participate with them in planning and implementing research-based improvements. All members of the staff hold themselves accountable for student learning and achievement.

6. *A safe and healthy school environment.* The school creates a climate in which students feel safe, supported, and motivated to learn. It has mechanisms for addressing any family and health problems that may hinder students' achievement.

7. *Ongoing professional development.* Professional development is embedded in the life of the school and is aligned with the goals in the school's improvement plan. Schools have opportunities to network with other schools using their particular model. Teachers seek to deepen their knowledge of content and how to teach young adolescents.

8. *Use of data to make decisions that impact learning.* Schools collect and analyze multiple sources of data on student, teacher, and school performance. Decisions to review or revise school and classroom practice are based on close study of this data. The data is carefully considered when setting measurable performance goals.

Three of the middle-grades CSR models have been operating for several years and have assembled a great deal of summative evaluation data:

- *Talent Development Middle School (TDMS) Model.*   Doug Mac Iver and his colleagues at Johns Hopkins University have carried out a number of rigorous research studies to determine the effects of the TDMS model on student performance. Most of these focus on the three original pilot schools in Philadelphia and their matched comparison sites. Using sophisticated modeling techniques, the researchers found that students in the TDMS program showed significantly greater growth in mathematics problem-solving, science, and reading achievement than did students in the comparison schools. The TDMS students have a much steeper growth rate, with effect sizes ranging from .18 to .33 depending on the subject, grade level, and years of engagement with the program. These effect sizes are not only statistically significant, but also educationally meaningful. The model's 8th grade U.S. History Program has also shown promising results (Balfanz, Byrnes, & Mac Iver, 2003; Mac Iver, Balfanz, Ruby, Byrnes, Lorentz, & Jones, in press; Ruby, 2003).

- *Turning Points.*   A number of studies also point to the positive impact of implementing the Turning Points principles. For example, a study conducted in 31 Illinois middle schools beginning in 1990 indicated a rise in student achievement and other measures of school improvement. The study compared groups of schools that differed in how comprehensively they had implemented the Turning Points principles as measured by a self-study survey developed by the University of Illinois's Center for Prevention Research and Development (CPRD). Students in highly implemented schools significantly outperformed their peers in mathematics, language, and reading, and their teachers also reported a significant decline in student misbehavior (Felner, Jackson, Kasak, Mulhall, Brand, & Flowers, 1997). An independent evaluation of 26 schools in Massachusetts (De Pascale, 1997) also showed positive results. Indeed, these schools had the highest gains of all the schools participating in a larger statewide reform initiative—and these improvements were at the low and high ends of the proficiency scale.

- *Michigan Middle Start.*   Qualitative and quantitative studies evaluations of Michigan Middle Start, conducted by the Center for Prevention Research and Development (1999) and the Academy for Educational Development (1998), show that schools implementing Middle Start for two or more years have greater gains than comparison schools in several important areas: (1) academic achievement,

(2) student behavior, (3) classroom practices such as interdisciplinary teaming, and (4) school capacity for continuous improvement.

The four other middle-grades models are relatively new to the middle-grades arena, and their summative evaluations have not been completed yet. Each of these models has shown positive results at the elementary and/or high school level, however, and early results from formative evaluations at the middle level show real promise.

LESSONS LEARNED

Findings from national studies, combined with the first-hand experiences of model developers, suggest that comprehensive school reform is a useful tool for bringing about deep transformation of middle-grades schools and accelerating student achievement. Whatever its approach, each model brings a set of well-honed principles, tools, and strategies designed to facilitate school improvement and student learning. In addition, each also provides human resources (outside facilitators or change agents) that can help the school identify its needs and assets, set goals and priorities, and provide a laser-like focus on implementing improvement plans.

Yet, not every model succeeds in every setting. In fact, evaluation studies reveal wide variation in both implementation and impact within and across models. CSR is not a magic bullet but a complex and time-consuming process involving many actors, none of whom controls the entire change process. Achieving results takes collaboration on the part of the model developer, the schools engaged in improvement, and the districts where the schools are located. Below, we describe some of the hard-won lessons that developers and researchers have learned about what it takes to achieve success in comprehensive school reform.

Lesson #1. Ensure Staff Buy-In!

The most important way to achieve results when adopting a CSR model is to make sure that those who must implement it—teachers and other school staff—are fully committed to the program from the very beginning. According to a number of researchers, schools perform better when the choice of model is freely made, well informed, and endorsed by a significant portion of the faculty (Bodilly, 1998; Fashola & Slavin, 1996; Stringfield, Millsap, & Herman, 1997). Put another way, even the best programs can be doomed to failure if the selection process is flawed (Bodilly, 1998).

While nearly half the models now require a 75% faculty vote before the start of program implementation (Borman et al., 2002), faculty "buy in," in and of itself, is not enough. The choice of model must also be well informed. Unfortunately, most schools examine a relatively small number of options before they select a specific program, according to Stringfield, et al., (1997). Several have no options at all; they are simply told by central office staff that the school will be receiving the same program as other schools in the district. The importance of free and informed choice cannot be overstated. When model developers ignore this well established truth, they often meet with unexpected resistance at the school and/or classroom levels that seriously impedes program implementation.

Communication about model expectations is also essential. Some schools do not fully understand the design when they choose it (Bodilly, 1998). When schools do not understand from the beginning what they are being called upon to do, considerable consternation and slippage in program implementation often ensue. Lack of clear communication about model requirements can result in lost time haggling over what should be done, or worse yet, doing nothing until everything is figured out. According to this researcher, the clearer and more fully prescribed the design, the easier it is to market, launch, and fully implement.

Some model developers enter into rather complex negotiations with districts and schools, attempting to adjust both services and fees to the specific needs of the site. Others present funding options clearly and do not negotiate over a customized package of services. In these cases, districts clearly know what they are getting and can agree to the package or not. Of course, it is easier for models with a long history of success to market a neat package with a fixed price than it is for promising, but relatively new, programs.

It is also important that the model match the particular needs of the school (CPRE, 1998.) Additionally, models must be aligned with both district and state mandates. For example, programs with a prescribed curriculum must ensure that the curriculum addresses state and local frameworks and performance standards. Districts that carry out their own systemwide professional development activities must coordinate these with the particular needs and interests of the CSR provider.

Early engagement is so important to CSR implementation and impact that New American Schools has developed a toolkit for engaging a design-based assistance provider entitled *Guidelines for Ensuring the Quality of National Design-Based Assistance Providers*. The guidelines encourage schools to take several steps to build support for comprehensive school reform before ever talking with an external provider. First, the school should assess its current situation with respect to students' learning and other accomplishments, the existing school program, and school-community support for improvement. Second, the school should determine if it is ready to make all the changes necessary to undertake a CSR effort. That is, does it have the will, capacity, and resources necessary to make comprehensive reform a success? Finally, the school should define its goals so that it can judge whether the design-based assistance provider can help the school meet them. The guidelines also suggest that schools form a representative group of individuals to evaluate the school's needs and select a provider from among the universe of possible designs. The team can talk with colleagues, attend conferences, review web sites and videos, and read brochures and other publications.

While a small group may take the lead in obtaining the information, all staff members need an opportunity to explore, discuss, and ask questions about implementing a design. Once all the information is assembled from various sources, the faculty can meet as a group to reach consensus to move forward with one of the designs.

A common mistake that districts make is to choose a particular model and impose it from above. Schools that are forced by the district to implement a specific design generally show lower levels of implementation (Bodilly, 1998). As several model developers have learned, this can cause serious repercussions—lack of ownership, externalization of responsibility for the program's success or failure, resentment of both the central office and the developer, and a lack of clear understanding of what is required to make the school improvement process work. If the district chooses a systemwide approach, it should actively involve large numbers of school personnel in the decision, make sure that the entire school faculty understands what is entailed, and find other ways to create a sense of ownership and buy-in.

Lesson # 2. It's a Partnership, not an "Intervention"

As noted above, the CSR legislation demands that schools employ proven methods and strategies based on scientifically-based research. In most cases, schools choose to adopt or adapt an externally-developed model. It is not uncommon for district and school administrators to view the school reform model as a quick fix—simply adopt the appropriate model and student performance will improve. But, as WestEd (2001) points out, "comprehensive school reform is not about implementing a model, it's about organizational change" (p. 3). The model itself is not the reform; it provides a framework, along with a set of structures, tools, and processes designed to facilitate change. To be effective, a model must be implemented with care and fidelity; it must be adapted to suit the particular needs of the school, its students, and the community; and schools must ultimately "own" the school improvement process. WestEd (2001) sums it up by saying, "It is important for everyone to make the distinction between a comprehensive school reform program and a school reform model. A model brings together strategies that the school can use to support its own comprehensive school reform program" (p. 3).

This distinction was underscored in the *No Child Left Behind Act*. The legislation notes that CSR sites must integrate a comprehensive design with aligned components; provide ongoing, high-quality professional development for teachers and staff; and include measurable goals and benchmarks for student achievement. Teachers, administrators and staff must support the reform, which must also provide for meaningful parent and community involvement in planning, implementing, and evaluating school improvement activities. Sites are responsible for evaluating implementation and student results and for identifying the resources to support and sustain the school's comprehensive reform effort. While the model can assist schools in meeting each of these requirements, the onus is on the school itself to actively engage in the transformation process, with support from the district as well as the model provider.

Lesson #3. Establish the Preconditions for Change

Both research and experience reveal schools where comprehensive school reform has failed despite the best efforts of the model developer. In order for comprehensive school reform to succeed, at least one of the following preconditions must be present: (1) a school leader who is committed to the model and willing to provide the time, resources, and support necessary to make it work; (2) a faculty that has respect for the school leader and is willing to experiment with new ideas and practices; and/or (3) a faculty that has the will and capacity to change in spite of weak leadership at the top. Even weak leaders can become energized and empowered through intensive leadership development and ongoing advice and support from external change agents—assuming they are willing to learn and change. In fact, some of the greatest "turnaround" stories come from schools where lackluster principals acquired the knowledge, skills, and dispositions needed to successfully transform their schools. Moreover, a school's faculty can compensate for weak leadership at the top by assuming shared responsibility for the reform effort. For this strategy to work, however, the assigned leader must provide at least passive support—that is, he or she must be willing to get out of the way and not set up any insurmountable roadblocks.

Change at the middle-grades level is especially difficult due to the size and departmentalized nature of these schools and the unique developmental needs of their students. The most critical precondition for success at the middle level is creating small, personalized learning communities through interdisciplinary teaming (Mertens & Flowers, 2003). Interdisciplinary teaming typically refers to a group of teachers from different subjects who work together to coordinate and integrate curriculum and instruction for a shared group of students. By breaking the school into smaller houses or clusters, teaming enables students and teachers to get to know each other well and for teachers to better understand and respond to the needs and interests of their students. Teaming also promotes school safety and discipline by bringing students together under the watchful eye of teachers who not only know them well, but also share the same part of the building. Even more important, it allows teachers to generate coordinated lesson plans, discuss student progress, meet as a group with parents, address common problems and issues, integrate curriculum and instruction, and reflect on their own practice (Ames & Miller, 1994; Epstein & Mac Iver, 1990; Erb, 2001; George & Alexander, 1993; Pate, 1997). Where teaming and its associated practices are in place, teachers and students report more positive and productive learning environments (Mertens & Flowers, 2003). What's more, a number of large-scale and comprehensive studies reveal that teaming has a positive effect on student outcomes.

Simply creating interdisciplinary teams is not enough, however. Research and first-hand experience suggest that teams must have regular common planning time during the school day to carry out their collective work (Erb & Doda, 1989; Flowers, Mertens, & Mulhall, 1999, 2000; George & Alexander, 1993; Howe & Bell, 1998; Warren & Muth, 1995). When teachers fully engaged in teaming have high levels of common planning time, a number of positive benefits result, including self-reported reductions in student depression and behavioral problems and increases in self-esteem and academic efficiency (Mertens, Flowers, & Mulhall, 1998). Most important, student achievement scores improve dramatically, particularly in schools with high concentrations of low-income students (Mertens & Flowers, 2003).

Many middle-grades models ask schools to create interdisciplinary teams as the first step in school reform. Yet, all too often these teachers have little or no experience in working together to design interdisciplinary curriculum, identify research-based instructional strategies, conduct their own action research, look at student work, or reflect on their own and others' practice. Without adequate training and ongoing support, team meeting time can turn into a gripe session with teachers dwelling on an immediate crisis or problem with no clear process for finding a solution, or become just another period of the day for individual planning. Experience shows that interdisciplinary teams must also have the skills needed to collaborate if they are to effectively support student learning and healthy development.

Lesson # 4. Focus, Focus, Focus!

According to the National Forum to Accelerate Middle-Grades Reform (1999), successful middle schools establish a clear focus that is widely shared by faculty and others in the school community. In the words of the Forum, "A shared vision of what a high-performing school is and does drives every facet of school change...."

Research on various CSR models confirms the importance of having a defined purpose. According to Bodilly (1998), the more school reform models focus on the core of schooling—curriculum, instruction, assessment, and professional development—the more likely they are to be highly implemented, at least in the early years of reform. Those teams that attempt to introduce other elements at the same time, such as district governance, parent involvement, and integrated social services are less likely to achieve their own implementation goals within the first two years.

Bodilly (1998) suggests three reasons for these findings: (1) addressing a larger number of elements is, in itself, a more challenging implementation task; (2) some of the systemic design elements require extensive interaction with other groups and individuals that are not under the control of the school itself; and (3) changing some elements in order to build collaboration and capacity for self-transformation simply takes more time. For example, aligning curriculum with state or local standards, building the capacity of teams, and developing integrated action plans all require a great deal of time and effort before any changes in curriculum, instruction, assessment, and student performance are likely to take place. Bodilly (1998) concludes that:

> Focusing on the core elements has high initial payoff in getting teachers to implement the design. Focusing on other areas as the means of entering into discussions of how to change the core elements might help set the stage for later important changes and for self-improvement. But it also presents initial implementation barriers that take time to overcome and that may have a domino effect on the implementation of other elements. (p. 72)

Bodilly (1998) goes on to note that it is too soon to judge which approach is better in the long run, but this finding still presents a conundrum for CSR models, which are supposed to be comprehensive by their very nature and label. Bodilly and her colleagues provide two examples where the marriage of core and comprehensive designs has worked especially well. In both cases, a more comprehensive, systemic approach was coupled with a specific approach to curriculum and instruction.

The middle-grades models provide additional examples of how CSR designers attempt to find focus within a comprehensive reform effort. For instance, Middle Start is a comprehensive, systemic reform model, focusing on school governance, parent-community involvement, comprehensive services, and other design features. Yet, it has worked in close partnership with a variety of colleges, universities, and professional development organizations to ensure that participating schools have focused professional development. So, too, Different Ways of Knowing, AIM at Middle-Grades Results, and Turning Points use various strategies for helping teachers identify and implement research-based strategies in reading, writing, and mathematics. These include providing prototype curriculum units along with professional development, ongoing support, and tools that model research-validated strategies that help students develop essential skills and deepen their understanding across the curriculum. At the other end of the spectrum, Talent Development Middle School (TDMS) and Success for All focus primarily on curriculum, instruction, assessment, and professional development. Yet, each of these models also introduces other comprehensive reform elements such as leadership development, supportive school services, and looping.

In sum, academic excellence is at the heart of the matter. At the same time, for all middle-grades students to achieve at high levels, they must have a developmentally appropriate context for learning. That means a safe and nurturing learning environment, instructional strategies tailored to their unique needs and interests, and a broad array of supports to ensure their success in meeting high standards. Without both these elements, few middle-grades schools are likely to achieve success with all their students, particularly those that are traditionally underserved due to race, ethnicity, or low socioeconomic status.

Lesson #5. The Nature and Extent of the External Support Matters

As noted above, the CSR legislation requires schools to use high-quality technical support and assistance from an external partner with experience and expertise in school-wide reform and improvement. This requirement dovetails with one of the Forum's Schools to Watch Criteria: "The school is not an island unto itself. It draws upon others' experience, research, and wisdom; it enters into relationships such as networks and community partnerships that benefit students' and teachers' development and learning" (National Forum, 1999).

The nature of that support matters. The CSR legislation and the Schools to Watch criteria both call for ongoing, high-quality, content-rich professional development that is connected to reaching and sustaining the school vision. According to research, such professional development does make a difference: the more intensive the support and the better the relationship with the site, the greater the chance of model implementation and impact. For example, based on their meta-analysis of 29 CSR models, researchers at CRESPAR found that:

> Reforms that provide on-site and other assistance to help schools implement the model, maintain frequent contact with the school after CSR implementation, and provide useful benchmarks and tools for helping schools assess the progress of their implementation promote stronger effects. The effects were most pronounced in schools that had implemented the model for five years or more, had a higher model developer support rating, and were characterized by higher personnel costs in the first year. (Borman et al., 2002)

Bodilly (1998) also found that design teams that provided intensive support—e.g., through whole-school training, facilitators, extensive training days, quality checks, and material—had higher levels of implementation The AIM at Middle-Grades Results (AIM) team discovered the critical importance of whole-school training during its pilot test of the program. In five of the seven pilot schools, the entire faculty received training in the core elements of the design, including how to teach for understanding and function effectively as a faculty inquiry team. For a variety of reasons, the leadership in AIM's two large urban schools could not arrange for the entire faculty to attend the model's summer institute or the other professional development programs. As a result, there were sharp differences in the degree of implementation across the seven schools.

For those designs that rely heavily on providing on-site support on a regular basis, the frequency of site visits and the nature of the relationship between the developer and the school faculty make a critical difference (Bodilly, 1998). Among the seven CSR models that focus on the middle-grades, three place heavy emphasis on external change agents that provide ongoing support to CSR schools: AIM at Middle-Grades Results, Turning Points, and Middle Start. For these models to achieve success, the external change agent must be knowledgeable about the context in which the school functions and establish an honest, respectful working relationship with administrators and teachers. He or she must be seen as a resource, guide, and mentor in moving toward established improvement goals. AIM's Glenda Copeland notes that a critical role of the external change agent is to help the group identify areas for improvement, determine priorities, and develop a plan with benchmarks to guide their efforts (personal communication, August 6, 2003). If there is turnover, if the external change agent lacks the full skill set necessary for this position, or if the relationship doesn't "click" for some reason, both program implementation and impact may suffer.

Some models bypass the external change agent and encourage schools to hire their own internal coaches or facilitators. While representatives from the model make monitoring visits throughout the year, the internal staff person is largely responsible for ensuring program implementation. This is the approach chosen by Different Ways of Knowing, Talent Development Middle School Model, Success for All, and Making Middle Grades Work. This strategy has several benefits: it (1) builds the internal capacity of the school to continue and sustain the improvement effort; (2) guarantees a high level of intensity since the individual is present every day; and (3) ensures that the change agent understands the local context and the key players. For this approach to be successful, however, the coach must have the knowledge and skills to be an effective change agent, understand and internalize the philosophy and key features of the model, and have the legitimacy to serve as a critical friend and catalyst for change. Simply training one or more "lead teachers" to work with others in the school does not work well as a whole-school change strategy (Bodilly, 1998).

According to Felner et al. (1997), the nature and extent of service may be especially important in schools with large numbers of students at risk of educational failure. Their analysis showed that for all students to be successful in schools with high concentrations of poor students and students of color, the assistance provided must be substantial, implementation must be rigorous and in-depth, and significant resources must be allocated.

Lesson #6. Schools Must Build the Internal Capacity for Continuous Improvement

While the model itself and the external change agent are critically important to comprehensive school reform, nothing is as important as what goes on within the school itself. Models can help shape the vision and provide structures, processes, and materials to support the change process, but administrators, teachers, parents, and students must engage in the everyday work of continuous school improvement. School restructuring involves making *major* changes in the school's organizational rules, roles, and relationships in order to obtain improved results (Corbett, 1990). Successful and sustainable school reform requires: (1) a positive school culture that supports continuous improvement, (2) shared leadership, and (3) a high-performing learning community in which learning is everyone's job.

This is especially true in the case of comprehensive school reform because it is designed to serve the lowest-performing schools. All too often, these schools are characterized by inexperienced teachers, out-of-field placements, chaos, low expectations, distrust and despair, racial tensions, high staff turnover, and a hunkered-down, siege mentality. In such schools, blame is usually the name of the game—whether it is high-stakes tests, the central office, the principal, other teachers, parents, or students' apathy and misbehavior. For these schools to succeed, they must first build the internal capacity for change. Internal capacity can be analyzed in terms of three factors: school culture, shared leadership, and high-performing learning communities.

School Culture. A number of researchers have found that school culture is a critical factor in school improvement efforts and affects the behavior and achievement of students (Deal & Kennedy, 1982; Patterson, Purkey, & Parker, 1986; Sarason, 1982). In the words of the National Forum to Accelerate Middle-Grades Reform (1999), successful schools are learning organizations that establish norms, structures, and organizational arrangements to support and sustain their trajectory toward excellence. Particular cultural norms facilitate school improvement, including norms of critical inquiry, continuous improvement, a widely shared sense of purpose, and shared decision making (Barth, 1991; Louis & Miles, 1990; Saphier & King, 1985). Successful change efforts also promote honest self-assessment, looking carefully at both strengths and weaknesses, as well as the beliefs, actions, and underlying assumptions that affect teaching and administration (Dreyfuss, Cistone, & Divita, 1992; Fine, 1991). Successful CSR models help promote such norms.

Shared Leadership. Someone in the school must have the responsibility and authority to manage the school improvement process on a daily basis, as well as to provide overall coordination, strategic planning, and communication (Berends, Bodilly, & Kirby, 2002; Bodilly, 1998; National Forum, 2003). Among the roles that effective leaders perform are: (1) developing and articulate a vision of what students should know and be able to do; (2) engaging in planning and providing resources (including supportive organizational arrangements as well as time, people, equipment, space, and assistance); (3) arranging for/provide ongoing professional development; (4) engaging in monitoring and evaluation using a wide variety of aggregated and disaggregated data at the school, classroom, and student levels; and (5) engaging in ongoing consultation, coaching, and problem-solving (Hord & Huling-Austin, 1986; Louis & Miles, 1990).

Traditionally, the leadership role has been played by the school principal and his/her assistant principals. Even the most skillful and charismatic leader cannot sustain the school improvement process after he or she departs, however. Thus, high-performing learning communities develop a system of shared leadership and an environment in which everyone takes responsibility for continuous school improvement. In such schools, the principal is an instructional leader, but his or her first priority is to identify strengths and interests among the faculty, assign roles and responsibilities, and mentor others so that everyone has the skills needed to carry out their assigned tasks. The broader and more skilled the school's leadership, the better the chance for success (Lambert, 1998).

A number of models emphasize collaborative leadership—creating a school improvement team that shares responsibility for the improvement effort. Such teams learn how to work together as a group by setting norms, creating structured and purposeful agendas, listening actively and communicating effectively, conducting action research, and coming to consensus. In addition, they learn how to collect and analyze data from a variety of sources and how to use those data to make decisions about goals, priorities, and effective school improvement strategies. The National Forum (2002) has created a two-day Instructional Leadership Module that integrates a variety of the tools and strategies the models use to build the capacity of administrators and school leadership teams.

High-Performing Learning Communities. Effective schools are high-performing learning communities (Boyd, 1992a, 1992b; Boyd & Hord, 1994; Kruse & Louis, 1993). Such organizations consist of people who see themselves as connected to each other and the world, where creative thinking is nurtured, and where people are engaged in learning how to learn together (Senge, 1990). According to Sergiovanni (1992), in a school learning community, members experience a sense of connectedness that "resembles what is found in a family, a neighborhood, or some other closely knit group..." (p. 47). Johannesen (in press) defines such communities this way:

> The whole school community collaborates in designing the work of the school, shares responsibility for data-driven decision-making, and conducts reflective, professional dialogue using the Norms of Collaborative Work.

Johannesen (in press) goes on to note that this emphasis can be seen in the way time is organized to provide for common planning, and is found in leadership that facilitates small learning communities and encourages teacher dialogue about lessons, strategies, and support to ensure student success and continuous improvement.

Schools that embrace shared leadership and create a high-performing learning community are more likely to implement CSR and achieve their goals for several reasons. First, such schools hold themselves accountable for their students' success rather than blaming others for their shortcomings. Second, they insist upon evidence and results, and they purposefully use them to reconsider their vision and practices as appropriate. Finally, in these schools, the notion of continuous improvement is deeply embedded in the life of the school, and learning, experimentation, and reflection are the norm.

Lesson #7. Districts Must Provide the Necessary Resources and Support

The external change agent of a CSR improvement effort provides a consistent focus on improvement plans and helps a school maintain a focus on progress toward its goals. Leadership and support at the district level, however, are extremely important as well. Both research and experience show that they can accelerate or halt the work at a given school.

According to Berends et al. (2002), the most critical factor is stability of district leadership, especially when that leadership is supportive of the CSR model, backs the reform, and views the reform as central to the district's school improvement efforts. The researchers also found that implementation levels were higher when there was a strong and trusting relationship between the school, the district, and the union leadership; a coherent program of reform; significant resources that are dedicated to the reform effort; and a high degree of school autonomy. WestEd (2001) outlines a number of things that districts can do to provide active support, including giving CSR schools control over their own hiring decisions, textbooks, and materials; (2) clarifying up-front the district's expectations and the role it will play in the reform effort; and (3) serving as a resource broker, starting with providing time, materials, and assistance in finding the right model. Above all, districts should let schools choose the model, while they supply the necessary support.

In addition to turnover in district leadership, budget crises, major school redistricting (something AIM at Middle-Grades results experienced in New York City), and the reconfiguration of individual schools can significantly impede CSR efforts (Berends et al., 2002). The number one reason that schools pull out of comprehensive school reform, however, is lack of funding. All too often, districts and schools underestimate the costs of comprehensive school reform. The design fees, which average $85,000 in the first year, are only one-third of the actual costs. Other costs include the costs of district and administrator support, school-based coaches, materials and equipment, and, above all, teachers' time and effort.

Another barrier to implementation is a sudden change in direction at the district level. For example, in the face of high-stakes testing, which puts a heavy premium on basic skills, many districts have elected to adopt a systemwide curriculum intervention or a focused professional development program that serves all teachers in the district. If that program conflicts with the CSR design or reduces the faculty's time to participate in model-sponsored professional development activities, the result can be lower levels of implementation. Such midstream changes also serve to jeopardize hard-won working relationships among district administrators, model staff, and school faculty who often feel caught in the middle.

CONCLUSION

Many of the new and veteran middle-grades reform models hold promise for helping middle-grades schools improve school and classroom practice and student results. Yet CSR is not a panacea for middle-grades school improvement. Even the most effective model can fail if the right conditions are not present. The following are seven important conditions.

1. School faculty must buy into the model after looking at a range of options and making a free choice.
2. The school must assume responsibility for making the model work, recognizing that it is a partnership, not an intervention.
3. Schools must also have the basic organizational structures to support change. In the case of middle-grades schools, that means creating interdisciplinary teams that strengthen adult-student relationships and providing teams with common planning time so that they can meet regularly and work together to improve teaching and learning.
4. Those schools that focus on curriculum, instruction, and assessment and provide the professional development to support classroom changes are more likely to see results faster.
5. The nature and extent of the external support matters. Frequent visits, high-quality training and technical assistance, staff consistency, and a focus on whole-school change are all key ingredients to successful school reform.
6. External change agents are not enough. For CSR to be implemented fully and sustained over time, schools must build the internal capacity for continuous improvement. This means creating a culture in which learning is everyone's business, ensuring that leadership is widely and skillfully shared, and constructing a learning community in which planning, action, and reflection are the norm.
7. Schools cannot go it alone. District leadership is essential in creating an enabling context for change; providing time, financial resources, and other forms of support; and eliminating any barriers to comprehensive school reform. While some districts play an extremely positive role in ensuring the success of CSR efforts, others take actions that undermine even the most promising CSR initiative.

REFERENCES

Academy for Educational Development (1998). W.K. Kellogg Foundation Middle Start Initiative, Cluster Evaluation Report, 1997–1998, Working Paper #4. Progress of the Middle Start Comprehensive School Improvement Schools.

Retrieved   August   25,   2003,   from   http://www.middlestart.org/cluster_report4.pdf

Ames, N., & Miller, E. (1994). *Changing middle schools.* San Francisco: Jossey-Bass.

Balfanz, R., Byrnes, V., & Mac Iver, D.J. (2003). *The implementation and impact of evidence based mathematics reform in high poverty middle schools: A multi-site, Multi-year study.* (in press).

Barth, R.S. (1991). Restructuring schools: Some questions for teachers and principals. *Phi Delta Kappan, 73*(2), 123–128.

Bernends, M., Bodilly, S.J., & Kirby, S. (2002). *Facing the challenges of whole-school reform: New American Schools after a decade.* Santa Monica, CA: Rand Corporation.

Bodilly, S.J. (1998). *Lessons from New American Schools' scale-up phase: Prospects for bringing designs to multiple schools.* Santa Monica, CA: Rand Corporation.

Borman, G.D., Hewes, G.M., Overman, L.T., & Brown, S. (2002, November). *Comprehensive school reform and student achievement: A meta-analysis* (Report 59). Baltimore, MD & Washington, DC: Center for Research on the Education of Students Places at Risk.

Boyd, V. (1992). *School context: Bridge or barrier to change?* Austin, TX: Southwest Educational Development Laboratory.

Boyd, V., & Hord, S.M. (1994). *Schools as learning communities: Issues about change, 4*(1), Austin, TX: Southwest Educational Development Laboratory. Retrieved August 25, 2003, from http://www.sedl.org/pubs/catalog/items/sch11.html

Center for Prevention Research and Development. (1999). *Executive summary of Phase I Report.* Institute of Government and Public Affairs, University of Illinois. Retrieved August 25, 2003, from http://www.cprd.uiuc.edu/

Consortium for Policy and Research and Development. (1998). *Policy briefs: States and districts and comprehensive school reform.* Philadelphia: University of Pennsylvania. Retrieved October 20, 2003, from http://www.CPRE.org/Publicatons/rb24.pdf

Corbett. H.D. (1990). *On the meaning of restructuring.* Philadelphia, PA: Research for Better Schools.

Deal, T., & Kennedy, A. (1982). *Corporate cultures.* Reading, MA: Addison-Wesley Publishing.

De Pascale, C.A. (1997). *Education reform restructuring network: Impact documentation report.* Cambridge, MA: Data Analysis and Testing Associates, Inc.

Dreyfuss, G.O., Cistone, P.J., & Divita, C. (1992). Restructuring in a large district: Dade County, Florida. In C.D. Glickman (Ed.), *Supervision in transition* (pp. 77–96). Alexandria, VA: Association for Supervision and Curriculum Development.

Epstein, J.L. (1996). Advances in family, community, and school partnerships. *New Schools, New Communities. 12*(3), 5–13.

Epstein, J.L. & Mac Iver, D. J. (1990). *Education in the middle grades: National practices and trends.* Columbus, OH: National Middle School Association.

Erb, T.O. (2000). *Do middle school reforms really make a difference?* Washington, DC: The Clearing House.

Erb, T.O. (2001). Transforming organizational structures for young adolescents and adult learning. In T.S. Dickinson (Ed.), *Reinventing the middle school* (pp. 176–200). New York: RoutledgeFalmer.

Erb, T.O., & Doda, N.M. (1989). *Team organization: Promise-practices and possibilities.* Washington, DC: National Education Association.

Fashola, O., & Slavin, R.E. (1998). Schoolwide reform models: What works? *Phi Delta Kappan, 79*(5), 370–378.

Felner, R.D., Jackson, A.W., Kasak, D.T., Mulhall, P., Brand, S., & Flowers, N. (1997). The impact of school reform for the middle years: Longitudinal study of a network engaged in Turning Points-based comprehensive school transformation. *Phi Delta Kappan, 78*(7), 528–550.

Fine, M. (1991). *Framing dropouts: Notes on the politics of an urban public high school.* Albany: State University of New York Press.

Flowers, N., Mertens, S., & Mulhall, P. (1999). The impact of teaming: Five research-based outcomes of teaming. *Middle School Journal, 31*(2), 57–60.

Flowers, N., Mertens, S., & Mulhall, P. (2000). What makes interdisciplinary teams effective? *Middle School Journal, 31*(4), 53–56.

George P.S., & Alexander, W.M. (1993). *The exemplary middle school* (2nd ed.). Fort Worth, TX: Harcourt Brace Jovanovich College Publishers.

Hord, S.M., & Huling-Austin, L. (1986). Effective curriculum implementation: Some promising new insights. *The Elementary School Journal, 87*(1), 97–115.

Howe, A.C., & Bell, J. (1998). Factors associated with successful implementation of interdisciplinary curriculum units. *Research in Middle Level Education Quarterly, 21*(2), 39–52.

Johannesen, L.A. (in press). *A different way of growing.* **Publisher?**

Lambert, L. (1998). *Building leadership capacity in schools.* Alexandria, VA: Association for Supervision and Curriculum Development.

Louis, K.S., & Kruse, S.D. (1995). *Professionalism and community: Perspectives on reforming urban schools.* Thousand Oaks, CA: Corwin Press.

Louis, K.S., & Miles, M.B. (1990). *Improving the urban high school.* New York: Teachers College Press.

Mac Iver, D.J., Balfanz, R., Ruby, A., Byrnes, V., Lorentz, S., & Jones, L. (In press). Developing adolescent literacy in high poverty middle schools: The impact of Talent Develoment's reforms across multiple years and sites. In P.R. Pintrich & M.L. Maehr (Eds.), *Motivating students, improving schools: The legacy of Carol Midgley, Vol. 13, Advances in motivation and achievement.* Greenwich, CT: JAI Press.

Mertens, S.B., & Flowers, N. (2003). Middle school practices improve student achievement in High poverty schools. *Middle School Journal, 35*(1), 33–43.

Mertens, S.B., Flowers, N., & Mulhall, P. (1998). *The middle start Initiative, Phase I: A Longitudinal analysis of Michigan middle-level schools.* Urbana: University of Illinois at Urbana Champaign.

National Forum to Accelerate Middle-Grades Reform. (1999). *Schools to watch criteria, organizational supports.* Retrieved August 25, 2003, from http://www.mgforum .org/Improvingschools/STW/STWcriteria.asp

New American Schools. (NAS). A toolkid for engaging a design-based assistance provider: Guidelines for ensuring the quality of national design-based assistance. Washington, DC: NAS. Retrieved August 25, 2003, from http://www.nasschools.org/uploadedfiles/guidecharter.pdf

No Child Left Behind Act. (2001). Retrieved October 20, 2003, from http://www.ed.gov/offices/OESE/compreform/2pager.html

Pate, E. (1997). Teaming and decision making. In T.S. Dickinson & T.O. Erb (Eds.), *We gain more than we give: Teaming in middle schools* (pp. 425–442).

Patterson, J.L., Purkey, S.C., & Parker, J.V. (1986). *Productive school systems for a nonrational world.* Alexandria, VA: Association for Supervision and Curriculum Development.

Ruby, A.M. (in press). *Science reform within whole school reform.*

Ross, S.M., Sanders, W.L., Wright, S.P., & Stringfield, S. (1998). *The Memphis restructuring initiative: Achieving results for years 1 and 2 on the Tennessee Value-Added Assessment System (TVAAS).* Unpublished manuscript, Center for Research in Educational Policy, Memphis, TN: University of Memphis.

Ross, S.M., Wang, L.W., Sanders, W.L., Wright, S.P., & Stringfield, S. (1999). *Two- and three-year achievement results for the Tennessee Value-Added Assessment System for restructuring schools in Memphis.* Unpublished manuscript, Center for Research in Educational Policy, Memphis, TN: University of Memphis.

Saphier, J., & King, M. (1985). Good seeds grow in strong cultures. *Educational Leadership, 42*(6), 67–74.

Sarason, S.B. (1982). *Culture of the school and the problem of change* (2nd ed.). Boston, MA: Allyn & Bacon.

Senge, P.M. (1990). *The fifth discipline.* New York: Doubleday Currency.

Sergiovanni, T.J. (1992). *Moral leadership: Getting to the heart of school improvement.* San Francisco: Jossey-Bass.

Stringfield, S., Millsap, M.A., & Herman, R. (1997). *Special strategies for educating disadvantaged children: Findings and policy implications of a longitudinal study.* Washington, DC: U.S. Department of Education.

Warren, L.L., & Muth, K.D. (1995). The impact of common planning time on middle grade students and teachers. *Research in Middle Level Education, 18*(3), 41–58.

West Ed (2001). Comprehensive school reform: Perspectives from model developers. Retrieved August 25, 2003, from http://www.WestEd.org/online_pubs/csrdperspective.pdf

CHAPTER 9

STATE-LEVEL POLICY DEVELOPMENT

David A. Payton

INTRODUCTION

On Thursday, July 17, 2003, after eighteen months of study and deliberation, the New York State Board of Regents unanimously approved a new Regents Policy Statement on Middle-Level Education. This chapter traces the evolution of this initiative and offers insights as to how a large bureaucracy—one that serves multiple constituencies which often have competing agendas—successfully managed a significant policy development process.

FOUNDATIONAL IDEAS

Two foundational ideas helped direct and shape the middle-level education policy development process in New York State. Understanding them before reading this chapter will help contextualize and explain much of what happened:

1. Educating and informing policymakers—slowly but methodically—are crucial aspects of policy development. The probability that poli-

Reforming Middle Level Education: Considerations for Policymakers, pages 155–188
Copyright © 2004 by Information Age Publishing
All rights of reproduction in any form reserved.

cymakers will enact "good" policy increases when the policymakers know and understand well the topic under consideration.

2. Educating, informing, and meaningfully involving the educational community are crucial aspects of policy development. Policymakers enact policy; the educational community executes policy. The probability that the educational community will comply with the policy increases when those who must implement it know and understand it well and have been involved in its development.

THE NEW YORK STATE BOARD OF REGENTS

The Regents of The University of the State of New York were established by the New York State Legislature on May 1, 1784, and as a consequence is the oldest, continuous state education entity in America. The University of the State of New York is the nation's most comprehensive and unified educational system. It consists of all elementary, middle, secondary, and post-secondary educational institutions, libraries, museums, public broadcasting stations, records and archives, professions, Vocational and Educational Services for Individuals with Disabilities, and other such institutions, organizations, and agencies as may be admitted to The University. The concept of The University of the State of New York is a broad term encompassing all the institutions, both public and private, offering education in New York State (New York State Board of Regents).

The Board of Regents consists of sixteen members elected by the State Legislature for five-year terms and is responsible for the general supervision of all educational activities within New York State, presiding over "The University" and the New York State Education Department:

> Subject and in conformity to the constitution and laws of the state, the regents shall exercise legislative functions concerning the educational system of the state, determine its educational policies and, except, as to the judicial functions of the commissioner of education, establish rules for carrying into effect the laws and policies of the state, relating to education, and the functions, powers, duties and trusts conferred or charged upon the university and the education department. (New York State Education Law 207)

Regents are unsalaried and are reimbursed only for travel and related expenses in connection with their official duties.

Background

State boards of education craft educational policy. State-level policy, taken at its most basic level, has two primary functions:

- Guiding and directing, but not necessarily requiring, local action and practice (voluntary compliance)
- Supporting new or existing law and regulation (mandatory compliance).

Usually, State-level policy is not based upon the notion of the "quick fix." Rather, it provides direction for long-term change, mandated or volitional.

The utility of the first purpose of policy—guiding and directing local actions—is almost completely dependent upon "buy-in" by those who are responsible for its actual implementation. Districts and schools must not only accept and support the direction and substance of non-mandated policy but also be willing and able to provide, voluntarily, both the will and the supports needed to implement it well. As a result, those schools and districts with the most discretionary resources are the ones that benefit most in this situation. They can evaluate policy objectively and, with their resources, implement it with fidelity over time should they decide it is in their best interests.

On the other hand, in situations where there are numerous competing priorities, persistent staff turnover, constantly changing leadership, and a variety of organizational impediments, finding sufficient where-with-all to implement policy well—regardless of its perceived value and potential but for which there are no official negative consequences for noncompliance—is difficult. The situation is especially problematic in those schools and districts where there are few, if any, discretionary resources and where all available energy must be directed at resolving immediate, "solve-me-now" problems.

Simply put, State-level policy, regardless of how well written or compelling it is, without the power and authority of law or regulation, operates at the whim of local circumstances. In those places where conditions are favorable, State-level policy can have a significant influence on local practice. In other places, where circumstances are unfavorable, State-level policy has little or no effect unless it can be leveraged to address an immediate local issue.

For maximum impact, State-level policy must be buttressed by law or regulation. Without a clear legal mandate (and, on occasion, even where there is a clear mandate), there is differential implementation. Those with means are able, should they wish, to translate policy into practice; those without means, regardless of need or desire, are left without the necessary leverage or resources to implement.

Raising Consciousness and Documenting Need

Creating new policy is daunting work. It is not a task to be taken lightly. Governing boards need compelling reasons for initiating the process. In New York State, the initial impetus for establishing new State policy for the middle grades came from two sources: student achievement results on the State's new standards-based assessments administered at the end of grade eight and student dropout rates in high school.

Student Achievement. By the end of the 2000–01 school year it was apparent that significant numbers of students leaving the middle grades and entering high school were at risk of not meeting New York State's commencement-level requirements and graduating:

- Less than half of the eighth grade students (44.9%) in both 1999–2000 and 2000–01 had met the English language arts intermediate-level (middle grades) standards;
- Only two out of five eighth grade students (40.3% in 1999–2000 and 39.4% in 2000–2001) had met the mathematics intermediate-level standards (New York State Education Department, 2001, September).

In schools and districts with large numbers of disadvantaged students, the percentages of middle grades pupils at risk were significantly higher than the State averages (NYSED, 2001, September). Members of the Board of Regents and the staff of the State Education Department were convinced that what was happening in many middle grades classrooms was not working for large numbers of young adolescents.

Dropout Rates. Middle grades students in New York State, unless they have been retained several times, cannot legally drop out of school. What they can do, though, is to give up trying to succeed in school and drop out at the first opportunity. Students who have made the decision to "educationally disconnect" often exhibit a particular pathology. Alienated from the educational system, they perceive no value in participating in the formal educational process or in conforming to the mores of the school. They are frequently discipline problems—disruptive, abusive, destructive, and truant.

While a cursory examination of student dropout data suggests that the problem is primarily a high school phenomenon, a closer look at what causes students to abandon hope and forgo further formal education makes it abundantly clear that its genesis can often be found in the middle grades. TURNING POINTS (1989) described the problem and its link to the middle grades:

Young adolescents face significant turning points. For many youth 10 to 15 years old, early adolescence offers opportunities to choose a path toward a productive and fulfilling life. For many others, it represents their last best chance to avoid a diminished future. . . .

Middle grade schools—junior high, intermediate, and middle schools—are potentially society's most powerful force to recapture millions of youth adrift, and help every young person thrive during early adolescence. Yet, all too often these schools exacerbate the problem of young adolescents. . . .

A volatile mismatch exists between the organization and curriculum of middle grade schools and the intellectual and emotional needs of young adolescents. Caught in a vortex of changing demands, the engagement of many youth in learning diminishes, and their rates of alienation, substance abuse, absenteeism, and dropping out of school begin to rise. (Carnegie Council on Adolescent Development, 1989, pp. 8–9)

Until recently, the dropout issue had limited significance for educational policy in New York State and elsewhere. Tolerance for an "acceptable level of educational casualties" enabled many schools and districts, without recrimination, to avoid acknowledging and addressing the problem. The No Child Left Behind (NCLB) federal legislation changed everything when it made high school completion a national priority and a measure of school success (United States Department of Education, 2000). Overnight, dropouts and dropout prevention—and their clear link with the middle grades—became everyone's concern.

By the end of 2001, the Board of Regents, prompted by deep concerns about student achievement and dropouts, had identified middle-level education as an area requiring its attention and study. What made the need to take a careful and systematic look at middle grades education in New York State so compelling to the Regents was that it was based on two critically important student concerns and not on partisan adult issues.

Informing and Educating the Policymakers

Having established a compelling need for action, the next task was to educate the policymakers about the middle grades and middle-level education. The last substantive discussion the Board of Regents had that dealt with middle-level education occurred in 1989. This resulted in the development and adoption of a Regents Policy Statement on Middle-Level Education and Schools with Middle-Level Grades (New York State Board of Regents, 1989). Unfortunately, by 2001, not a single Regent who helped create the 1989 policy statement was still on the Board.

The immediate challenge was to ensure that each of the sitting Regents (as well as the larger educational community) had a complete and accurate understanding of middle-level education—what it was and what it was not.

The Board of Regents, thoroughly familiar with the middle-level education philosophy, would be well positioned to develop an informed and justifiable middle grades plan of action and the educational community, similarly knowledgeable, would be more accepting of a thoughtful, well-constructed approach to strengthening the middle grades and more disposed to implementing the policy.

The education of the Board of Regents and New York State's educational community began in December 2001 with a formal report to the Regents prepared by the State Education Department (NYSED, 2001, December, b) and proceeded gradually and systematically for the next year and a half. In this first of what became a series of presentations on middle-level education, Department staff targeted five topics for discussion.

DEFINING MIDDLE-LEVEL EDUCATION

It was important at the very beginning to define clearly "middle-level education" and provide the Regents with a detailed description of the common characteristics of schools with middle-level grades where student performance is high. These attributes, catalogued by the State Education Department in 2000 in a document titled the "Essential Elements of Standards-Focused Middle-Level Schools and Programs," were organized into seven discrete categories (NYSED, 2000):

- A philosophy and mission that reflect the intellectual and developmental needs and characteristics of young adolescents;
- An educational program that is comprehensive, challenging, purposeful, integrated, and standards-based;
- An organization and structure that support both academic excellence and personal development;
- Classroom instruction appropriate to the needs and characteristics of young adolescents provided by skilled and knowledgeable teachers;
- Strong educational leadership and a building administration that encourages, facilitates, and sustains involvement, participation, and partnerships;
- A network of academic and personal support available for students; and
- Professional training and staff development that are ongoing, planned, purposeful, and collaboratively planned.

ESTABLISHING A RESEARCH BASE

A second need was to establish a strong New York State-specific research connection among the seven Essential Elements and student achievement. In early 2001 the State Education Department had completed a research study to gauge the degree to which high performing middle-level schools and low performing middle-level schools were implementing the seven Essential Elements (Middle-Level Education Program, 2001). The results were instructive:

1. High achieving schools were implementing each of the Essential Elements to a greater degree than low achieving schools. The data also showed that, for the most part, the more schools implemented the Essential Elements, the higher student achievement.

2. Most middle schools in New York State, despite their name, had not implemented effective middle-level practices (i.e., the Essential Elements) to any great degree. Those that had were able to demonstrate higher student achievement than those that had not. These data, by validating the pervasive lack of implementation of the Essential Elements, helped counter the claims of those in the educational community who argued that the middle-level education philosophy was not effective in improving student achievement.

EXPLAINING GRADE CONFIGURATION EFFECTS ON STUDENT ACHIEVEMENT

The third priority was to address directly the question of grade configuration and its relationship to effective middle grades education. As Chart 9.1 indicates, In New York State, schools with middle-level grades have been, and continue to be, organized in a variety of grade configurations (MLEP, 2003).

Since none of the grade configurations had demonstrated that it was inherently the best when the measure was student achievement, it was critical at this time to establish the idea that more important than grade configuration was what was actually happening within the school—the school's vision, the alignment and rigor of the curriculum, the organization of staff and students, the purposefulness and effectiveness of classroom instruction, leadership in the building, student support systems, and ongoing professional learning.

**Chart 9.1.   Grade Configurations of New York State Schools
with Middle-Level Grades 1981–1982 through 2002–2003**

Grade Span	1981–1982	1991–1992	2001–2002	2002–2003	21-Year Change	
K/1–5	452	789	1,147	1,172	+720	(+159.3%)
K/1–6	1,468	981	570	547	–921	(–62.7%)
K/1–8	71	60	106	106	+35	(+49.3%)
5–8	50	87	99	98	+48	(+96.0%)
6–8	162	292	463	473	+311	(+192.0%)
6–9	34	30	13	11	–23	(–67.6%)
6–12	16	30	45	48	+32	(+200.0%)
7–8	120	93	75	73	–47	(–39.2%)
7–9	211	78	25	23	–188	(–89.1%)
7–12	227	224	156	146	–81	(–35.7%)
9–12	398	470	595	604	+206	(+51.8%)
10–12	109	36	21	16	–93	(–85.3%)

DIFFERENTIATING THE MIDDLE GRADES
FROM OTHER GRADES

A fourth purpose of this initial report was to explain why education in the middle grades, regardless of where these grades are actually housed, must be different from education in elementary schools and high schools (e.g., students in the middle grades are fundamentally different from elementary and high school students; the educational expectations for the middle grades are different than they are for elementary schools and high schools; and in New York State, time requirements for the different subjects in the middle grades, and especially in grades seven and eight, are more restrictive and prescriptive than for any other grades or level).

SHARING NEXT STEPS

The report concluded with a series of coordinated next steps for improving middle-level education that was a logical extension of an ongoing statewide effort to strengthen the middle grades that began in 2000 when the State Education Department, prompted by student performance of the State's intermediate assessments, began to develop a long-range plan to strengthen middle-level education. As a first step, Department staff completed a review of the most recent research and literature on middle-level education (MLEP, 2001, March, b) determined the key issues a Statewide middle-level reform initiative must address to be successful (MLEP, 2001, March, a) and identified the various agencies, organizations and constituencies within the State interested in the education of young adolescents. Once the information sharing phase was finished, Department staff, working closely with a blue-ribbon Middle-Level Education External Advisory Council, prepared a draft of the State's long-term Agenda to Improve Middle-Level Education (NYSED, 2001, December, a). This plan had two parts. The first part detailed the activities directly related to changing middle-level schools and middle-level schooling; the second part contained the activities associated with actually managing the initiative. The "Agenda" was a comprehensive, multi-year plan that also included specific, immediate actions designed to engage middle-level practitioners and the larger educational community in meaningful dialogue focusing on a series of seminal questions organized around the Essential Elements:

1. What is the purpose or mission of middle grades education? Should it be academic excellence? Should it be to support each student's development—providing opportunities for students to plan their futures, make choices, and explore a variety of topics and interests that will help them develop their identities and discover their abilities? Or, should it be a balance of the two, and, if so, what should the nature of the balance be?

2. What should comprise the middle grades curriculum? What's important and necessary for middle-level schools to teach? What's "nice" but not essential? What's an acceptable level of "rigor" for the middle-level curriculum—what should students leaving grade eight know and be able to do (and to what proficiency) to be successful in high school and later in life? What are the implications for existing Commissioner's Regulations?

3. Can all middle-level schools in New York State—especially those in urban areas—develop the organization and structures that research has shown foster student learning (i.e., small schools, teacher teams, etc.)? What is needed, locally and at the State level, if schools are to construct the enabling infrastructure of an effective middle-level school?

4. Do middle-level teachers have the content knowledge to teach their subjects to high standards? Are veteran teachers skilled in teaching young adolescents? Are teacher preparation programs providing the content knowledge and the pedagogical skills to teach young adolescents to high standards, especially those who traditionally have been relegated to the "local diploma" track? If there is a problem, what is the solution?

5. What can be done to prepare the next generation of middle- level principals who can lead a middle-level school to excellence? What are the essential skills and knowledge a middle-level administrator needs to succeed? What needs to happen to encourage capable educators to desire to be middle-level administrators?

6. What works for middle grades students who are at risk of not meeting the State's intermediate (middle grades) learning standards in English language arts and mathematics? How can these effective practices be identified? How can they be "transported" to other middle-level schools?

7. What programs are being implemented in middle-level schools that are reducing "barriers to learning" and reconnecting disaffected students who are at risk of dropping out once they become "age-eligible?" Why are they working? What is required for these programs to be implemented in other sites?

8. What should professional learning for middle-level educators—both administrators and classroom teachers—emphasize? What are the attributes of an effective staff development program—what makes it work? How might the new 175-hour requirement for ongoing professional learning for newly certified classroom teachers be used to support middle-level improvement?

The systematic and early education of both policymakers and the larger educational community about middle-level education was critically important. This preparatory work—tedious, time-consuming, and often mundane—was the basis on which the policymakers made informed decisions affecting the middle grades that were understandable to middle-level educators and others interested in the education of young adolescents.

SECURING BUY-IN FROM THE LARGER EDUCATIONAL COMMUNITY

With the Board of Regents fully engaged in a discussion of middle-level education following the December 2001 report, it was time for the State Education Department to involve the educational community in a meaningful way in the conversation. In spring of 2002, the Education Department, working closely with middle-level educators and others with an interest in the education of young adolescents, held a series of eleven Regional Forums around the State on middle-level education. The purposes of these Forums were to:

1. Stimulate a Statewide discussion of the Essential Elements of Standards-Focused Middle-Level Schools and Programs and recent research on middle-level education;
2. Share the most effective middle-level instructional practices and programs that are based on research and theory and that lead to improved student achievement;
3. Explain the steps the Board of Regents and the State Education Department proposed to take to strengthen the middle grades and seek support for the activities;
4. Solicit field comment and advice on current middle-level mandates;
5. Explore ways to remove barriers to learning in the middle grades through the implementation of best practices; and
6. Promote continuing interagency collaborative efforts on behalf of middle-level schools and young adolescents.

More than 2700 people from more than 500 school districts participated in the discussions. Representative comments taken from the evaluation forms submitted by those who attended the Forums indicated that:

1. Participants, overwhelmingly, found the sharing of best practices and the showcasing of effective programs the most beneficial aspects of the Forums and wanted more. Practitioners were eager for opportunities to share experiences and best practices and to network and interact with peers and colleagues, including those outside their local area.
2. The Education Department's Essential Elements of Standards-Focused Middle-Level Schools and Programs document represented a vision of schooling that the education community supported and embraced.
3. The State's plan for improving middle-level education and its proposed activities were generally supported by those attending the Forum. There were those who requested that the activities be further defined to be clearer to practitioners.
4. Timely, accurate, two-way communication with the field was a key to future efforts to strengthen education in the middle grades.
5. The field was looking for the Department (and the Regents) to provide statewide leadership to improve middle-level education.
6. The State's intermediate-level (middle grades) standards-based assessments and their perceived influence, positive or negative, direct or indirect, on good middle-level practices, remained issues with practitioners.

7. Specific course requirements for the middle grades, while a concern of some constituent groups, did not receive inordinate attention or discussion during the Forums.

Engaging the educational community early on in substantive discussions (rather than one-way information-sharing sessions) vested them as informed and contributing partners in the Regents' effort to improve middle grades education.

SUSTAINING THE MOMENTUM

The Regional Forums not only offered large numbers of practitioners and others an opportunity to join in the middle grades discussion but also informed the deliberations of the Board of Regents. In a June 2002 public report to the Regents on the recently completed Forums (NYSED, 2002, June) the Education Department shared five "Lessons Learned" from the experience.

Lesson #1. There must be a clear recognition and balance in the middle-level program between strong academics and youth development. Schools that do not address both will ultimately fail to get students to meet standards, pursue their education, and develop the respect and responsibility needed to be successful in high school and beyond. Further, for many students, the academic and personal experiences they have in the middle grades directly affect their decision to stay in school and to drop out before completing their diploma requirements. Schools will often need to collaborate with other service providers to meet the needs of young adolescents.

Lesson #2. There are successful curriculum and instructional approaches that are effective at the middle level. They emphasize in-depth projects and learning that are tied to the standards and are interdisciplinary. They are not drill and practice, repetitive approaches and test preparation. In some cases, accelerated learning approaches are being used.

Lesson #3. The organization and structure of middle-level schools in New York State vary widely—by grade level, how courses are organized, and how teachers are assigned. Even the certification system results in teachers with different skill sets teaching at the middle-level—those who are trained as generalists ("common branch") and those who are trained as content specialists. The curriculum and the instructional program need to be flexible enough to fit different organizational structures and subject matter expertise. It is unclear whether State mandates are a problem; most people cite the importance of all of the State's 28 learning standards, but find some of the mandated time requirements constraining to effective programming. Participants also recommended looking at requirements in a grades 5–8 context rather than just grades 7 and 8.

Lesson #4.   School leadership at all levels is vitally important to effective middle-level programs. Yet, there seemed to be very little attention given to preparation and continuing education of school leaders to the unique challenges of leading at the middle level.

Lesson #5.   There is a hunger for more professional conversation and exchange of ideas on effective middle-level programs. The Regional Forums were oversubscribed and most participants wanted more opportunities to continue the discussion and learn more.

Ongoing Education of the Policymakers.   In addition to sharing the results of the Regional Forums and the five "Lessons Learned" with the Board of Regents, the State Education Department continued its efforts to educate the policymakers (and the educational community) about the middle grades and to build support for reform (NYSED, 2002, June). Taking advantage of the attention being focused on middle-level education, Department staff shared with the Regents:

1. A brief history of middle-level education in New York State, beginning with the adoption of the Regents Policy Statement on Middle-Level Education and Schools with Middle-Level Grades in March 1989. This provided context and additional legitimacy for the middle-level initiative and established that the State Education Department, working closely with middle-level practitioners and others interested in the growth and education of young adolescents, had developed a solid foundation to support long-term, systemic middle-level education reform.

2. Recent research conducted with principals of schools with middle-level grades that illustrated the dynamic nature of middle-level educational change and strongly supported the Lessons Learned from the Regional Forums. One study examined the experiences and perceptions of 252 middle-level principals in New York State concerning the State's intermediate-level (middle grades) assessments (MLEP, 2002) and found:

   • The State's new standards-based assessments were having a positive effect on the middle grades curriculum (89.9% of respondents).

   • The new State tests were having a positive effect on instructional delivery (69.7% of respondents).

   • Remediation programs had been positively affected by the State's new intermediate-level assessments (65.9% of respondents).

   • The new tests had had a positive influence on student learning (65.3% of respondents).

- Instructional time had increased in the middle grades (49.3% of respondents).
- Time for exploratory courses (e.g., art, music, home and career skills, technology education) had decreased (41.7% of respondents).
- Time for advisory programs had been reduced (30.2% of respondents).
- Middle-level principals had very little formal coursework related to middle-level education. Half of the respondents had never taken a graduate course dealing specifically with middle-level education; 79% of respondents had had two or fewer courses.

Actions taken since the December 2001 Regents report and a series of discrete and immediate next steps designed to move the middle-level improvement effort forward that included:

1. Revising and refining the State Education Department's long-range plans for strengthening the middle grades;
2. Reviewing Commissioner's Regulations pertaining to the middle grades and proposing changes to reflect the "Lessons Learned" in the Regional Forums;
3. Creating a Statewide Network of Middle-Level Education Support Schools that were implementing the Essential Elements of Standards-Focused Middle-Level Schools and Programs and were demonstrating high student achievement;
4. identifying and disseminating successful middle grades curriculum and instructional practices;
5. Creating a comprehensive, coordinated strategy for helping schools create positive youth development programs that involves interagency partnerships with adolescent service providers; and
6. Developing strategies to recruit teachers and quality leaders to serve in middle-level schools.

After six months of informed discussions, the Regents were conversant and comfortable with middle-level education and its issues. They proceeded to make it a Regents priority and authorized the Education Department to pursue its immediate plans to strengthen middle grades education. Establishing middle-level education as a Regents priority and supporting the Department's improvement plan, while more token than substantive actions, were the Board of Regents' first public commitments to middle-level educational reform—commitments that would culminate in the approval of a new Regents Policy Statement on Middle-Level Education.

SHARPENING THE FOCUS

The Education Department, with the full support of the Regents, continued to pursue its middle-level reform efforts and in October 2002 again reported to the Board (NYSED, 2002, October). This report, like the others, was focused and purposeful. Its goals were to inform and to educate. First, it provided the Regents with an update on the Department's activities relative to middle-level educational reform (to indicate that progress was being made in developing both a Statewide and a local capacity to initiate and sustain middle grades reform).

The second section shared the most recent intermediate-level (middle grades) assessment results in English language arts and mathematics (to indicate that the problem of student achievement was still a pressing issue, especially in schools with large numbers of disadvantaged children). While middle-level schools were making significant progress in addressing the educational needs of students at risk of not meeting the State's English language arts and mathematics learning standards, they were having limited success, especially in language arts, improving achievement of the rest of the middle grades student population.

The third part of the report described in some depth the Department's vision for middle-level education, the research-based Essential Elements of Standards-Focused Middle-Level Schools and Programs (to indicate that the Department had a clear goal for its middle-level reform efforts).

The fourth section analyzed the current regulations related to the middle grades using a series of guiding questions to frame the discussion (to indicate the issues and concerns the educational community had with the present mandates and requirements).

The next to the last section summarized the substance of the December 2001 and June 2002 reports to the Regents (to indicate a systemic and logical progression and to provide background and context for the most recent report):

1. The December 2001 report was informational. It provided a context for beginning an informed discussion of middle-level issues as well as the next steps to support middle-level change.

2. The June 2002 report was also informational—a continuation and an extension of the first report. It provided additional information about the status and future of middle-level education in New York State.

The final section laid out specific actions the Department proposed to begin in 2002–03—activities taken directly from the Department's long-term plan to improve middle-level education—to lead and support positive change in middle-level schools and the tangible outcomes of these actions (another indication that the Department had a thought-out plan of action to strengthen the middle grades):

1. Revise Commissioner's Regulations as they relate to the middle grades.

2. Establish a Statewide Network of Middle-Level Education Support Schools that would serve as a support system for middle-level school change.

3. Publish a registry of middle-level schools that were successfully addressing positive youth development.

4. Prepare a catalogue of successful middle-level Academic Intervention Services (AIS) programs.

5. Document successful middle-level curricular and instructional practices;

6. Employ new strategies to recruit quality teachers and leaders to serve in middle-level schools.

7. Conduct follow-up regional sessions—an outgrowth of the Regional Forums—to encourage extended local conversations about the education of young adolescents.

This third report was both important and strategic because it kept middle-level educational reform on the Regents' "radar screen" at a time when the Board was dealing with a myriad of issues, including the recently enacted No Child Left Behind federal legislation; reinforced the fact that the middle grades student achievement "problem" was not yet solved and needed the Regents' continued attention; indicated that there were real and pressing concerns with the current regulations and requirements related to the middle grades; offered tangible hope and eventual success in the form of an improvement plan—a series of coordinated, thoughtful, long-term actions proposed by the Department; committed the Education Department to a series of immediate next steps designed to produce tangible results; and ensured that the Regents would continue to receive status reports that would keep middle-level educational reform on the Regents agenda and in the public eye for the foreseeable future.

ENGAGING THE REGENTS AS LEADERS IN THE EFFORT TO STRENGTHEN MIDDLE GRADES EDUCATION

The first two reports to the Board of Regents (December 2001 and June 2002) were primarily "stage setting" and preparatory—informational and educational—ensuring that the policymakers and the educational community were informed and knowledgeable about middle-level education. The third report (October 2002), while also informational and educational, had another purpose: to invite an informed and knowledgeable Board of Regents to assume an active leadership role in strengthening middle grades education.

Up until this time, the members of the Board of Regents had been students of middle-level education, receiving periodic reports on current research as well as on the actions and activities of the Education Department and others to strengthen middle grades education. Their role was by and large passive, getting and processing information. It was at the October 2002 meeting that the New York State Commissioner of Education suggested that the Regents, as the educational policymakers for the State, become more active and assume a proactive leadership role in middle grades reform.

The Regents have rich material before them on middle grades. The challenge is to make sense of it all to prepare the ground for better results. [The] Deputy Commissioner . . . and his colleagues have defined seven elements of middle grades programs that work, and deduced five lessons from the regional discussions of last year. . . . Where do we go from here?

1. The whole point is to raise student achievement of the standards. What we do should build local capacity to accomplish that.

2. We now have research, local commentary, and rising performance in some quarters that can support a crisp redrafting of our vision. This can take the form of a new Regents policy statement on middle grades education. It would be concise, practical, and a guide to both local practice and any future regulatory change. . . .

3. Regulation may be a barrier to improvement or a lever for change. Let's think about regulation but only after the Board has reflected on the above points, and considered the questions posed in the analysis of regulations before we talk about the regulations themselves. (Mills, 2002, October)

The Regents agreed, and the effort to develop a new Regents Policy Statement on Middle-level Education began in earnest. The Education Department's role also changed at this time. Previously, it had assumed the primary leadership role for the State's middle-level reform effort, while routinely keeping the Regents informed of its work. Now, the Department not only would be sharing the leadership mantle with the Regents but also would be serving in a direct support capacity to the Board of Regents as it developed the new policy. The text introduction to the October 2002 and December 2002 illustrate the change in dynamics and leadership responsibility.

October 2002	The State Education Department (SED), working closely with the field, is taking purposeful actions to strengthen middle grades education and to improve student performance on the State's intermediate assessment. The attached report—a follow-up to the December 2001 and June 2002 reports to the Regents—describes what the Department has done and is doing to address the problems at the middle level (NYSED, 2002, October).
December 2002	The New York State Board of Regents and the State Education Department, in collaboration with the field, are engaged in a series of actions designed to strengthen middle grades education and to improve student performance on the State's intermediate assessments. The attached discussion item is the fourth in a series of reports to the Board of Regents dealing with middle-level education.... In October, the Board agreed to revisit and revise the 1989 Regents Policy Statement on Middle-Level Education and Schools with Middle-Level Grades.... At its December 2002 meeting, the Board will discuss the proposed core contents of a revised policy statement. Board members were asked to submit suggestions on the overall content or topics to be included in the policy statement.... With [the Regents] concurrence on the core contents of the policy statement, a draft of the proposed policy statement will be submitted to the Board.... to attain approval for soliciting public comment.... A revised policy statement reflecting public comment will be submitted to the Board for approval... (NYSED, 2002, December, a).

The Board of Regents' task was now focused, purposeful, and declarative: develop a new policy statement on middle-level education. In his report to the Regents in December, the State Education Commissioner reiterated the Regents' charge:

The Regents will define middle grades policy this spring. This work will be presented in the context of the current concerns about enabling all students to meet the standards. It's clear, for example, that the seeds of dropping out are sown in middle grades. In order to meet the graduation standards, students cannot be allowed to fall behind in these grades.

The Regents policy discussions on this topic have been and will continue to include all interested parties. The work has included research on effective practice, regional meetings, and identification of essential elements of successful middle grades programs. After their policy decision, Regents will change regulations and the State Education Department will certify model programs in local schools to enable others to learn from them. (Mills, 2002, December)

It began its work by reviewing the 1989 Regents Policy Statement on Middle-Level Education and Schools with Middle-Level Grades to provide an historical context and a beginning point for discussions and by discussing the proposed core contents of the new policy statement which were organized around the seven research-based Essential Elements and reflective of the five "Lessons Learned" at the spring 2002 Regional Forums on middle-level education. The Education Department proposed three sets of key questions to guide and structure the Regents' conversation and shape the final policy statement (NYSED, 2002, December, b).

Questions #1. Are the seven identified core topic areas (Philosophy, Educational Program, Organization and Structure, Classroom Instruction, Educational Leadership, Student Academic and Personal Support, and Professional Learning) sufficiently encompassing and inclusive? Are there other concerns that cannot be accommodated by the seven identified areas and need a separate designation?

Questions #2. How specific should the Regents policy statement be? What level of detail is needed to guide regulatory revision and to provide direction to local schools and districts? Should the policy statement be prescriptive and directive? Or, should it be more general with the specifics needed by schools to implement the policy statement be provided by Commissioner's Regulations and Department publications such as the Essential Elements of Standards-Focused Middle-Level Schools and Programs?

Questions #3. Should the Regents policy statement be written from the perspective of the school and the adults in the school? Or, should it be written from the perspective of the student, the young adolescent?

The answers to the three sets of guiding questions were critical, because they became the decision rules or "design principles" that Department staff would use to prepare the draft language of the proposed middle grades policy. The Regents, after thoughtful deliberations, agreed that the new Regents policy statement would be a revision and update of the 1989 Regents Policy Statement on Middle-Level Education and Schools with Middle-Level Grades (in deference to, and recognition of, the careful, thoughtful work done by earlier Regents) and would reflect the following design principles (NYSED, 2003, February):

1. be written from the perspective of the young adolescent;

2. address the dual needs of young adolescents: academic achievement and personal development;

3. reflect the most recent research on the educational and personal needs of young adolescents;

4. include the following seven core topics (which mirror the seven Essential Elements and provide a clear connection to the Education Department's research-based vision for middle-level education): Philosophy, Mission, and Vision; Educational Program; Organization and Structure; Classroom Instruction; Educational Leadership; Student Academic and Personal Support; and Professional Learning; and

5. be concise but sufficiently substantive and precise so as to guide and inform the review of Commissioner's Regulations related to the middle grades.

The nature of the design principles was critically important to the development of policy. While they provided clear direction, they were sufficiently broad to provide the degree of flexibility Department staff needed to draft a comprehensive policy statement. Any more specificity in the design principles (e.g., what classroom instructional practices) must be included or the actual length of the policy statement) would have constrained the development of policy by limiting what options or language would be considered acceptable.

CRAFTING LANGUAGE FOR A DRAFT POLICY STATEMENT

During December 2002 and January 2003, Department staff labored to write a draft Regents Policy Statement on Middle-Level Education for consideration by the Board in February. They used the design principles agreed to by the Regents. In February 2003, the Department presented the Regents with proposed draft language for a new middle grades policy statement that conformed to the decision rules and design principles established by the Board (NYSED, 2003, February).

In addition, and possibly more important, Department staff accompanied the draft language with a concisely written document that provided a thoughtful rationale—grounded in a solid middle grades/young adolescent research base—for what was presented in the draft policy statement. This provided not only a justification for the policy contents but also a focus for much of the discussion. Subtly but effectively, it broadened the subsequent discussions from primarily a conversation about "what" was in the policy to a more thoughtful dialogue that balanced the "what" with the "why" of the proposed language. The conversations among the Regents and in the educational community became less focused on what was written and more a discussion of why it was written.

SOLICITING PUBLIC REACTION TO THE DRAFT POLICY
STATEMENT LANGUAGE

Once the Regents accepted the proposed draft language in principle, they directed the Education Department to engage the educational community and other relevant constituencies in an extensive and inclusive public review of the draft Regents policy statement on middle-level education

(Chart 9.2). This Statewide public engagement effort began in mid-February 2003 and continued through April 2003. To ensure that every public engagement session had certain common characteristics and desired outcomes that allowed for comparisons among sessions, the Education Department prepared a Public Engagement Tool Kit that contained all the necessary information and materials to conduct a successful session (e.g., who to invite, session agendas, supporting documents, structured response questionnaires, information on where to send the results of the discussions, etc.) and made it available on its website. The use of a set agenda, a uniform information solicitation process, and a common survey instrument allowed for the collection of comparable information across the State.

Chart 9.2. Plan for Public Engagement Related to the Review and Critique of the Draft Regents Policy Statement on Middle-Level Education

Target Groups	Process
Local School District Teams	Thirty-three BOCES, individually or regionally, convened 30 public engagement sessions where local school district teams met and discussed the draft Regents Policy Statement on Middle-Level Education. Each session involved participants who were broadly representative of the educational community and others interested in the education of young adolescents.
Big Four City School Districts	The Department solicited reactions to and insights about the draft policy statement from the Buffalo, Rochester, Syracuse and Yonkers City School Districts. Rochester, Syracuse, and Yonkers joined with a local BOCES to conduct their public engagement sessions; Buffalo conducted its own forum.
New York City	The Department solicited reactions and comments from the Chancellor's Office of the New York City Public Schools and staff of the New York City Department of Education. New York City School Support Center staff met with building leadership teams in three Boroughs to solicit comment and reaction to the draft policy statement.
Students	The Department's Student Support Services Unit, working closely with the Coordinated School Health and Wellness Centers and the Regional School Support Centers and using a specially designed survey instrument, conducted several regional forums upstate involving middle-level and high school students. In New York City, Young Citizens, Inc. hosted a student forum involving middle-grades students.
Parents	The Department, working closely with the NYS PTA, a Big Four City School District, and the United Parents Associations of New York City and using a specially-designed survey instrument, solicited comments and insights from the parents of young adolescents on their opinions and concerns about education in the middle grades.

**Chart 9.2.   Plan for Public Engagement Related to the Review
and Critique of the Draft Regents Policy Statement
on Middle-Level Education (Cont.)**

Target Groups	Process
Middle-Level Teachers	The New York State Council of Educational Associations (NYSCEA), with the support of the Department, held a public engagement session that involved not only organizations whose constituency consisted of teachers from the disciplines where there were no intermediate State assessments, but also organizations whose constituency consisted of teachers from disciplines where there were intermediate State assessments.
Organizations, Agencies and Other Groups	The Department provided a series of opportunities (e.g., conference sessions, special meetings, on-line surveys, etc.) for organizations, agencies, and other groups both within and outside the educational community to provide commentary on the draft policy statement.
Statewide Educational Groups and Organizations	The Department solicited public testimony via a structured statewide hearing in Albany on Tuesday, April 29, 2003. Twenty-four people, representing a variety of perspectives (e.g., the Arts, Technology Education, District Superintendents, New York State United Teachers (NYSUT), NYS School Boards Association, NYS Middle School Association, NYS Parent-Teachers Association, Family and Consumer Sciences, United Federation of Teachers (UFT), Middle-Level Principals, Public Television, Gifted and Talented Education, Higher Education, Physical Education, Second Language, etc.), presented testimony.

In addition to the series of meetings and discussion sessions that engaged the various groups, the Education Department provided additional avenues for interested parties to share their views and ideas. Available on the Education Department's website was a structured, on-line survey for individuals who were unable to attend a scheduled session but wished to complete a formal survey. The Department also provided a dedicated e-mailbox for people who wanted to express a point-of-view or provide open-ended commentary. More than 2300 people participated in the scheduled public engagement sessions held around the State. One hundred eighty-two respondents completed the on-line survey and 84 individuals submitted comments via the dedicated e-mailbox.

HONORING THE RESULTS OF THE PUBLIC ENGAGEMENT PROCESS

The public comments and reactions fell into six general groupings (NYSED, 2003, June):

1. General reactions to the draft policy statement. By and large the overall reaction to the draft policy statement was extremely positive ("This is a good, general statement for middle school education."). Only a few disagreed with the basic content.

2. Specific language suggestions for additions, deletions, or modifications to the draft policy statement. Language changes ranged from specific word changes to more general recommendations ("Pare down to essentials."). Department staff used the following guidelines to review and evaluate suggested language changes:
   • The suggestion addressed policy issues (reflecting broad-based philosophy and purpose) rather than regulation (specific mandates or requirements) or implementation (practical "how-to's").
   • The suggestion was research based and substantiated.
   • The suggestion added value to the policy (clearer wording, new concept, etc.).

3. Thoughts and ideas about how to best implement the policy statement. Many of the comments and suggestions focused not on the policy language but on how it should be implemented. While these were not immediately useful, they were to become extremely valuable in later discussions once the Regents policy was approved.

4. Potential barriers to the implementation of the policy statement. Again, also common were references to potential barriers to the implementation of the policy. These, too, were not immediately useful, they were very helpful in informing later discussions once the policy language was adopted.

5. Suggestions for specific regulations in support of the policy statement. Many respondents used the opportunity for public comment to propose that the Regents take specific regulatory action, often in support of—or at the expense of—a particular discipline or curricular area. Other suggestions were more general, geared at increasing flexibility and local options. These comments and reactions, while not germane to the immediate discussions, were of value in later conversations related to the promulgation of new regulations.

6. Concerns ancillary to the policy statement. These included comments that, while tangentially related to the policy statement discussions, could not be easily classified ("Hold State accountable for funding.").

The intensive and extensive public engagement process generated a number of significant modifications to the draft policy statement. The revised draft policy statement, modified to reflect public reactions, was presented to the Board of Regents in June 2003 (NYSED, 2003, June). It was at this June meeting that the Department provided the Regents with additional professional learning about middle-level education to inform further their final deliberations. Dr. Robert Felner, Chair of the School of Education at the University of Rhode Island and a nationally-renowned expert on middle-level educational reform and school improvement, especially in districts with large numbers of disadvantaged students, discussed with the Regents in an open session the realities and nuances of systems change and educational reform. Dr. Felner's presentation was extraordinarily important at the time as it had the effect of personalizing middle grades reform and, at the same time, putting a human "face" on the middle-level education research canon. The Regents had one final chance to talk face-to-face with a leading expert and researcher in middle-level education and ask any last questions prior to the formal vote on the approval of the proposed policy statement that was scheduled for July 2003.

The July 2003 report included, along with the final proposed language of a new policy statement on middle-level education, a recapitulation of the work of the last eighteen months and an "anticipatory set" describing in broad terms what needed to happen next to sustain the Statewide middle-level educational reform initiative following the adoption of a new policy (NYSED, 2003, July):

> The Board of Regents and the State Education Department are involved in an ongoing, comprehensive, and systematic effort to strengthen and improve education in the middle grades. This initiative has three distinct phases:
>
> - Phase One: Reviewing and discussing the literature and research on middle-level education to develop a knowledge base for making informed decisions; engaging the educational community and others interested in the education of young adolescents in a broadly-based discussion of middle-level education; and revising the 1989 Regents Policy Statement on Middle-Level Education and Schools with Middle-Level Grades to reflect current research, best practice, and public input.
> - Phase Two: Reviewing Commissioner's Regulations related to the middle grades; engaging the educational community and others interested in the education of young adolescents in a discussion of Commissioner's Regulations; and, finally, aligning Commissioner's Regulations as closely as possible with the newly adopted Regents Policy Statement on Middle-Level Education;
> - Phase Three: Developing guidance and support materials and resources (e.g., Essential Elements of Standards-Focused Middle-Level Schools and Programs with self-assessment rubrics, a Statewide Network of Middle-Level Education Support Schools, promising practices) that will assist school districts and school with middle-level grades in implementing the new Regents Policy Statement on Middle-Level Education and Commissioner's Regulations related to the middle grades.

This outline, along with a definitive timeline for Phase Two activities made it very clear that the official adoption of the Regents Policy Statement on Middle-Level Education was both the culmination of a set of specific, planned activities and the beginning of a new series of immediate, short-term actions (all of which were part of a larger, more extensive and comprehensive, long-term initiative designed to strengthen middle grades education). The prospectus made it clear that the Board of Regents would have a continuing and critical role in the middle-level initiative.

APPROVING THE REGENTS POLICY STATEMENT
ON MIDDLE-LEVEL EDUCATION

In July 2003, after Department staff had made a few refinements in the language in response to suggestions by the Regents, the Board of Regents, with little discussion and almost anticlimactically, officially adopted a new Regents Policy Statement on Middle-Level Education (NYSED, 2003, July). Accompanying the proposed policy statement, as an item of information, was a detailed comparison among the 1989 Regents Policy Statement on Middle-Level Education and Schools with Middle-Level Grades and the 2003 Regents Policy Statement on Middle-Level Education. This comparison made it very clear to the Regents that their actions had kept faith not only with themselves and their obligation to the educational community to craft a dynamic new policy that reflected current realities and provided a clear direction for the future but also with previous Regents by building on and extending, rather than dismissing, their 1989 policy statement.

REFLECTING ON THE PROCESS

Looking Back.   In eighteen months, the Board of Regents and the State Education Department, working closely with the State's educational community developed—systematically, methodically, and according to schedule—a new Regents Policy Statement on Middle-Level Education that directly affects State mandates and local practice in the middle grades:

Time Frame	Activity	Purpose(s)
December 2001	First discussion by the Board of Regents: Report on Middle-Level Education in New York State	Informational and educational
February–May 2002	First series of public discussions by the larger educational community	Informational, educational, invitational, participatory, and instructive
June 2002	Second discussion by the Board of Regents: Status Report on Middle-Level Education in New York State	Informational and educational
October 2002	Third discussion by the Board of Regents: Status Report on Middle-Level Education in New York State	Informational and educational
December 2002	Fourth discussion by the Board of Regents: Draft Outline of a Middle-Level Education Policy Statement	Informational, educational, and participatory
February–May 2003	Second series of public discussion by the larger educational community	Informational, educational, invitational, participatory and instructive
June 2003	Fifth discussion by the Board of Regents: Proposed Regents Policy Statement on Middle-Level Education	Clarification and reconciliation
July 2003	Sixth discussion by the Board of Regents: Regents Policy Statement on Middle-Level Education	Final Approval

Hindsight is a wonderful teacher. A thoughtful look back at the year and a half of work suggests several key ideas to consider in developing educational policy:

1. Take advantage of every opportunity to educate policymakers and the larger educational community: educated decision-makers make informed decisions; an educated public understands informed decisions.

2. Have a long-term plan that provides context, but take short progressive steps: While people generally tend to focus on the most immediate actions, they need to know that their efforts are purposeful and part of a comprehensive long-range plan.

3. Engage the educational community early in meaningful conversation: people are much more ready to accept a decision if they have had a substantive role in the discussions leading up to the decision.

4. Make the process and outcomes as transparent as possible: the more understandable the endeavor—both process and results—the greater the likelihood it will be accepted by those whom it affects most.

5. Use research to substantiate need, buttress decisions, and depersonalize debate: This helps to objectify the discussion, moving it away from opinion and personal preference and to data and documentation.

6. Take every opportunity to recapitulate: people need periodic reminders of what has happened (progress to date), why it has happened (rationale), and where it is leading (eventual outcomes).

7. Keep discussions centered on what is best for young adolescents and avoid debating adult issues: the conversation needs to remain focused on addressing student needs rather than adult concerns.

8. Never rush the process: people need to feel comfortable and informed when crafting policy.

9. Listen carefully to the educational community: the immediate experiences of different constituencies provide valuable perspectives and insights.

10. Five policymakers a strong research-based rationale for their decisions: this allows them to defend their positions with facts and authority.

Looking Ahead.   The approval of the Regents Policy Statement on Middle-Level Education marked the end of a beginning. More difficult work lies ahead. Policy, if it is to have maximum impact, needs to be both enacted and executed. At the end of eighteen months of study and discussion, the New York State Board of Regents enacted a well-researched, thoughtfully discussed middle-level policy. Two defining challenges now face the New York State Regents and the State Education Department if the new policy is to have maximum impact:

1. The substance of the new policy statement must be translated into mandates and regulations that have the power of law.

2. Useful supports and positive enticements that increase the likelihood that the educational community will take seriously and implement, completely and with fidelity, the sum and substance of the new policy need to be developed and readily available to schools and districts.

So easy to say; so difficult to do. Stay tuned....

Supporting Young Adolescents: Regents Policy Statement on Middle-Level Education July 2003

INTRODUCTION

Young adolescents from ages 10 to 14 are undergoing personal transformations—physical, intellectual, emotional, social and psychological. The Board of Regents believes that the time these students spend in the middle grades, 5 through 8, is critical to both their personal growth and development and their success in high school.

Based on a series of statewide discussions with many groups and a thorough review of the research on effective middle-level education practices, the Regents and the State Education Department have identified seven essential elements of standards-focused middle-level schools and programs. This policy statement reflects these seven key factors.

The challenge to middle-level education is to make the change from childhood to adolescence and from the elementary grades to the high school a positive period of intellectual and personal development. For many students, this is a hopeful time of life. However, for some youngsters emerging adolescence is a stressful time. These personal difficulties may be exacerbated in cases where either the home or the community (including the school) in which the young person lives and learns offers limited opportunities for positive role models, employment, and a satisfying lifestyle.

Educators, parents, families, and communities must recognize that they need to work together to assist students in a changing society. Educators need to recognize and assume a shared responsibility not only for their students' intellectual and educational development, but also for their students' personal, social, emotional, and physical development. The entire school community must share responsibility for the success of all students, assuring high-quality instruction, course content, and support and other services in the middle-level grades, and promoting high expectations for all students, regardless of disability, limited English proficiency, religion, sex, color, race, or national origin.

The following seven essential elements must be in place in standards-focused schools with middle-level grades if young adolescents are to succeed academically and develop as individuals:

1. A philosophy and mission that reflect the intellectual and developmental needs and characteristics of young adolescents;

2. An educational program that is comprehensive, challenging, purposeful, integrated, relevant, and standards-based;

3. An organization and structure that support both academic excellence and personal development;

4. Classroom instruction appropriate to the needs and characteristics of young adolescents provided by skilled and knowledgeable teachers;

5. Strong educational leadership and a building administration that encourage, facilitate, and sustain involvement, participation, and partnerships;

6. A network of academic and personal support available for all students;

7. Professional learning for all staff that is ongoing, planned, purposeful, and collaboratively developed.

In a standards-focused middle-level school or program, the goals of academic achievement and personal development for each student are not in conflict or in competition. Rather, they are compatible, complementary, and mutually supportive. From a young adolescent's perspective, the essential elements of a successful standards-focused middle-level school or program must contain the following components.

Philosophy, Mission, and Vision

Every young adolescent deserves a school that values academic achievement and personal development and provides a supportive environment free from violence, bullying, harassment, and other negative behaviors. Students in the middle grades are in a unique period of development, a period of rapid intellectual, physical, social, and emotional change. The philosophy, mission, and vision of a school with middle-level grades must reflect the dual purposes of middle-level education (academic achievement and personal development). They must also stress the positive development of the individual and affirm the school's responsibility to assist all students in making a successful transition from the elementary grades to high school and from childhood to adolescence.

Educational Program

Every young adolescent needs a challenging, standards-based course of study that is comprehensive, integrated, and relevant. They need an educational program that is enhanced by genuine involvement of students, their parents, their families, and the greater school community. Further, they need an educational program that emphasizes and promotes the requisite academic knowledge and skills needed to succeed in school—both middle-level and high school—and in later life. The educational program should be fully aligned with the State's 28 learning standards and emphasize the natural connections and linkages among the standards. Middle grades instruction must build upon the foundational knowledge and skills of the elementary grades and, in doing so, prepare students for success in high school.

Literacy and numeracy are key to the educational program. English language arts—reading, writing, listening and speaking—and mathematics are emphasized across the subject areas with expectations for performance that are consistent across and within the disciplines and commonly understood by both teachers and students. Strategies for reading are applied in all the content areas and writing experiences are provided in a variety of forms. Mathematics instruction builds on basic skills and emphasizes conceptual understanding and problem-solving skills. The educational program also promotes both an understanding and the use of the concepts of technology; fosters an understanding and an appreciation of the arts; teaches how to access, organize, and apply information using various media and data bases; helps students understand and apply positive health concepts and practices and participate in healthful physical activities; and develops skills to explore new subject areas.

The educational program also encourages students to pursue personal interests, engage in school and community activities (e.g., sports, clubs, etc.), explore potential futures and careers, and develop useful social, interpersonal, and life skills needed to live a full and productive life. It also offers opportunities for the development of personal responsibility and self-direction.

Up-to-date learning aids (e.g., textbooks, current adolescent literature, laboratory equipment, etc.), instructional materials, and instructional technology are used to support the educational program. Targeted and timely academic intervention services must be provided so that students do not fall behind in meeting the learning standards. These additional academic instruction and/or student support services that address barriers to learning are critical in the middle grades to ensure that all students achieve the State's learning standards and graduate from high school. Such services are particularly important to students with disabilities and those who are English language learners to ensure they are successful in the general academic program.

Organization and Structure

Young adolescents learn and develop best in a school that is organized and structured to promote both academic achievement and personal development. Organizational effectiveness and school success are not contingent upon a particular grade or school configuration. What is critical is that a school is organized and structured to help young adolescents make the transition from the elementary to the high school grades, from childhood to adolescence.

The organization and structure should help make all students, staff, parents, and families feel secure, valued, and respected as significant contributors to the school community. Teachers must be provided with regular opportunities to interact and collaborate to ensure that instruction is consistent and interrelated across and within the subject areas. Scheduling flexibility is necessary to provide a comprehensive educational program, interdisciplinary curricula, targeted and timely academic intervention services, co-curricular and extracurricular activities, and opportunities for students to engage in leadership and community service projects.

The organization and structure connect youngsters to adults and to other students in the school and community and provide opportunities for increasingly independent learning experiences and responsibilities within a safe and structured environment. Each student needs a caring adult advocate in the school who knows that student personally and well. The organization and structure provide time during the school day that is necessary to ensure opportunities for additional instruction and personal support are available for students who need extra help to meet the State's standards.

Classroom Instruction

Every young adolescent requires skilled and caring teachers who have a thorough understanding of their subject(s) and of the students whom they teach. Young adolescents learn and develop best when they are treated with respect, involved in their learning, engaged with challenging content that has meaning and connections for them, and receive assurances that they are capable, worthy people. Teachers need to recognize and understand the changes that are occurring within their students, design and deliver a challenging curriculum based on the State's learning standards, and accept responsibility for each student's learning and development. They need to have an extensive understanding of their subject matter and of different approaches to student learning. A variety of successful instructional techniques and processes that reflect best practices (e.g., differentiated instruction, cooperative learning, etc.) must be used and capitalize on the unique characteristics and individual needs of young adolescents.

Teachers must provide instruction that is purposeful, challenging, relevant, integrated, and standards-based and use classroom assessments that are useful indicators of individual student growth and performance to monitor each student's progress and to plan instruction. They ensure that performance expectations are consistent and interrelated across and within subject areas. Student data, both personal and achievement, are used to make curricular and instructional decisions and technology and other instructional resources support and enhance learning. Teachers use flexible grouping based upon pupil needs, ways of learning, and interests, and employ interdisciplinary approaches to help students integrate their studies and to fulfill their potential. Opportunities are created for students to develop social, interpersonal, and leadership skills in addition to academic proficiency.

Teachers consult with each other and with other school personnel about instructional, curricular, and other student-related issues. They also inform and involve parents in their children's education by helping them understand the instructional program, their children's progress, and how to help their children at home with schoolwork, school decisions, and successful development through early adolescence.

Educational Leadership

Every young adolescent should be educated in schools that have knowledgeable, effective, and caring leaders. Students learn and develop best when the adults in the school community have high expectations for students and staff, share and support a common vision, and work together to achieve common purposes. The personnel in effective schools with middle-level grades share leadership responsibilities. For the school to prosper, those in positions of leadership must know and understand the needs and developmental characteristics of young adolescents and the essential elements of a standards-focused, high-performing school with middle-level grades. They must articulate and maintain high standards for classroom instruction and student performance and support and encourage teachers to take risks, explore, question, and try new instructional approaches. They must also ensure and facilitate inter-school cooperation, collaboration, and communication with feeder elementary schools and receiving high schools.

Educational leaders promote school/community partnerships and involve parents and other members of the community in school activities and initiatives that benefit students. They create, promote, and sustain a school culture and climate of mutual support and collective responsibility for the educational and personal development of every young adolescent. They also ensure students are provided with opportunities to assume significant and meaningful leadership roles in the school.

Student Academic and Personal Support

Every young adolescent needs access to a system that supports both academic achievement and personal development. Caring adults are a significant positive influence for young adolescents. To ensure a comprehensive network of academic and personal support is available for students and their families, schools with middle-level grades must maintain two-way communication with parents and families and ensure that all students and their families have access to counseling and guidance services to make educational, career, and life choices. Trained professionals (including school counselors who know and understand the needs, characteristics, and behaviors of young adolescents), special prevention and intervention programs, and community resources must be available to support those who require additional services to cope with the changes of early adolescence and/or the academic demands of middle-level education, especially students with disabilities and those who are English language learners. Students also need to be provided with opportunities to have access to adult mentors and positive role models. Parents, families, and community groups must be informed of the essential role they play in ensuring students attend school and access available services, expanding and enhancing venues for significant learning, promoting youth development, and supporting positive school change.

Professional Learning

Every young adolescent deserves an educational setting that values continuous improvement and ongoing professional learning. Young adolescents need highly qualified, well-trained, knowledgeable, caring teachers, administrators, and other school staff if they are to succeed. Schools with middle-level grades need to be professional learning communities where adults in the school engage in programs of growth and development that are ongoing, planned, purposeful, and collaboratively developed. At the core of professional growth should be specific subject area expertise, a knowledge and understanding of the linkages among the 28 learning standards, research-based instructional practices that have proven successful in raising student achievement and, at the practical level, the developmental characteristics of young adolescents. School staff must understand, not only theoretically but also operationally, how to implement the essential elements of a standards-focused, high-performing school with middle-level grades.

Summary

The University of the State of New York and all of its resources are unified in the mission to raise the knowledge, skill, and opportunity of all people in the State. The Board of Regents believes that the middle-level grades, grades 5 through 8, are a vital link in the education of youth, a critical period of individual growth and development, and a key to success in high school. A high performing, standards-focused school with middle-level grades addresses both academic performance and personal development. It ensures that young adolescents are prepared and ready to make a successful transition to high school, academically and personally. Creating effective schools with middle-level grades will necessitate systemic change and require a philosophy and mission committed to developing the whole child, a challenging and rigorous educational program, a supportive organization and structure, skilled and knowledgeable teachers who use effective instructional practices, strong leadership, a network of support appropriate to the needs and characteristics of young adolescents, ongoing professional learning, and a strong will to succeed.

CHAPTER 10

CREATING COMMON MIDDLE-LEVEL KNOWLEDGE

A New York Story

Jeannette Stern and Sandra L. Stacki

INTRODUCTION

A favorite cartoon about the middle level shows two middle school students, a girl speaking to a boy, as they are about to enter the middle school on the first day of school. The caption reads "Did you ever wonder what we're in the middle of?" This question seems apt not only for the students but also sometimes for the teachers and administrators. With typical certification providing licenses for K–6 and 7–12, a certification in the middle has been less available, creating a vacuum in middle-level specialized knowledge, skills, and dispositions (McEwin & Dickinson, 1998). Although many states created regulations to allow separate certification for the middle grades, now including New York (www.emsc.nysed.gov), many teacher education institutions still do not offer a distinct program that would license students for teaching in the middle grades, typically grades 5–9. Some teacher educa-tion faculty rationalize that pre-service students will be better served with a certification in grades 7–12: even though these students may start teaching

Reforming Middle Level Education: Considerations for Policymakers, pages 189–203
Copyright © 2004 by Information Age Publishing
All rights of reproduction in any form reserved.

in a middle school or junior high school, they may want to "move up" to the high school at a later time. The preferred status of high school versus middle school is clearly evident in this rationale. Likewise the education of middle school administrators is usually not a distinct route. Some administrators who have already successfully lead at the high school level or who planned on working at that level find themselves in a middle school knowing little of what the middle school foundations and developmental foci are really all about. In 1989, the Board of Regents of the State of New York issued their *Regents Policy Statement on Middle-Level Education and Schools with Middle-Level Grades* (Board of Regents, 1989). In that policy were broad concepts of what should be present in a school where young adolescents between the ages of 10 and 14 were being educated. The policy clearly stated that education at the middle level should be unique and not like that found in the elementary or high school. While the 1989 Regents Policy was quite specific in explaining what school personnel should know and do, the information to teach the staff of the middle-level building to accomplish these goals and to create a successful middle school was simply not available. In short, the policy was not operationalized into a plan of action. This chapter will discuss the difficulties of establishing and providing distinct education at the middle level and focus on New York's journey to create common middle-level knowledge and skills for teachers and for administrators. As active participants in the statewide middle-level movement, we will report on the ongoing collaborative efforts of the New York State Education Department (NYSED), the Board of Regents, the New York State Middle School Association (NYSMSA), and the Statewide Network of Middle-Level Education Liaisons, an advisory group, to meet the challenge of narrowing this policy-practice gap for both teachers and administrators.

PAST PRACTICE: GAPS AT THE MIDDLE LEVEL

With the 1989 Regents Policy Statement on middle-level education, educators throughout the state had a guideline that in numerous ways echoed the foundations and concepts of key documents in the middle-level movement (Carnegie Council on Adolescent Development, 1989; National Middle School Association 1995). In summary, the document acknowledged the physical, intellectual, social, and psychological changes that occur during the chronological period associated with the middle grades. Emphasis was also given to the type of philosophy, organization, instruction, student support, and staff development that would best meet the needs of the students and staff at this level. The policy clearly delineated that teachers at this level needed to involve students in learning experiences, use flexible grouping and a variety of classroom strategies and activities, employ interdisciplinary instruction throughout the school, consult with colleagues on student progress, and actively involve parents as partners in the learning process. The document also envisioned administrators who understood the need for the new formats and would support the students, staff, and parents in fostering the academic success and positive personal and social development of the students at this juncture of their lives (Board of Regents, 1989).

A middle-level configuration as outlined in this Regents policy statement gained popularity throughout the next thirteen years. According to a report issued by the State Education Department, using the 1981–82 school year as a base, the number of schools with grades 6–8 increased more than 185.8% through the 2001–2002 school year. Schools with a 5–8 configuration also had an increase of 98% (www.emsc.nysed.gov/rscs/MiddleLevel/gradelevelreorginnys.htm). However, while changing the grades in a particular school can give the impression of change, few modifications in policy or practice will result without funding. Throughout the 1990s, schools with grade configurations between 5 and 8 attempted to reach the outlined goals but with various degrees of success. Many of the suggestions (i.e., teaming, advisory programs, etc.) were expensive items for school budgets and not part of any state-aid incentive package. Furthermore, no statewide study had been completed to confirm the value of this new middle-level format as opposed to what was currently in place.

Thus, many districts declined to add to a school budget that already increased each year due to new reading and writing programs in the elementary schools and new electives and state mandates in the high school. Even when districts wished to move to a middle school format (some for fiscal reasons since their elementary schools were becoming overcrowded, or because they felt that this type of school culture would better meet the needs of their students), the lack of knowledgeable administrators or teachers trained in these concepts hindered the transition. While an abundance of teachers needed jobs, the institutions of higher learning were still turning out educators (both teachers and administrators) who had "secondary certification" in one subject, with little or no knowledge of the different needs of the early adolescent in the middle.

In the past, when new philosophies, strategies, or "best practices" have been introduced, most central office and building-level school administrators turned to the teacher education colleges and universities to set the standard and provide the appropriate training. Today, many colleges and universities have established partnerships with school districts so that prospective teachers have a "laboratory" where they can observe and have hands-on experience in practicing their learning under the eyes of mentors and university personnel. The participating schools gain the insight and expertise of the university personnel, have extra sets of hands to help with student learning, provide staff development for their staff, and are kept current on many new developments in educational practice. For many new strategies such as cooperative learning, brain-based strategies, and interdisciplinary instruction, new teachers entering the field and having just benefitted from university research become the mentors for the more veteran staff and provide valuable help for the building administrators.

This was not the case with middle-level education, because few courses focusing distinctly on this level were available in the state. Institutions of higher learning followed the patterns of certification and tenure areas set up by the NYSED, with only two levels identified—elementary (K–6) and secondary (7–12). Teachers learned general strategies to teach information to students between the ages of 11 and 18, with little differentiation explained or suggested. As McEwin and Dickinson (1998, p. 4) stated, "This pattern of neglect continues despite more than 75 years of calls in the literature for specialized preparation of middle-level teachers and other educators who serve young adolescents." Thus, even though the Board of Regents of the state of New York had identified and explained in the Policy Statement why students between these ages were vastly different developmentally and needed to be taught using strategies more appropriate to their maturity, most schools maintained the status quo, teaching these young adolescents in the "mini-high school" format.

In addition to the gap in expertise to teach and nurture students at this level, the increased requirements in curriculum and new statewide assessments in New York at both the elementary and high school levels also had negative impacts on education in the middle. High school Regents exams changed in format and students were no longer able to graduate from high school with a local diploma: all students must now strive for a Regents diploma and take state exams. Almost at the same time, elementary schools were required to give assessments in math, English Language Arts (ELA), science, and social studies. These exams immediately became high-stakes as results were published in the local papers, providing the public a broader look at their schools' successes or perhaps failures and making district and school administrators more accountable and more nervous. Poor results on these tests also mandated "Academic Intervention Services" (AIS) with curricular and financial implications. In trying to ensure that scores would be the best they could be, many districts began sending their best teachers to those levels, leaving gaps in the staffing in the middle. Very often, when districts hired new staff, they were sent first to the "middle-level building" to prove themselves. If they were successful, they were then moved to the high school. Not until the intermediate assessments finally began in 1999 did districts realize that this may not have been the best plan in the long-term. Because these 8th grade assessments began several years later than the high school and elementary exams, many of the key teachers who had shown their expertise in enabling middle-level students to achieve were already entrenched in the other two levels.

AN INSTRUCTIONAL MODEL:
THE ACADEMY AND ESSENTIAL ELEMENTS

New York needed a plan of action that operationalized the State Education Department's goals into successful school organization and classroom practice. This plan must include how to educate teachers and administrators and then evaluate good practice. In the administrator's role as instructional leader, he or she would need to have the same knowledge about good teaching and learning practice that the teacher does. Providing teachers and administrators this commonly needed training *together* would create a team approach and would result in the creation of a collaborative building culture. Dr. David Payton, the Supervisor of Middle Level for the NYSED and the key link to the Middle-Level Liaisons (an advisory group of middle-level leaders who meet with the State Education Department twice a year) and the NYSMSA began to identify what key elements should be common knowledge for all middle-level educators. The result of this collaboration was the New York State Middle-Level Education Academy, a program including standards, performance indicators, and outcomes that represent the foundation of what each middle-level administrator and teacher should know to provide the best opportunities for the success of their students. This Academy structure has been copyrighted by the Middle School Association and has been successfully conducted in schools and districts across the state in various formats—in-serivce courses over a semester, week-long full-day courses, or daylong sessions separated by time. Since 1999, more than 30 Academies have been successfully completed across the state from Buffalo to Long Island, providing a common set of understandings that serve as foundations for middle-level educational programs around the state.

The Academy curriculum has six major divisions. The first provides a general introduction and foundation upon which the other sessions build. In this session, a brief history of the middle-level movement, including a cadre of documents, forms the foundation. Participants then are introduced to the essential elements of an effective middle-level program and how they can be gradually implemented into a school. Finally, the interdependent characteristics of the middle-level child are explored, making sure that all involved understand the implications for the instructional program.

The second section deals with appropriate instructional strategies. Students at this point in their development have certain cognitive, social, emotional, and physical needs and a successful educational program must be customized to meet them. Once educators understand the developmental needs of students, creating an age-appropriate program to meet these needs can begin. Participants are introduced to Bloom's *Taxonomy*, Maslow's *Hierarchy of Needs*, brain-based research, multiple intelligences, cooperative learning, alternative forms of assessment, and hands-on strategies that research has shown work best with students at this stage of development. Time is provided for the creation of new activities that are in sync with what was learned.

Structures to help meet primarily the affective needs of students are addressed in sections three and four of the Academy program. Sample structures for teams, suggested functions, and roles of teachers and administrators are explored. Teaming enables the teachers to share information on students with the rest of the staff not on their team, to identify concerns earlier that might hamper social or academic success and to suggest a course of action, and to create appropriate learning opportunities (Forte & Schurr, 1993; Rottier, 1996). Advisor-Advisee programs, community service, service learning, and developing student responsibility are the crux of section four. All of these programs deal with the positive personal development goal of middle-level education. None of these are ever evaluated with paper and pencil assessments. Yet students who do not first feel comfortable or confident in their abilities will not perform academically to their level of potential. Various models of advisories are identified (Cole, 1992; Forte & Schurr, 1993). Creating time for students and staff members to develop a non-subject-based relationship enables students to ask questions that they would not normally ask and receive the important information they need. Establishing student-adult interactions of this kind enables students to see teachers as role models and real people, not just human fonts of knowledge. Providing service learning and links to adults in the community who can provide positive role models or opportunities to experiment with future careers are also addressed in this section (Fertman, White, & White, 1996; McPherson, 1977). Positive youth development has been shown to be tantamount to student success and this part of the Academy not only explains how to foster affective development but how it relates to the school and instruction.

The fifth section deals with instruction, beginning with New York State's 28 learning standards and their relevance to middle-level education (www.emsc.nysed.gov). The need for teachers to be aware of *all* the standards rather than the few that are directly related to a subject they might have primary responsibility for is stressed. General skill acquisition, interdisciplinary instruction and reinforcement of learning, and multiple assessment strategies are some of the elements included here (Beane, 1993; Schurr, 1999; Vars, 1993). The goal is to create learning communities where common skills and information are consistently apparent and emphasized and the students see learning in real-life situations and not as fragmented and isolated activities. The final section is designed to provide each participant with the opportunity to apply what has been learned to his or her actual school setting. In this way, learning becomes readily applicable to the school setting in which the participants are currently a part. Long and short-term goals, implementation plans, the creation of a model that would work in their school, and strategies to see their plans through to fruition are developed.

Since its inception, this Academy program has been used successfully with individual schools, groups of schools, and as part of a university program. While it provides a firm foundation for a middle-level program, other mechanisms need to be in place to support the translation of the newly acquired information into good classroom practice within the format of whatever building configuration exists. Thus, administrators need help to obtain updated, timely information and to provide the best leadership for the staff in terms of professional development and instructional support.

To further the efforts of providing a plan of action, in 2000, The Board of Regents and the NYSED, with input from the Middle-Level Liaisons and NYSMSA, issued *The Essential Elements of Standards-Focused Middle-Level Schools and Programs.* Clearly supporting a balance of academic and affective goals, this document explained that a good middle-level program consisted of two major goals: "the intellectual development and academic achievement of all students, and the personal and social development of each student" (Board of Regents, 2000, p. 1). In addition, this document set forth seven essential elements that should be part of a successful program. Closely aligned with the Academy outline, the first four of these elements address philosophy and mission, the educational program, the organization and structure of the school, and classroom instructional needs. The other three identify the need for educational leadership, a network of academic and personal support, and professional training and staff development. Recognizing the importance of educated administrators who can be effective in multiple roles, the middle school Essential Elements advocate "strong educational leadership and a building administration that encourages, facilitates, and sustains involvement, participation, and partnerships" (Board of Regents, 2000, p. 8).

Professional Development: Sharing the Message Locally

Providing professional training and staff development should involve contextualizing to participants' knowledge and needs. The Middle-Level Academy is available for districts or groups of districts. However, before deciding, some type of preassessment can ascertain what the staff and administrators already know. The NYSMSA has developed a Likert-scaled questionnaire for New York middle schools to use to determine the extent to which the Essential Elements are present in their program. A similar questionnaire could be developed to ascertain how much is known about each of the seven elements. After this information is analyzed, a staff development program could be developed to capitalize on what is already known and to introduce new information. Any professional training program for middle-level educators should provide information such as what is provided through the Academy, dealing with the numerous aspects of the Essential Elements and the 28 learning standards within the confines of the individual district and its constraints.

Some middle-level educational opportunities are available on the state or regional level. NYSMSA hosts an annual conference and various regional meetings throughout the year where middle-level information is shared. Practitioners and national presenters are invited to discuss their best practice with the conference attendees, who go home with new strategies to be tried the next school day and hopefully shared with colleagues. However, many of these opportunities are "one-shot" presentations, leaving the support and sustainability to the district and building administration to accomplish. Middle-level list-serves also facilitate collaboration and information gathering among teachers and administrators.

ABOVE AND BEYOND: THE LEADERSHIP

Wanted: Administrators Appropriate for Middle Level

Regardless of the quality or quantity of the professional development or the number of conferences or other opportunities teachers have for acquiring new information, the success of any program rests in large part with the building principal. As many researchers have reported, the principal plays a pivotal role in the success of any school improvement plan. Ernest Boyer, Ann Lieberman, and Lynne Miller all found in their research that the principal often made the difference between success and failure of building culture or program change (Dufour, 1991). In fact, Goodlad (1984) reported that schools were not able to solve their problems if the principal lacked good leadership skills. Lipsitz (1984) claimed that every survey dealing with the effectiveness of a school shows that strong leadership is the key factor for a school to be excellent. The National Association of Secondary School Principals (NASSP), in their 1985 statement, *An Agenda for Excellence at the Middle Level*, also emphasized the importance of a strong, knowledgeable principal to have a successful school program.

Yet knowledge of leading at one level is not immediately transferable and applicable to another level. Some school districts in New York, to counter the growing negative reputations of the middle-level buildings in a district, transferred some of their successful high school administrators to these buildings. The hope was that these principals' previous track records would enable them to improve the learning and climate in these buildings. Yet the mistake was to send them before or without first providing them with training so they could better work with students of this age group and teachers committed to middle-level philosophy and practice. Once there, based on their own expertise and experience, middle-level buildings were run as high schools, with smaller and younger students, with little if any increase in achievement level or social success. These administrators, as well as the teachers, needed to understand the vast differences in students between the ages of 10 and 14 as opposed to 14 and 18. Delivery of instruction, discipline, extracurricular offerings, and the entire structure of the day should be different for a 6th or 7th grader than for a junior or senior in high school.

Over time, many school district personnel who worked with the "middle-level youngster" saw minimal success using the existing models: administrators and teachers needed education specific to the characteristics and needs of the early adolescent. Certainly philosophy, curricular and affective strategies, and other topics connected to the development of a solid program for the 10 to14 year-old would be beneficial for everyone in the building to learn. However, while this common knowledge was critical in creating meaningful and clear expectations for students, staff, and parents, the administrators in the building needed additional training, beyond that which deals with classroom instruction and climate.

Providing these strong leaders who can sustain the newly-learned middle-level knowledge has been difficult in many places, because many of the administrators were not trained in middle-level education themselves. In a survey conducted between 1981 and 1983, 54% of the administrators participating in the survey reported that they did not have any formal middle school training. In the 2001–2002 school year, a new State Education Department survey again targeted principals. The purpose of this survey was to inform the State Education Department about the professional development of the leaders in middle-schools or schools with middle grades (for instance a 7–12 junior-senior high school) as well as to gather their opinions of the new state assessments. Statewide organizations dealing with curriculum and middle level were asked to encourage the targeted group of principals to complete the online, anonymous survey.

A total of 222 principals submitted completed surveys. This represented about one fourth of the principals eligible across the state. The results indicated that 50% of the principals responding to the survey reported having no courses dealing with middle-level education (NYSED, 2002). While one might not be surprised with the fact that over half of the middle-level administrators responding in the early 1980's had no formal middle-school training, findings indicating the same dearth of education only last year indicate the need for further action. Programs must be established to increase the number of middle-level principals who have participated in distinct coursework facilitating knowledge and skills at the middle level.

Specific Administrative Skills

Successful middle-level administrators need to possess four skills, according to George, Stevenson, Thomason, and Beane (1992):

> Leaders must possess a clear understanding of the characteristics and needs of young adolescents and must translate that understanding into a vision of an appropriately organized and effective middle-level school.
>
> They must be able to make recognizable progress toward the realization of that vision by organizing staff members, students, programs, time, and the building in such a way as to create a unique and effective learning environment based on the characteristics of young adolescents.
>
> Leaders must understand what tasks need to be accomplished during the reorganization process and possess the skills of "change agentry" necessary to bring those tasks to a successful completion.
>
> They must be able to engage the stakeholders (teachers, parents, students, board members, and central office staff) in a process of shared decision making in the continued long-term maintenance and improvement of the school(s). (p.111)

While the last two skills are necessary for success on any level of administration, the first two identify a specific knowledge-base that a successful middle-level leader must possess. In his article entitled, "30 Things Great Middle Level Principals Do," Little (2000) shared the results of his research on the middle-level principal, a person whom he says is one of the least studied parts of a middle-level program. His research with experts in the field of middle-level education identified seven roles for an exemplary middle-level principal: a person, a visionary, an instructional leader, a leader in an educational organization, a problem solver, a manager, and a school-community facilitator (pp. 25–28).

Even more specifically, topics such as discipline, parental roles, extracurricular activities, lesson construction, teacher evaluation, and scheduling describe the varied areas for which the principal, as the instructional and institutional leader, must be responsible and have adequate training

(Anfara, Jr., Brown, Mills, Hartman, & Maher, 2001). In addition, and perhaps even more important, the principal needs to understand more about the foundations of a good middle-level education model and be able to adapt what is good practice to what is possible in the specific building he or she leads. This ability to synthesize what is known and to create a vision that is possible to achieve, given the resources of the district, is critical for success (DuFour, 1991).

Creating Common Vision and Shared Leadership

Learning along with the staff and creating a common vision are the first steps. Learning how to work with the staff to develop a common language, common expectations, and a vision of how middle level will look in their school makes the end goals identifiable and attainable. Administrators should also know how to work with each other and with staff to translate that vision into changes in daily practice. Modeling the integration of the newly-acquired knowledge and vision helps principals to show that they believe in the changes and are not just mouthing the beliefs of others.

A principal must be a team leader, yet at the same time, be a member of the team in order to assure success. A philosophy of shared leadership must pervade the school as all staff is supported in existing or new leadership roles. Administrators still lead middle schools, but they allow for others to take on different facets of the leading process, allowing for a more collaborative culture, similar in some aspects to the same culture the teachers are being asked to establish in their classrooms. An environment must exist in which creative thoughts, suggestions, and questioning of existing practice—keeping the common vision as a framework for all change—are encouraged. This mutual responsibility and accountability often build the cohesiveness needed to make fundamental changes in buildings and programs.

A key role of the principal is to facilitate the learning and leadership of others. A good middle-level administrator should expand leadership roles, allowing teachers to take on more responsibility for their own learning and professional growth. Team leaders need to be trained in positive leadership strategies so that the team meetings will be productive and result in success for students. Committees need to have responsibilities and the opportunity to suggest changes. Administrators need to take risks and allow others to do the same, without blame if the results are not what had been expected. If a high trust level exists in a middle school, when situations develop in the blink of an eye, and administrators must make quick decisions, teachers will trust these decisions. Teachers need to feel supported and know that the building administrators trust them and are fair in their policies and processes. Working with middle-level students following the September 11 terrorist attack in New York City demanded that administrators and teachers shared leadership and trusted each other's decisions. This incident allowed some administrators to assess the level of shared leadership in their buildings.

Colleges and universities must also share the vision and the responsibility for the specialized education at the middle level that both teachers and administrators need. All teacher education institutions are changing their curricula in response to the new teacher certification requirements taking effect in 2004 in New York. Around the state, educators are realizing that a university curriculum needs to include a middle-level component (Phillips, 2003). Many universities have revised their programs in response to the new middle-level certificate in New York, grades 5–9, and within a few years, pre-service students in these programs will graduate with more concentrated knowledge and skills for the middle level. Some institutions have also designed new programs for dual certification in elementary and middle level—a few even incorporating special education certification. However, some teacher education institutions have not responded to this new call and prefer to maintain their middle-level extension programs which allow a 7–9 extension to an initial certification in K–6 or a 5–6 extension to an initial certification in 7–12 (www.emsc.nysed.gov).

Yet the changes in the state certification regulations to allow for the distinct certification in middle level indicate the success of the various groups in the state, such as NYSMSA and the Middle-Level Liaisons, in working with the state toward more recognition and distinction for the middle level. Teacher education institutions must institute more informal and formal partnerships with local middle schools to insure that university professors, teachers, and administrators share their own knowledge and share the responsibility for knowledgeable new teachers and administrators who will enter middle schools. More field experiences in a middle school for both aspiring teachers and administrators will increase their practical knowledge and lessen the theory-practice gap. This will result in new teachers and administrators entering the middle-level classrooms again having the state-of-the-art knowledge and again providing examples for the veteran staff.

The Future: New York State's Plan

In response to the need for administrative support so that they, in turn, can provide the foundation for good middle-level practice in the buildings, many regions in New York have created middle-level principals' groups who meet regularly to allow for exchange of information and informal mentoring. These groups will continue to enhance collaboration and shared knowledge of the middle level. Furthermore, NYSMSA is just beginning to pilot a Middle-Level Academy for administrators, designed not only to teach the elements of middle level, but also to provide strategies and suggestions for changing building culture, providing internal mentoring, and building sustained instructional change. Cohorts of administrators new to middle level can create peer support groups and an informal helpline to assist each other when a new situation or problem develops. This networking will be especially important for newer administrators because many of their experienced and wise, older colleagues will be retiring. The principals responding to the NYSED survey on training and assessment in 2001–2002 (approximately 25% in the state) indicated that 60% of them were 50 years old or over. Thus, high rates of retirement are expected over the next five to ten years (NYSED, 2002).

The format of an Administrative Academy is to infuse the philosophy of middle level education with that of good leadership skills and to provide examples of everyday situations for the participants to tackle within the framework of what is seen as good middle-level practice. The long-term goal of this program is to provide all administrators, whether new to the field of administration or new to this level of administration, with a solid background in how to translate good middle-level practice into every building—regardless of grade configuration, building size, or location.

The year 2003 was a pivotal year for middle-level education in New York as the Board of Regents continued its process of approving a new policy statement and regulations on Middle-Level Education. In 1989, middle-level education as an entity separate and apart from secondary education was a new idea. The introduction of the 1989 policy statement included a significant amount of information about child development at this juncture, specifically identifying changing physical, social, emotional, and intellectual characteristics that normally occur during the time of early adolescence. The 2003 version is much shorter, with none of the introduction to early adolescence. Instead, the policy speaks to the need to provide a challenging education that meets the needs at this time, separate and apart from elementary and secondary programs.

This policy, which has been discussed in public meetings and was approved in July 2003, includes several areas where emphasis on specific components is different—less or more—than the 1989 version. Yet notable in this new version are the sections on staff development and educational leadership. While the 1989 version addresses professional training and staff development, the newer version addresses professional learning—emphasizing the need for everyone, especially educators, to be lifelong learners providing support for all students. The strengthened education leadership section states the following:

Every young adolescent should be educated in schools that have knowledge-able and effective leaders. Students in the middle grades learn and develop best when the adults in the school have high expectations for students and staff, share and support a common vision and work together to achieve common purposes. The personnel in effective middle-level schools share leadership responsibilities and work to create, promote, and sustain a school culture of mutual support and collective responsibility for the educational and personal development of every young adolescent. The district and building administration encourages, facilitates, and sustains involvement, participation, and partnerships that enhance student learning and development. (Board of Regents, 2003, p. 5)

As middle-level education becomes more of an entity unto itself, the need for expanded professional learning for teachers and for administrators will become even more apparent. The new teacher certification in grades 5–9, effective in 2004, and the new Middle-Level Academy for administrators highlight the continuing plan of action and the continuing awakening of middle-level education in New York. Colleges, universities, professional organizations, and local districts will all be looking for more and more information to support both academically and socially the nearly one million New York children "in the middle" (NYSMSA, 2003).

REFERENCES

Anfara, V.A., Jr., Brown, K. M., Mills, R., Hartman, K., & Maher, R. J. (2001). Middle level leadership for the 21st century: Principals' views on essential skills and knowledge; Implications for successful preparation. In V. Anfara (Ed.), *Handbook of Research in Middle Level Education* (pp. 183–213). Greenwich, CT: Information Age Publishing.

Beane, J. (1993). *A middle school curriculum: From rhetoric to reality.* Columbus, OH: National Middle School Association.

Board of Regents of the State of New York. (2003). *Supporting young adolescents: Regents policy statement on middle-level education (DRAFT).* Albany: Author.

Board of Regents of the State of New York. (2000). *Essential elements of standards-focused middle-level schools and programs.* Albany: Author.

Board of Regents of the State of New York. (1989). *Regents policy statement on middle-level education and schools with middle-level grades.* Albany: Author.

Carnegie Council on Adolescent Development. (1989). *Turning points: Preparing American youth for the 21st century.* Washington, DC: Carnegie Corporation of New York.

Cole, C. G. (1992). *Nurturing a teacher advisory program.* Columbus, OH: NMSA

Dufour, R. P. (1991). *The principal as staff developer.* Bloomington, IN: National Educational Service.

Fertman, C., White, G. & White, L. (1996). *Service learning in the middle school.* Columbus, OH: National Middle School Association.

Forte, I. & Schurr, S. (1993). *The definitive middle school guide.* Incentive Publications.

George, P., Stevenson, C., Thomason, J., & Beane, J. (1992). *The Middle School—And Beyond.* Alexandria, VA: ASCD.

Goodlad, J. (1984). *A place called school.* New York: McGraw-Hill.

Lipsitz, J. (1984). *Successful schools for young adolescents.* New Brunswick, NJ: Transaction Books.

Little, A.L. (2000). 30 things great middle level principals do. *Middle Ground, 4*(1), 25–28.

McEwin, C.K., & Dickinson, T.S. (1998). Preparation of middle-level teachers: A call to action. *Action in Teacher Education, 20*(3), 4.

McPherson, K. (1977). Service learning: Making a difference in the community. *Schools in the Middle,* Jan/Feb, 9.

National Association of Secondary School Principals, (1985). *An Agenda for excellence at the middle level.* Reston, VA: Author.

National Middle School Association. (1995). *This we believe: Developmentally responsive middle level schools.* Columbus, OH: Author.

New York State Education Department. (2002). *New York state survey of principals of schools with middle-level grades: School year 2001–2002.* Albany: Author.

New York State Middle School Association. (2003). *Position paper: Part 100.4 regulations middle school requirements.* Pleasantville, NY: Author.

Phillips, T.J. (2003). *Teacher preparation must include middle level education.* SAANYS Journal, *32* (1), 7–12.

Rottier, J. (1996). *Implementing and improving teaming: A handbook for middle level leaders.* Columbus, OH: National Middle School Association.

Schurr, S. (1999). *Authentic assessment using product, performance, and portfolio measures from A to Z.* Columbus, OH: National Middle School Association.

Vars, G. (1993). *Interdisciplinary teaching: Why and how.* Columbus, OH: National Middle School Association.

CHAPTER 11

A NEW VISION FOR PROFESSIONAL LEARNING

Stephanie Hirsh

INTRODUCTION

High-quality professional development supports the goals, objectives, and standards of states, districts, and schools. Sustained, intellectually rigorous staff development is essential for everyone who affects student learning. This not only means teachers, principals and central office, but also includes policymakers, school board members, state department personnel, and support staff.

The core of a new vision for professional development is teacher participation on learning teams. Learning teams meet every day and focus their attention on improving the quality of teaching in classrooms and the learning of students. Learning team meetings begin with a review of the upcoming standards students will be expected to master and moves into a discussion of the underlying concepts teachers must understand in order to teach the standards. Together teachers plan and develop powerful lessons, and as the unit evolves, they critique students' work to see if their intentions are met. Over time the team determines the areas in which additional learning or external assistance is required. Members of learning

Reforming Middle Level Education: Considerations for Policymakers, pages 205–229
Copyright © 2004 by Information Age Publishing
All rights of reproduction in any form reserved.

teams take collective responsibility for the learning of all students represented by team members.

Throughout the school and system, additional learning teams are organized to facilitate other facets of school improvement. School and district teams, representing all stakeholder groups, set direction and monitor progress toward improvements. Central office administrators study and learn together to strengthen knowledge and skills essential for supporting school-based improvements. Administrators meet in small teams to facilitate their learning. They learn ways to strengthen their role as instructional leaders, to assist teachers in improving the quality of student work, to critique one another's school improvement efforts, and to develop their skills in areas such as data analysis and consensus building.

In order to play its part in increasing student learning in the middle grades, Sparks (1997), executive director of the National Staff Development Council, advocates for staff development that is results-driven, job-embedded, and standards-based.

RESULTS-DRIVEN

Results-driven professional development is focused on the answer to the question: "what do we want our middle-level students to know and be able to do?" Professional development is designed to focus on the particular knowledge and skills teachers need to enable students to achieve success. Covey (1990) admonishes people to begin with the end in mind. Results-driven professional development is about focusing on the end. Unfortunately, most professional development systems organize around courses or content offered in a smorgasbord approach to educators. Professional development effectiveness is measured by course completion or workshop satisfaction scores. Professional development is viewed as potentially helpful to one's performance as opposed to essential. Few expectations exist for the district's investment, and as a result, in most cases the investment is minimal.

Renyi (1996), executive director of the National Foundation for the Improvement for Education (NFIE), which is a foundation of the National Education Association, writes that the goal of professional development in schools must be to improve results in terms of student learning, not simply to enhance practice. In a system that recognizes the value of professional development, there is alignment among individual, team, school, and system learning plans. Participants at each level consider the outcomes sought for students, the knowledge and skills required by themselves, and the professional development that will enable them to assist the system to achieve its goals.

JOB-EMBEDDED

Little (1997) writes that while research of the past decade confirms the link between professional development and student learning when it is implemented as teachers working in professional communities within the school, staff development is still typically thought of as something external to the ongoing work of teaching. It is described as something that one "does" or that is "provided" in the form of activities or events. Sparks and Hirsh (1999) ask that educators imagine schools in which teams of teachers meet almost every day, for an hour or more, to discuss ways to improve their teaching and student learning. These teams of teachers are assigned a group of students and share responsibility for their students' success. Renyi (1996) reports that when professional development is built into the daily, weekly, and yearlong job of teaching, it results in changed practice and student success.

McRobbie (2000), referencing a speech delivered by Linda Darling-Hammond, writes, "The most critical change for supporting high-quality professional development is to structure teachers' workweek so they do not spend virtually all their time teaching, but instead have adequate preparation, consultation, and collaboration time" (p. 1).

All professional development is not created equal. Years of experience have taught us that "one-shot workshops" do not help teachers acquire new skills and put them into practice in the classroom. Instead, teachers will use about 10% of what they hear in a workshop. If we want higher levels of implementation, then plans need to extend beyond the adult "pull out" model of staff development.

Job-embedded professional development makes professional learning a part of every teachers' workday. Job-embedded forms of learning include team learning, classroom observations, peer coaching, and classroom-based assistance from master teachers. Teachers have access to the tools and assistance they need to improve on a daily basis.

While this vision for professional development is absent in most middle schools, some embrace it. These schools recognize that the goals of middle school reform are not achieved without a serious commitment to ongoing professional learning on the part of all educators.

STANDARDS-BASED

Four kinds of standards contribute to effective professional development. Standards for student learning delineate expectations for students and provide direction for the content of professional learning. Standards for teachers and standards for leaders offer performance expectations and provide additional direction and content for staff development. Standards for staff development guide the planning of professional development that produces improved practice for educators and learning for students.

Fortunately, research separates effective and ineffective forms of professional development. The standards, advanced by the National Staff Development Council (NSDC) and developed in collaboration with the nation's leading professional organizations including the National Middle School Association, represent a consensus regarding the characteristics of staff development that contributes to improved student learning. These standards delineate the qualities of staff development essential to advancing improved educator practice and student performance. The standards offer assistance with planning, implementing, and monitoring staff development. The standards are organized into three areas. These areas are:

- *Context Standards.* The context standards address organizational factors necessary to support high-quality professional development. These standards are most relevant to the planning phase of staff development.
- *Process Standards.* The process standards provide direction for designing and delivering professional development that impacts daily practice of educators.
- *Content Standards.* The content standards address the knowledge and skills educators acquire through professional development.

Systems must attend to all three kinds of standards simultaneously if the desired results are to be achieved.

STANDARDS FOR STAFF DEVELOPMENT PROMOTE QUALITY

According to Hayes Mizell (2001), Distinguished Senior Fellow of the National Staff Development Council (NSDC), "...the standards are grounded in the belief that students must benefit from a teacher's investment in professional development. Each standard begins with the premise: "Staff development that improves the learning of all students..." (p. 19). This emphasizes the important connection between implementing the standards and producing better results for students. Understanding the rationale and research that support each standard and implications for middle-grades practitioners contributes to the design and implementation of more powerful professional development.

Context Standards

Context standards provide the framework for successful staff development. They address the structural issues that must be in place for new learning to have its intended impact. The quote "place a good person in a bad system and the system will win every time" emphasizes the necessity of paying attention to system-level issues. The three context standards put the building blocks in place to lay the necessary foundation for each professional development endeavor.

Learning Communities

"Staff development that improves the learning of all students organizes adults into learning communities whose goals are aligned with those of the school and district" (NSDC, 2001, p. 8). Louis (2002) addresses a group of middle-grades reform advocates and leaders on the importance of professional development in middle grades. She states that an increasing body of research suggests that real change in schools requires the development of strong professional learning communities (p. 23). Brandt (2003) states that a school culture that invites deep and sustained professional learning will have a powerful impact on student achievement.

Hord (2003) has studied, researched, and written extensively about learning communities. She offers these characteristics of professional learning communities:

1. Shared leadership by a principal who invites staff input,
2. A shared vision that represents a commitment to student learning and is consistently articulated and referenced for the staff work,
3. Collective learning and problem solving among staff,
4. Supportive physical and emotional conditions, and
5. Shared practice involving peer visitation and review of each teacher's classroom to support individual and school wide improvement.

Middle-grade schools that successfully implement this first standard exhibit these characteristics. In addition, teachers meet during scheduled times within the school day with learning teams. Teachers participate in subject matter and interdisciplinary teams. Within team learning time they develop lesson plans, examine student work, discuss student progress, and identify future needs for professional learning. These teams pay attention to how their work aligns with the school and district goals. Additionally individuals and teams participate in local, state, regional, and national networks to extend their individual and group learning.

Principals participate as members of the school-wide learning community as well as in additional district, regional, state, and/or national networks. They build a school culture that exemplifies trust, encourages risk taking, and celebrates accomplishments. The principal builds the structures to support regular school-wide and team sharing and ensures that the teacher facilitators have the skills and knowledge to support the learning process.

Fullan (2000) summarizes the importance of this staff development standard with this statement, "School improvement will never occur on a wide scale until the majority of teachers become contributors to and beneficiaries of the professional learning community" (p. 584).

Leadership

Staff development that improves the learning of all students requires skillful school and district leaders who guide continuous instructional improvement (NSDC, 2001, p.10). Cross and Rice (2000) observe, "where schools are successful, one will find a principal who places academics first and who knows how to motivate staff and teachers" (p. 62).

Leadership is a very broad term. The NSDC standard on leadership focuses on the importance of instructional leadership and the advocacy responsibilities of teachers and principals. Schools characterized by this standard are schools where teachers promote the importance of professional development with colleagues, the principal, key district leaders, community leaders, and other policymakers. Teachers articulate the connection between improved student learning and effective professional development. Selected teachers serve on the instructional leadership team and experience opportunities to develop skills that will assist them. Leadership responsibilities may include serving as a school improvement team member, committee chair, curriculum writer, lead teacher, instructional coach, and mentor for new teachers. These teachers participate in the assessment, design, monitoring, and evaluation of professional development needs and initiatives.

The Council of Chief State School Officers (1998) concludes in a report to middle-grades policymakers that without a doubt, the single most influential person in a school building is the principal. Principals in effective schools keep instruction as the priority. They create a plan with the faculty that supports ongoing school wide and team learning and improvement. The principal demonstrates this commitment by ensuring all actions, meetings, conversations, and discussions are focused on the goals of the plan. Distractions are minimized. The principal participates in professional development that aligns with the instructional priorities of the school. In turn, the principal creates structures that allow teacher leaders to participate in related professional development and then immediately practice the new learning in leadership roles in their school. Like the teacher, the principal regularly articulates the importance of professional development and advocates for its priority status with all staff, central office personnel, school board members, and community.

Barth (2001) suggests that leading by example is perhaps the purest form of leadership and the one over which each of us has the most control. The leadership standard is about the responsibility each individual has for providing the leadership and support so that staff development efforts produce the desired results. Perhaps Albert Schweitzer said it best, "Example is not the main thing in influencing others. It's the *only* thing."

Resources

"Staff development that improves the learning of all students requires resources to support adult learning and collaboration" (NSDC, 2001, p. 12). Former Secretary of Education Richard Riley (1999) suggests that giving time and support for professional learning is critical if the nation expects teachers to help students achieve higher standards. Shortly thereafter, the Education Commission of the States (2000) notes, "states and districts should ensure that all schools have the resources, time and money, to participate in effective professional development" (p. 17). Elmore (2002a) observes, "I don't think policymakers at the state and local level have any conception of the investment in professional development that's going to be required to pull this off" (p. 42). When it comes to high-quality professional development for all staff, resources are essential. The amount and application are both critical to producing the results sought from staff development.

Teachers recognize that time, dollars, and expertise are scarce and that they have a responsibility to make effective use of each. The standard on resources call for teachers to spend 20 percent of the workweek in learning and collaboration with colleagues focusing on school wide priorities, instruction, curriculum, assessment, and technology applications. Teachers access internal and external experts to assist with instructional priorities, develop identified knowledge and skills, and solve problems. They apply staff development resources according to school guidelines that ensure alignment with school priorities.

Principals also value their four primary resources: dollars, time, staff, and external support. School improvement goals and understanding of what it takes to achieve them guides the allocation of resources. They understand the importance of limiting school goals to a small number of priorities to achieve the benefit of concentration and focus. This ensures resources do not get diverted from what is most important. Organizing teachers into learning communities who support each other in the development and implementation of new skills ensures that an investment is well spent. Principals recognize that investments in one shot workshops are a waste of valuable and precious dollars. Instead, school schedules are structured to provide teachers quality time each day for collaborative team learning and planning. Principals recognize and view staff knowledge and skills as an important resource to the improvement process. Finally, new purchases of technology and/or curricular materials are planned and implemented with an understanding of what it takes to see them used well.

Process Standards

Process standards answer the staff development questions that begin with the word: How? How do we use data to assist with staff development planning? How do we evaluate the impact of professional development? How do we assess needs and plan for a diverse audience? When followed appropriately, process standards ensure that adults acquire intended new knowledge and skills, are able to use them successfully on the job, and the intended outcomes of professional development are achieved.

Data-Driven

"Staff development that improves the learning of all students uses disaggregated student data to determine adult learning priorities, monitor progress, and help sustain continuous improvement" (NSDC, 2001, p.16). As one superintendent says, "In God we trust, all others bring data." Effective professional development relies on the careful use of data.

Teacher practice characteristics of this standard includes teachers' use of disaggregated student data to determine their own learning needs. This is in contrast to the traditional teacher needs assessment tools that prioritize a list of "popular" topics. Data are disaggregated so middle-grades teachers know which students are being successful and which are not. Teachers ask whether results differ according to socioeconomic status, gender, race, or classrooms. Discussions are held at the school as well as team levels. Teachers explore these important issues to determine what they can learn that will help their students. Data are continuously reviewed and used to monitor programs and initiatives so that adjustments can be made when deemed necessary.

Principals in these schools place the same priority on the analysis and discussion of data. According to DuFour (1999), "Principals must be constantly in search of meaningful data. They must analyze results critically. If the principal of a school disregards, dismisses, or denies data that suggest a problem, there is little hope the school will ever improve" (p. 15). The principal brings data to the attention of the entire faculty and assists the staff in understanding the implications. Multiple sources of data provide a rich and inclusive picture of what is occurring in the middle school. Such data include student participation in extracurricular activities, disciplinary referrals, suspension rates, grade retention, customer satisfaction surveys, student recognitions, as well as test scores. Such data are disaggregated to ensure that all student groups are experiencing similar opportunities to benefit from the school's most challenging programs and that no student group is being singled out for either positive or negative reasons. This information contributes to the selection of school improvement goals and priorities for staff learning. The Council of Chief State School Officers (1998) agrees, "Acquiring the ability to use information can be one of the most important tools for reforming a middle school" (p. 24).

Evaluation

"Staff development that improves the learning of all students uses multiple sources of information to guide improvement and demonstrate its impact" (NSDC, 2001, p.18). In addition to using data for planning and monitoring, effective staff development uses data to demonstrate its impact. Schorr (2000) reports in *Education Week*, "We must be thinking more rigorously, realistically, and precisely about why we do what we do, what ends we hope to accomplish, and how we can document our successes achieving those ends."

Little (1997) states, in a paper for the Office of Research and Improvement, that professional development might be judged by the collective contributions that teachers and other professionals make to one another's work, to the school or district in which they work, and to a wider professional community. In this conception, professional development is linked to collective responsibilities for the improvement of teaching and learning. Elmore (2002b) suggests, "Those who engage in professional development should be willing to say explicitly what new knowledge and skill will be manifested in their professional practice, and what specific activities will lead to this learning" (p. 8).

Teachers contribute information to the evaluation of professional development. They identify the changes in knowledge and skills they experience. They collect data regarding the impact of new practices on student behavior and learning. They offer perceptions regarding the impact of changes on school culture and other organizational structures. They recognize that they have a responsibility to collect, contribute, and analyze such data. They know the value of professional development evaluations for the purpose of maintaining their improvement efforts.

Principals also recognize the value of multiple forms of data to determine the impact of professional development investments. They work with their staffs to develop a comprehensive plan for evaluating all improvement efforts and ensure that the plan is implemented successfully. While district level data are valuable for benchmarking, principals recognize the value of studying thoroughly their own data and involving all stakeholders in discussions concerning the implications. Principals use both formative and summative evaluation structures to assist in the collection of data and share information broadly so that process and outcomes are owned by all stakeholders.

Research-Based

"Staff development that improves the learning of all students prepares educators to apply research to decision making" (NSDC, 2001, p. 20). In 2001 the Federal Government passed the *No Child Left Behind Act* (NCLB) calling for more sophisticated use of scientific research to generate better results in schools. While the "jury" is still out on the requirement, more schools are questioning the scientific basis of proposed staff development programs. Unfortunately, there is limited staff development research that meets the government's "gold standard" definition. In the meantime, middle-level educators should use all available research and best practice to assist with planning. Establishing a reasonable basis for decisions is key to designing successful professional development.

This staff development standard calls on teachers to be critical consumers of research when selecting among options for professional learning. Teachers can interview educational researchers, conduct site visits, and determine whether necessary structural supports are in place or accessible to produce the results promised by a program. Teachers know how to interpret research and, when research is unavailable they can collaborate with others to set up small-scale pilots to test their assumptions.

Principals also have a responsibility for regularly reviewing and understanding research. They can also conduct staff development for their staff and community to enhance skills in reading and discussing research. The American Federation of Teachers (AFT) (2000) suggests that putting proven reforms in place is more than sound educational policy, it is a moral imperative and that we must resist the lure of unproven programs that offer no track record of success. Research-based decision making is essential in getting the expected results from professional development.

Design

"Staff development that improves the learning of all students uses learning strategies appropriate to the intended goal" (NSDC, 2001, p. 22). "A school's instructional capacity is enhanced when its programs for student and staff learning are coherent, focused on clear learning goals, and sustained over a period of time" (NSDC, 2001, p. 22). King and Newmann (2000) write "high capacity requires strong individual staff competence directed toward focused and sustained collective purposes and supported through reflective collaboration and empowerment of the full staff" (p. 32).

NEA Foundation for the Improvement of Education (NFIE) cites, "Schools where teachers focus on student work, interact with colleagues to plan how to improve their teaching, and continuously bring new skills and knowledge to bear on their practice are also schools that produce the best results for children" (p. 1). One of the most comprehensive studies of the impact of professional development reveals that professional development that focuses on academic subject matter (content), gives teachers opportunities for "hands-on" work (active learning), and is integrated into the daily life of the school (coherence), is more likely to produce enhanced knowledge and skills.

For many educators, staff development is synonymous with training, workshops, and courses. They are unaware that teacher and administrator professional learning can occur through means as diverse as collaborative lesson design, the examination of student work, curriculum development, the immersion in the work of experts, case studies, action research, study groups, and professional networks, to name a few such processes (Loucks-Horsley, Hewson, Love, & Stiles, 1998). Yet these strategies should not be used without careful consideration of the desired outcomes of the staff development. Loucks-Horsley, et al. (1998) state, "It is important to select . . . strategies wisely, (as) it helps to know that some strategies fulfill some purposes better than others. For example, some strategies (such as workshops) are more appropriate for building knowledge, whereas others (such as case discussions) help teachers think deeply about learning and teaching" (p. 45).

The influence of the design standard in teacher work occurs when teachers engage in collaborative interactions in learning teams and participate in a variety of activities chosen specifically for expected outcomes. Different learning strategies can include examining student work, curriculum writing, developing classroom assessments, and observing and critiquing lessons. Teachers recognize that substantive improvements in their practice require many practice sessions, follow-up sessions, support group participation, and feedback from coaches and colleagues, and it may take many years. As the result of a three-year instructional and professional development study, researchers Finley, Marble, and Ferguson (2000) conclude, "Dialogue, inquiry, and reflection can promote teacher learning and growth. Teachers are professionals who construct their own knowledge of teaching . . . and, as such, can and should be partners in generating knowledge of teaching. Finally, teachers can learn to focus their decision-making on students and learning. Professional development should support them in their efforts" (p. 39).

Principals also recognize the importance of connecting their goals to the appropriate learning strategy and offering opportunities to staff that align with desired outcomes. Principals recognize that substantive change requires a multiple year commitment and express that understanding through words and actions to the faculty. In an effort to support school wide consistent implementation of new practices, the principal also works with staff and program experts to create rubrics that add definition and clarification to the expectations associated with new programs.

Learning

"Staff development that improves the learning of all students applies knowledge about human learning and change" (NSDC, 2001, p. 24). Research on teacher learning shows that fruitful opportunities to learn new teaching methods share several core features. These features are ongoing (measured in years) collaboration of teachers for purposes of planning; the explicit goal of improving students' achievement of clear learning goals; attention to students' thinking, the curriculum, and pedagogy; and access to alternative ideas and methods and opportunities to observe these in action and to reflect on the reasons for their effectiveness (Garet, Porter, Desimone, Birman, & Yoon, 2001).

NSDC standards (2001) highlight three important dimensions of adult learning and change: learning styles; feelings regarding change; and life stages. When teachers experience professional development tuned into these issues, they have the opportunity to experience and practice what they are expected to use in the classroom. They develop deep understanding of new concepts and strategies. They choose among a variety of opportunities to further their development as a professional. They experience modifications and alternatives to professional development plans based on their expressed needs and concerns.

Principals recognize the value in understanding the individual and organizational change process. They encourage teacher leaders to develop expertise. They ensure that all school leaders have opportunities to develop deep understanding of the changes their colleagues will be expected to make, and they will be asked to coach. The principals discuss with teacher leaders how to vary opportunities for learning and leadership according to different career stages and interests of faculty. Principals regularly assess concerns and feelings of staff so that modifications and alterations to plans can address faculty issues and accelerate movement toward goals.

Collaboration

"Staff development that improves the learning of all students provides educators with the knowledge and skills to collaborate" (NSDC, 2001, p. 26). Darling-Hammond (1999) writes, "Teachers need to know about collaboration: how to structure interactions among students; how to collaborate with other teachers; and how to work with parents to shape supportive experiences at school and home" (p. 1). Effective collaboration is essential for student achievement. Newmann and Wehlage (1995) point out that when the school has a collaborative work culture that supports a professional learning community among all stakeholders, uses data to inform decisions about instructional practices, and also links to external standards and provides support for staff development, student achievement increases substantially.

Teacher's collaboration includes a commitment to work together on improving practices and the achievement of all students. In addition to learning new content and practices, teachers commit to learn strategies that facilitate productive work and working relationships. They agree to use strategies to monitor group effectiveness and improve decision-making opportunities. Learning team facilitators apply effective meeting strategies, including consensus building and effective management of conflict.

Trust is essential to successful collaboration. Principals instill trust when their actions and words demonstrate their trust and respect for their staff. They listen attentively and encourage individuals to share different points of view without fear of retribution. Such collaboration requires a collective commitment to put the interests and needs of the students before the staff. Principals recognize that all staff members need opportunities to develop skills associated with effective group relations. They structure the opportunities and model the use of strategies in faculty and team meetings. Pogo said, "None of us is as smart as all of us." A commitment to collaboration and all the benefits of working together produces a school where improvement efforts are accelerated.

Cohen and Hill (1998) report that research shows that student achievement can be improved when professional development is a collaborative activity, involves capacity building (not just skill development), and relates to the everyday work of the teachers' subject area and activities. The Consortium for Policy Research in Education (1996) concludes, "Collegiality and collaboration among teachers can raise morale, increase work effort, and promote the sharing of ideas and practices" (p. 7).

Content Standards

Content standards address the categories of knowledge, skills, and dispositions of effective teaching. Staff makes these a priority to ensure student learning. Countless lists, adopted by states and/or districts, address what is included in the NSDC Content standards as well as other areas.

Equity

"Staff development that improves the learning of all students prepares educators to understand and appreciate all students, create safe, orderly and supportive learning environments, and hold high expectations for their academic achievement" (NSDC, 2001, p. 30). Noguera (1999) reports that although there are only a small number of schools where no achievement gap exists and where there are students who achieve despite the challenges they face, these islands of success provide educators opportunities to examine what could happen if there was a high quality equitable school for every child.

Such schools are characterized by teachers who adjust classroom instruction and support according to student backgrounds, culture, and socioeconomic status. These teachers recognize that their own backgrounds and understandings are powerful influencers on their beliefs and their practice. It is essential that they develop a deeper understanding of their students and their perspectives. They have the ability to communicate high expectations for all students. Students respond to such expectations because of the powerful relationships that are built with the teachers. Students feel emotionally and physically safe at school, and these feelings translate into greater success.

Principals hold high expectations for themselves, their teachers, and their students. They accept no excuses and work with staff to build systems to support outstanding levels of achievement. Permanent tracking is not an option. They attend to school schedules, curriculum, and use of staff time. They make professional development, focused on high expectations, a priority. While teachers take responsibility for assuring emotionally and physically safe classrooms, principals take responsibility for the school. They encourage school wide programs and themes that support respect, caring, diversity, and safety.

Former Memphis Superintendent House (2000) reports in *Education Week*, while discussing the Memphis reform effort, "We had to create a map that would guide whole systems of people to make the quantum leap necessary to turn all schools into student-centered, results-based learning environments where high achievement is the norm, regardless of race, ethnicity, or socioeconomic status." Reeves (2000) writes, "The most important resource any educational system has to allocate is the expertise of its teaching professionals. The assignment of teachers to different schools and courses, decidedly more sensitive and less convenient than the reallocation of financial resources, has the greatest opportunity for a profound impact on student equity" (p. 36).

Quality Teaching

"Staff development that improves the learning of all students deepens educators' content knowledge, provides them with research-based instructional strategies to assist students in meeting rigorous academic standards, and prepares them to use various types of classroom assessments appropriately" (NSDC, 2001, p. 32). Massell (1998) observes, "Standards-based reform requires teachers to know more about their subject, to teach in a more dynamic style, to respond to the knowledge and dispositions that their students bring into the classroom, to engage in continuous learning, and to assume new professional roles..." (p. 5).

Darling-Hammond (1997) concludes, "No other intervention can make the difference that a knowledgeable, skillful teacher can make in the learning process. At the same time, nothing can fully compensate for weak teaching that, despite good intentions, can result from a teacher's lack of opportunity to acquire the knowledge and skill needed to help students master the curriculum" (p. 8). There is an abundance of evidence that nothing has a greater impact on the success of students than the teacher's knowledge base (Haycock, 1998). Quality teaching is characterized by educators who recognize the importance of deep understanding of content knowledge and appropriate uses of research-based instructional strategies. Some instructional strategies are more effective with specific disciplines. This is the core of professional learning.

The principal designs and supports professional development that assists teachers in developing competency in curriculum, instruction, and assessment. For example, if the teacher on an interdisciplinary team teaches both language arts and social studies, then the teacher requires content expertise in both areas. While much of this learning can occur in daily team meetings, teachers with serious gaps in content preparation require more intensive training.

Learning to develop classroom-based assessments and performance tasks for students is powerful professional learning. Fullan describes successful schools as places where teams of teachers meet regularly to focus on student work through assessment and change their instructional practice accordingly to get better results (as cited in Schmoker, 2002). The National Alliance of Business (2001), along with the National Association of Manufacturers, and The Business Roundtable, state emphatically that improving student achievement will fail without high-quality teachers. These groups, collectively, understand that research has shown that teachers can make the critical difference in whether or not a student succeeds. Also, if students are to meet ambitious expectations, they must have superbly prepared teachers equal to the task. The quality of teaching is the most important change that must occur in schools.

Family Involvement

"Staff development that improves the learning of all students provides educators with knowledge and skills to involve families and other stakeholders appropriately" (NSDC, 2001, p. 34). Many school improvement plans identify increasing family involvement as a priority. Schools involve parents in a variety of ways. This standard focuses on providing teachers and principals with the skills to help families support student learning.

Teachers must learn to develop partnerships with families and other community stakeholders. In middle schools these partnerships organize community service programs led by students. They work with local businesses to develop partnerships that provide students opportunities to enhance skills and talents. They share with students and their families information about community activities that link to student interests and talents. Teachers also learn strategies to increase parental and caregiver involvement in support of at-home follow-up work. The school can offer parent education workshops with information about how to support homework, read progress notices, and how to interact with young adolescents. Where appropriate, teachers use technology to increase communication with parents.

Principals recognize the responsibility they have to this standard as well. Principals provide assistance to teachers in developing partnerships and after-school programming to support student learning. They support family education sessions. Sometimes teachers serve as faculty for workshops, and at other times the principal serves. Ultimately the principal assumes responsibility for school communication with families. NFIE (2000) reports, "When parents and community members learn along with teachers, they become advocates for professional development" (p. 3).

CONNECTING STAFF DEVELOPMENT AND STUDENT RESULTS

Educators frequently debate the connection between staff development and student results. Plausible arguments, presented as "theories of change," explain the link between high-quality staff development and student results. Such theories of change carefully describe the connection between intended goals for staff and students, the content and skills teachers use to address the goals, the support teachers receive in adopting new practices, and the measures that will assess teacher change in practice and student results. When careful design and data collection go hand in hand the connection is accepted. A growing number of studies, reports, and authorities are contributing to a substantive case regarding the link between professional development and student learning.

The Council for School Performance (1999) studied the connection between Georgia's investment in staff development and student achievement. The Council selected a sample of higher- and lower-achieving students across the full range of socioeconomic status and gathered data on professional development in the schools. They then tested the extent to which the characteristics of professional development varied between the two groups of schools. The major difference was that in lower-achieving schools, professional development was considered an activity with little connection to classroom results while in the higher-achieving schools, there was more collaboration on decisions about professional development, a greater focus on students and classroom teaching, more use of effective training processes, more support from school leadership, and a greater excitement about working together to find ways to increase student learning.

Weglinsky (2000) for Education Testing Services (ETS) reports that professional development activities or hands-on learning and higher-order thinking skills are associated with improved student performance. Weglinsky's study also finds that teachers who receive rich and sustained professional development geared toward higher-order thinking skills and concrete activities, such as laboratories, are more likely to engage in desired classroom practices. Schmoker (2002) writes, "There is substantial evidence that results are virtually inevitable when teachers, working in teams:

- Focus substantially—though not exclusively—on assessed standards.
- Review simple, readily available achievement data to set a limited number of measurable achievement goals in the lowest-scoring subjects or courses and target specific standards where achievement is low within that course or subject area.
- Work regularly and collectively to design, adapt, and assess instructional strategies *targeted directly at specific standards* of low student performance revealed by the assessment data (e.g., "measurement" in math; "voice" in writing; "sight reading" in music) (p. 11).

Garet et al. (2001) report, "Research on teacher learning shows that fruitful opportunities to learn new teaching methods share several core features: (a) ongoing (measured in years) collaboration of teachers for purposes of planning with (b) the explicit goal of improving students' achievement of clear learning goals, (c) anchored by attention to students' thinking, the curriculum, and pedagogy, with (d) access to alternative ideas and methods and opportunities to observe these in action and to reflect on the reasons for their effectiveness" (p. 917).

The Consortium for Policy Research (1998) finds that professional development that is grounded in the curriculum that students study, connected to several elements of instruction (for example, curriculum and assessment), and is extended in time influences teachers to change the ways they teach. Then their students perform better on curriculum-based assessments (p. 1).

Again, a number of studies and authorities attest to the important contribution staff development makes to improved educator practice and student learning. In the end, middle level educators can feel confident that professional development that focuses on academic subject matter (content), gives teachers opportunities for "hands-on" work (active learning), and that is integrated into the daily life of the school (coherence), is more likely to produce enhanced knowledge and skills (Garet et al., 2001).

AWARD WINNING SCHOOL DISTRICTS AND SCHOOLS: MAKING CONNECTIONS

The Consortium for Policy and Research in Education identifies five dimensions to organization capacity:

- Leadership that helps articulate and sustain a collective vision of excellence;
- Collective commitment to student learning and cultural norms that demand continual improvement;
- Access to knowledge (ensuring that staff members have access to ideas, strategies, and models that will improve their practice);
- Organizational structures that promote improvement (for example, a schedule that provides common planning time for collaborative efforts); and
- Resources (time, money, and people) that support improvement (O'Day, Goertz, & Floden, 1995).

Following on this theme, the United States Department of Education created the National Awards Program for Model Professional Development to recognize school systems and schools able to demonstrate a link between professional development efforts and student results. Over the course of six years, countless schools and districts have applied. An elite group was selected for national recognition. The winners represented urban, rural, and suburban districts, as well as primary, intermediate, middle, and high schools. Applicants documented how their district or school professional development plan complied with the following USDOE Principles of Professional Development (1999):

- Focuses on teachers as central to student learning, yet includes all other members of the school community;
- Focuses on individual, collegial, and organizational improvement;
- Respects and nurtures the intellectual and leadership capacity of teachers, principals, and others in the school community;
- Reflects best available research and practice in teaching, learning, and leadership;

- Enables teachers to develop further expertise in subject content, teaching strategies, uses of technologies, and other essential elements in teaching to high standards;
- promotes continuous inquiry and improvement embedded in the daily life of schools;
- Is planned collaboratively by those who will participate in and facilitate that development;
- Requires substantial time and other resources;
- Is driven by a coherent long-term plans;
- Is evaluated ultimately on the basis of its impact on teacher effectiveness and student learning; and this assessment guides subsequent professional development efforts (p. 2).

Eight award-winning programs were studied in 1997 to determine the characteristics of their success. All but one school included middle-level students. Conclusions drawn from the study included the following:

- Use clear, agreed upon student achievement goals to focus and shape teacher learning (Learning Community, Leadership);
- Provide an expanded array of professional development opportunities (Design, Learning, Equity, Teaching Quality, Family Involvement);
- Embed ongoing, informal learning into the school culture (Collaboration, Data Driven, Learning Community);
- Build a highly collaborative school environment where working together to solve problems and to learn from each other become cultural norms (Collaboration, Leadership, Research Based, Learning Community);
- Find and use time to allow teacher learning to happen (Resources); and
- Keep checking a broad range of student performance data. (Data Driven, Evaluation).

Each of the findings correlates to one or more staff development standard (WestEd, 2000).

While many studies report characteristics of successful schools, this study focused specifically on the professional development that contributed to the success. Resnick, while conducting research based on the Pittsburgh Public Schools, found that well-informed practice can overcome the achievement gap between white students and minorities. In schools with successful comprehensive reforms that aligned curriculum, instruction, assessments, and professional development focused on high-quality content, Black students outperformed white students who were in schools with poorly implemented reforms (cited in Lewis, 2001). Countless studies continue to document the essential role professional development plays in school and system reform.

STRATEGIES FOR ADVANCING QUALITY STAFF DEVELOPMENT STATES

In 2000 the Education Commission of the States issued its report on teaching quality. The Commission (2000) concluded, "It is the responsibility of state and district policymakers and educators to take the lead in making sure all teachers have the skills, knowledge, and support they need to succeed" (p. 28). Changing school systems is a tremendous challenge as well as an incredible responsibility. No one is in a better position to do this important work than school board members. State and local decision makers may consider the following strategies for advancing quality professional development in all middle schools. States can build the framework for improved professional development that supports advanced educator learning and student results by putting in place the following:

- Require the development of a statewide professional development system that aligns state, district, school, and team goals. Create a continuous improvement cycle that evaluates district, school, and team improvement plans according to student learning increases.

- Adopt standards for staff development that are then used as the basis for planning and evaluation of staff development efforts. Consider adopting NSDC's Standards for Staff Development. Encourage schools to use collaborative models and other powerful designs to meet their specific needs.

- Fund professional development adequately. Consider strategies employed by various states. Illinois appropriates $4 million of state funds for teacher professional development. Kentucky provides $23 per child, Florida spends $4 per child, and Massachusetts allocates, through a formula-driven system, $10 million for local districts. Missouri, in response to a court order to redesign its finance system, spends 2 percent of all K–12 funding on staff development (National Conference of State Legislatures, 2002).

- Allocate funding to programs that demonstrate results for students. As with everything else, not all staff development is of the same quality. Most states currently treat all staff development programs as equal, without an attempt to measure their productivity. States should insist that schools use research-validated staff development practices and that they require outside providers to present evidence that their programs work. Where appropriate, fund pilot projects to measure the effectiveness of new programs.

- Provide adequate time for all educators to learn during the school day. Examine the structure of the school year and school day. Search for options that ensure teachers have daily time for professional learning and time in the summer for curriculum development and more intensive study. These changes, which require extensive discussions among leaders, are likely to require significant modifications of collective bargaining agreements.

- Recognize that teachers need support and recognition throughout their careers. Differentiate expectations and support services for new teachers and experienced teachers. Develop comprehensive induction programs that include quality mentoring. Provide leadership opportunities for outstanding teachers, as well as other incentives for remaining in the classroom.

- Examine the current recertification structures for teachers and administrators. Many states require participation in professional development for certification. Most states perpetuate outdated ideas about what constitutes staff development by paying for seat time in courses or workshops (e.g., continuing education units). Yet research shows that collaborative school wide forms of staff development have more power to change the culture of a school and update teachers on better ways to help students learn (NCSL, 2002).

- Create rewards to recognize the implementation of effective staff development by school systems. States can utilize the models supplied by the Malcolm Baldridge Award and by the winners of the U.S. Department of Education's National Award for Model Professional Development. Recognized for their superlative professional development that raised achievement and/or enhanced productivity, these winners serve as models for others (NCSL, 2002).

- Realign the support structures in the statewide staff development system. Redefine the role of state departments, regional service centers, and other technical assistance providers. Acknowledge the new vision of professional development. Where resources are scarce, direct them toward high-poverty populations.

SCHOOL BOARDS OF EDUCATION

School board trustees have a different set of available strategies to influence the quality of professional development in schools.

- *Make high-quality professional learning a district priority.*   There is a wealth of research demonstrating the connection between student success and teaching quality. Within the context of district goal setting, school board members can include a statement regarding the importance of a well-qualified and well-trained staff.

- *Adopt staff development standards.*   Adopting staff development standards show commitment to ensuring quality professional development. Using the standards as the basis for decision making on issues that have staff development implications demonstrates an understanding of their value.

- *Fund professional development adequately.*   In addition to federal and state responsibilities for funding, school boards are also responsible for providing the money and time necessary for effective professional development. In addition to the NSDC standard on resources, the Council adopted a resolution that calls for school systems to dedicate at least 10 percent of their budgets to staff development and devote at least 25 percent of an educator's work time to learning and collaboration with colleagues (NSDC, 1999).

- *Support employee agreements that advance results-driven professional learning.*   Employee contracts can support work schedules that facilitate ongoing collaboration and daily learning time for teachers. They can establish recognition systems that reward school and district collaborative efforts that accomplish system goals for students. They can also create compensation systems that provide salary increments for demonstration of knowledge and skills as opposed to additional coursework and/or degrees.

- *Adopt a professional development district policy.*   School district staff development policies are grounded in research, best practice, stakeholder viewpoints, and goals for student success. A comprehensive district policy addresses purpose, mission, goals, standards, resources, requirements, positions, travel, stakeholder involvement, and recognition systems. It may include statements of purpose, mission, goals, and standards,

- *Function as a learning community.*   Leaders have responsibilities to teach by example. When a school board is serious about its commitment to continuous improvement you can see the trustees spending considerable time on developing deeper understanding of important issues, convening community conversations for purpose of study and dialogue, attending professional association meetings, reading professional literature, and listening to the voices of students, employees, and the community.

School board members are entrusted by their communities to provide a quality education for all students. Few decisions school boards make are more important than those that improve educator and student performance. As Dee Hock, the founder of Visa, once said, "It is no failure to fall short of realizing all that we might dream. The failure is to fall short of dreaming all that we might realize." When implemented according to standards, research, and best practice, professional development offers the solution to many middle-grades education issues. Teachers and principals find that professional development is the critical ingredient for transforming middle-level education and for giving it staying power (Council for Chief State Officers, 1998).

REFERENCES

American Federation of Teachers. (2000). Doing what works: Improving big city school districts. *Educational Issues Policy Brief*, No. 12., pp. 11–12.

Barth, R. (2001). Teacher leader. *Phi Delta Kappan, 82*(6), 443–449.

Brandt, R. (2003). Is this school a learning organization? *Journal of Staff Development, 24*(1), 10–16.

Cohen, D., & Hill, H.(1998). *State policy and classroom performance: Mathematics reform in California.* Policy Brief, Consortium for Policy Research in Education.

Consortium for Policy Research in Education. (1996). *Public policy and school reform: A research summary.* Report #36, p. 7.

Council for School Performance. (1999). *Staff development and student achievement: Making the connection in Georgia schools.* Atlanta,GA: School of Policy Studies, Georgia State University. Retrieved September 5, 2003, from http:// arcweb.gsu.edu/csp/csp_staffdev.htm

Council of Chief State School Officers. (1998). *State policies to support middle school reform: A guide for policymakers.* Washington, DC: CCSSO.

Covey, S. (1990). *The seven habits of highly effective people.* New York: Simon & Schuster.

Cross, C.T., & Rice, R.C. (2000). The role of the principal as instructional leader in a standards-driven system. NASSP *Bulletin, 84*(620), 62.

Darling-Hammond, L. (1997). Executive Director, prepared for the National Commission on Teaching and America's Future; *Doing what matters most: Investing in quality teaching*, p. 8.

Darling-Hammond, L. (1997). *Edutopica*, CA: The George Lucas Foundation.

DuFour, R. (1999). Help wanted: Principals who can lead professional learning Communities. *NASSP Bulletin, 83*(604), 12–17.

Education Commission of the States. (2000). In pursuit of quality teaching: Five key strategies for policymakers. Denver, CO: ECS, p. 17.

Elmore, R. (2002a) Building capacity to enhance learning. *Principal Leadership, 2*(5), 39–43.

Elmore, R. (2000b). *Bridging the gap between standards and achievement: The imperative for professional development in education.* Washington, DC: The Albert Shanker Institute, p. 8.

Finley, S., Marble, S., & Ferguson, C. (2000, October 24). Professional development and teachers' construction of coherent instructional practices: A synthesis of experiences in five sites.

Fullan, M. (2000). The three stories of educational reform. *Phi Delta Kappan, 81*(8), 584.

Garet, M., Porter, A., Desimone, L., Birman, B., Yoon, K. (2001). What makes Professional development effective? Results from a national sample of teachers. *American Educational Research Journal, 38*(4), 915–945.

Haycock, K. (1998). Good teaching matters...a lot: How well-qualified teachers can close the gap. *Thinking K–16, 3*(2), 3–14.

Hord, S. (2003). *Professional learning communities: Perspectives from the field.* New York: Teachers College Press.

House, G. (2000, April 5). Re-creating a school system: Lessons learned in Memphis about whole-school reform. *Education Week, 19*(30).

King, M.B., & Newmann, F.M. (2000). Will teacher learning advance school goals? *Phi Delta Kappan, 82*(8), 567.

Lewis, A.C. (2001). A performance test for districts and states. *Phi Delta Kappan, 82*(8), 567.

Little, J.W. (1997, March). *Excellence in professional development and professional community.* Working Paper Bench for Schools. Office of Educational Research and improvement.

Loucks-Horsley, S., Hewson, P.W., Love, N., & Sstiles, K.E. (1998). *Professional development for teachers of science and mathematics.* Thousand Oaks: CA: Corwin Press, Inc.

Louis, K. (2002). Teachers' professional development is vital for middle schools: What do we know and where should we go? Plenary Address, *National Educational Research Policy and Priorities Board's Conference on Curriculum, Instruction, and Assessment in the Middle Grades: Linking Research and Practice.* Washington, DC, p. 23.

Massell, D. (1998). *Some strategies for building capacity in education: Progress and continuing challenges.* Consortium for Policy Research in Education (CPRE) Research Report, p. 5.

McRobbie, J. (2000). *Career-long teacher development: Policies that make sense.* Based on a Presentation by Linda Darling-Hammonds to the WestEd Board of Directors in March 2000, San Francisco: CA: WestEd.

Mizell, H. (2001). How do we get from here to there? *Journal of Staff Development, 22*(3), 18–20.

National Alliance of Business. (2001). *Investing in teaching: A common agenda.* A report by the Business Roundtable, National Alliance of Business, and National Association of Manufacturers. Retrieved September 5, 2003, from http://www. nab.com

National Staff Development Council. (1999). Council resolution on funding. Oxford, OH: NSDC.

National Staff Development Council. (2001). *National Staff Development Council's standards for staff development.* Oxford, OH: NSDC.

NEA Foundation for the Improvement of Education (NFIF). 2000, Fall). *Engaging public support for teachers' professional development,* No. 3.

Newmann, F., & Wehlage, G. (1995). *Successful school restructuring.* Madison, WI: Center on Organization and Restructuring of Schools.

Noguera, P. (1999, April 10). Confronting the challenge of diversity in education. *In Motion Magazine.* Retrieved September 5, 2003, from http://www.inmotionmagazine.com

O'Day, J., Goertz, M.E., & Floden, R.E. (1995, December). *Building capacity for educational reform.* CPRE Policy Briefs.

Reeves, D.B. (2000). Standards are not enough: Essential transformations for For school success. *NASSP Bulletin, 84*(520), 16.

Renyi, J. (1996). *Teachers take charge of their learning: Transforming professional development for student success.* Washington, DC: NEA Foundation for the Improvement of Education.

Riley, R.W. (1999, June 24). *The challenge for America: A high quality teacher in every classroom.* Speech in South Carolina, Secretary of U.S. Department of Education.

Schorr, L. (2000, July 12). Commentary. *Education Week, 19*(42).

Schmoker, M. (2002). Up and away. *Journal of Staff Development, 24*(2), 232–238.

Sparks, D. (1997, September 21–23). A new vision for staff development. *Principal.*

Sparks, D., & Hirsh, S. (1999). Sit and get won't cut it. *Virginia Journal of Education, 92*(5).

U.S. Education Department. (1995). *Building bridges: The mission and principles of professional development.* Washington, DC: USDOE.

Weglinsky, H. (2000). *How teaching matters: Bringing the classroom back into discussions of teacher quality.* Princeton, NJ: Milken Family Foundation and Educational Testing Service.

WestEd. (2000). *Teachers who learn; Kids who achieve: A look at schools with model professional development.* San Francisco, CA: WestEd.

CHAPTER 12

WHAT OF THE FUTURE?

Deborah Kasak

INTRODUCTION

The late songwriter and performer Steve Goodman delighted fans with a catchy ditty called "The 20th century is almost over, it's almost over, and it's almost over, all over this world." In exuberant voice, he cleverly engaged audiences in not only speculation of the future about also reflection on the accomplishments in the 20th century.

Likewise, middle grades educators might be singing a similar tune, "A century of middle grades education is almost over, it's almost over, and it's almost over, all over this world." For it was around the turn of the 19th century that elementary education and secondary education were undergoing reform, and suggestions for specialized attention on young adolescents and schooling started to appear in the literature. G. Stanley Hall in the early 1900s "influenced Americans into believing that education should be based on psychology and that adolescence should be given scientific study" (cited in Eichhorn, 1966, 1987, p. 2). Its journey toward legitimacy has been referred to "the longest-running, most extensive educational reform movement in the United States (Lounsbury, 1991).

A century of middle grades education is almost over, so what does the future hold? The movement has just experienced its best decade in history. Three broad factors contributed to the acceleration and unprecedented

Reforming Middle Level Education: Considerations for Policymakers, pages 231–250
Copyright © 2004 by Information Age Publishing
All rights of reproduction in any form reserved.
231

attention on middle grades. First, several high profile foundations paid attention to the middle grades. The release of the Carnegie Corporation's report, *Turning Points: Preparing American Youth for the 21st Century* in 1989, and the follow-up publication, *Turning Points 2000: Educating Adolescents in the 21st Century* were the bookends for the last decade. These documents affirmed the need to significantly turn around the quality and function of middle grades education so millions of young Americans would reap the benefits of a productive future. Four major foundations stepped forward and dedicated significant grant making programs:

> While grounded in part in the vision put forth by middle school proponents, these funders (Lilly Endowment, Edna McConnell Clark, W. K. Kellogg and Carnegie) were dedicated to transforming the learning experiences of early adolescents regardless of what type of configuration their schools had. This commitment to fundamental reform was rooted in a vision of middle level education that married developmental responsiveness to academic excellence and reflected also a deep and abiding concern for equity. (Kronley & Handley, 2003, p. 17)

Each foundation had a slightly different twist to its purpose and mission of middle grades reform. One focused on the district central office and schools in multiple urban sites within one state, another funder concentrated on structural changes in its state-wide overall improvement plan which included urban, suburban and rural settings, yet another gave its attention to several major systemic changes at the district level in urban areas across the country, and the other pursued a state policy initiative across a cluster of states. In addition to the program benefits of these particular initiatives, the research-base accompanying the different grant initiatives filled a critical void and crucial need for documentation.

Simultaneously throughout the last decade, the National Middle School Association increased its presence and visibility as it grew in membership, diversified services and raised strategic initiatives to address more aspects of young adolescent education. Its publications alone had provided the primary source of technical information for middle grades education over the past several decades, and those materials became more extensive. In 1995, the revised edition of *This We Believe* set sale records. The Association's creation of the middle level guidelines for teacher preparation programs for the National Council for Accreditation of Teacher Education (NCATE) proved extremely influential in addressing the long acknowledged problem of inadequately prepared teachers for the middle level.

Finally in 1997, the creation of the National Forum to Accelerate Middle-Grades Reform, an affiliation of the country's top associations, foundations, researchers and practitioners concerned with the improvement of middle grades education, added value and credibility with its vision for middle grades. Members from various constituencies put aside organizational priorities in order to "speak with one voice" for the continuous improvement of schools with middle grades featuring a balance of academic excellence within developmentally responsive schools for the benefit of each and every student.

The last decade's activities heightened awareness about young adolescent learning and schooling; witnessed active, on-the-ground reform support from major foundations; and fostered a more favorable increased policy environment. The backdrop for those accomplishments was the foundation set by the work in preceding decades on behalf of a level of education historically overlooked by most educators and policymakers.

MAJOR TRENDS THROUGH THE DECADES

A quick snapshot of past trends and projections beyond the last decade will aid to enlighten the future. Forty years into the evolution of the junior high school in the 1940s, Gruhn and Douglass made six broad recommendations, including thirty-one suggestions, as they described what it would take to make the junior high school an educational institution capable of meeting the needs of youth in a changing society (Gruhn & Douglass, 1947, p. 455).

Foremost, they said the movement needed its philosophy, aims and functions better articulated so there was agreement among faculty concerning the basis of what they were to do and why; a specific curriculum for the middle grades, not one brought down from the high school, which was well rounded with fundamental skills yet included a breakdown of the artificial gaps across various subject areas; teaching materials that used good strategies for this age group; and as its 31st suggestion, "a program of professional education which prepared teachers for work at the junior high level since there was still a tendency to prepare teachers for either the elementary school or the secondary school, but with no particular attention to the demands of a junior high school program" (Gruhn & Douglass, 1947, p. 459).

Eichhorn (1966,1987) set forth his "functional model" about the "middle school" to counter the "failures of the junior high school." The recommendations in *The Middle School* were based upon "available knowledge derived from the related academic disciplines of psychology and sociology and the foundations of education and educational administration" (Eichhorn, 1966, 1987, pp. 104–105). It called for three distinct levels of schooling; state reimbursement formulas altered to account for the middle school needs; teacher certification standards; and district allocations done on what needs to happen at the middle level.

George and Malinka (1977) in *The Middle School: A Look Ahead* noted that middle school advocates have had to "fight for every inch of ground" in their attempts to implement an effective middle school program. They hypothesized that it would continue to be particularly true as the pressures of the late 70s put the movement to the test because of the hard financial times, accountability, and back-to-basics. Their major priority for the future survival was to establish and maintain the credibility for the middle school through communications, demonstration, and evaluation of effectiveness.

In a review of the middle school movement from 1964–1984, *Perspectives: Middle School Education* (Lounsbury, 1984) closed with an agenda for the next decade that would require "more than tinkering and more than new seat covers for the buggy." The ambitious collective agenda included:

- Seek continued growth of NMSA.
- Establish middle level programs in all schools that contain middle level grades.
- Extend efforts to educate the general public regarding the nature of early adolescents.
- Institute efforts to communicate beyond existing practitioners.
- Achieve recognition of both the humane and the academic responsibilities of middle schools.
- Break the hammerlock of departmentalization as the sole basis for organizing the curriculum.
- Secure leadership for the middle school in state departments of education.
- Achieve distinctive middle grades teacher certification and teacher education in every state.
- Promote the involvement of parents in the development of improved middle level programs.
- Institute one or more specific improvements in each and every middle school. (pp. 172–175)

The period from 1964–1984 was described as the "years of readiness—a necessary period for accumulation of an experiential background that has to precede major action" (Lounsbury, 1984, p. 171). One of the biggest challenges to accomplishing the collective actions set forth was the need to keep the emotion and commitment alive in order to stay on the cutting edge to institute reforms.

Epstein and Mac Iver (1990) conducted a national survey of practices and trends and used survey data from 1753 schools to identify past, present and future use of twenty-two recommended practices for middle grades schools. They identified underlying issues including the sobering fact that most schools with grade seven had not yet developed educational programs based on recommended practices for middle grades. In fact, principals in junior high schools reported using the fewest number of desirable practices. The trends projected in 1984 had yet to become universal by the late eighties.

In their study, Epstein and Mac Iver (1990) characterized possible "signature" practices and identified them as "trends." Principals predicted which trends were most likely to increase 10% or more in frequency within the next three years. Reported trends included higher use of interdisciplinary teams of teachers, common planning time, flexible scheduling, students assigned to the same homeroom or advisory teacher for all years in the middle grades, cooperative learning, exploratory and mini-courses, parent involvement in workshops on early adolescence, and parents as volunteers in the middle grades. Principals in separate middle grades buildings predicted they would be more likely to adopt these trends than principals in K–8 buildings.

Turning Points: Preparing American Youth for the 21st Century (1989) bolted onto the scene and captured national attention citing, "The volatile mismatch exists between the organization and curriculum of middle grades schools, and the intellectual, emotional, and interpersonal needs of young adolescents" (p. 32). Decades after the initial calls for change had been proposed; a glaring gap between knowledge and practice persisted, particularly for students of greatest need. The report declared, "*We do not lack the knowledge* to transform the education of young adolescents. What we need is the leadership and the will*" (Carnegie Corporation, 1989, p. 85). The report's eight recommendations set a comprehensive course of transformation and called for significant changes in governance and school structures which promote optimal learning environments; teacher preparation; adoption of effective practices including those of health; effective curriculum and instruction; and parental and community involvement.

As the age of Turning Points moved into the early 1990s, lively debate and inquiry occurred in many states about middle grades education, the progress of the reform process, and the issues and trends still confronting the transformation of middle grades schools. Publications of proceedings such as *Reform in Middle Grade Education: Current Status, Future Directions* (CCSSO, 1992) or *Middle Grades Education in an Era of Reform: Proceedings of a Seminar Series* (AED, 1993) typified the number of various organizations, agencies and groups discussing the issues confronting middle grades education and its future. Policy changes did occur in some states with common expectations of practice being set and upgrades in middle grades teacher preparation requirements developed.

At NMSA's William M. Alexander Memorial Lecture (1998), Paul George's speech, *A Middle School—If You Can Keep It,* took another look at the trends and progress of middle grades education. Twenty-five years earlier he had delivered a speech by the same title where he posed the central challenges of that time:

- Develop a clear definition of middle school;
- Forestall the potential conflicts with advocates for the junior high school and critics from the senior high school;
- Implement a program that matched the 60s vision out of which middle school education grew;
- Abolish what was commonly called the star system;
- Improve the poor articulation and lack of continuous progress between middle, elementary and high schools;
- Correct the absence of virtually any university middle school teacher education programs or state certification for that level.

In the new speech, George updated the challenges and trends of concern to the future of the middle grades movement.

- Ensure broad and permanent implementation of the middle level components;
- Help high schools adopt effective practices such as personalization through teams, advisement, and integration;
- Redouble efforts toward the establishment of more middle school teacher education programs;
- Find a way to make advisor/advisee relations and programs work well;
- Know the middle grades program is not about boundaries and grade configurations but about the effects that are possible because of long-term relationships;
- Commit to social equity in middle schools, to teach all the children well and advocate for it;
- Differentiate instruction on a regular and widespread basis;
- Fight to establish a curriculum that is truly based on the living concerns of youth and be more than narrowly focused on test scores.

In 1999, the Office of Education Research and Improvement (OERI) for the U.S. Department of Education, held a conference of distinguished researchers and experts because it recognized the need to support more research and improved strategies. At the close of the meeting, the participants concluded:

Despite the research, too few schools serving young adolescents are implementing these practices. Research at the middle level needs to focus on how to best help practitioners develop the capacity and will to implement practices that are known to produce positive outcomes for students. Suggestions for this research include: emphasize middle level reform rather than middle school orthodoxy; embed a shared and common vision for high-performing middle grades schools; reduce the size of schools that serve young adolescents, instill necessary leadership; and create unified, broader approach to middle level reform. (National Association of Secondary Principals, 1999, p. 160).

One of the other emerging trends for the 1990s was the realization that collective action across organizational boundaries was proving more effective than individual efforts for affecting change. Berliner (1997) suggests that alliances in education became popular and were motivated by "the decades-long reckoning with the complexity of broad-scale school reform and the prevailing wisdom was that no single organization can transform schools into successful learning communities" (p. 1). This is precisely the reason for the creation of the National Forum to Accelerate Middle-Grades Reform. Its strategy is to leverage resources, raise issues, address public policy, articulate needs and lend credibility through the unified voice of key organizations and leaders.

Turning Points 2000: Educating Adolescents in the 21st Century provided in-depth analysis and description of the experiences and research resulting over the previous decade in order to envision what can happen in middle grades education in the 21st century. The challenges and opportunities included discussions on deep elements of teaching and learning; relationship, collaboration and decision-making; community connections; and excellence and equity (Jackson & Davis, 2000).

Kronley and Handley (2003) reported on their investigation of the role of the major foundations in affecting middle grades improvement. They highlight the next steps as maintaining the middle grades vision: creating challenging curricula; strengthening teacher quality; fostering change; and sustaining leadership and conclude by saying the "middle grades reform movement has reached a crossroads in its continuing journey where sustaining the accomplishments and promoting achievement for early adolescents requires a new generation of targeted investments" (Kronley & Handley, 2003, p. 83).

The themes of trends through the decades have a familiar and even repetitious quality. Decade after decade there is a push for public recognition of the movement and its age-level needs; wider and effective implementation of proven practices across all types of schools responsible for educating young adolescents well; continued priority for appropriately prepared teachers; adequate distribution of resources; tailored, engaging curriculum and instructional practices; and attention to the value of advocacy and personalization.

The effectiveness of the overall movement through the last century might rate a 4 or 5 on a 10-point scale. It has been the longest-running grassroots movement. Yet, after the most admirable efforts to make successful schools for young adolescents the norm, not the exception, an uphill battle looms ahead. Widespread implementation of high quality middle grades practices has not been fully realized.

Speaking with One Voice states that sustainable middle-level school reform is achievable; however it "cannot be achieved on the run, distractedly, shallowly, or piecemeal." There are important strategies to employ to attain overall improvement, but "the loss of intensity and focus has been the single greatest barrier to comprehensive and sustained middle-grades reform" (Lipsitz et al., 1997, p. 538).

Dickinson and Butler in *Reinventing the Middle School* (2001) assert that:

> In school after school the word 'middle school concept' has become a phrase mindlessly uttered, but with no understanding of the real meaning of the phrase. What misleads many middle level educators, what the movement has not made a forceful argument over, is that the original concept is a totally integrated ecology of schooling. It is an organizational, curricular, instructional and relational environment that cannot be parsed or broken (Felner, Jackson, Kasak, Mulhall, Brand & Flowers, 1997). Any attempt to do so, as in many well-intentioned schools, leads to the condition of arrested development. (Dickinson & Butler, 2001, p. 8)

If the challenge of making changes happen and be sustained in schools is not demanding and stressful enough, this current decade adds new pressures. The immediate future has all the markings of a very tough time for the further evolvement of middle grades education. The federal legislation, No Child Left Behind Act of 2001 (NCLB), presents both opportunities and challenges for middle grades education. It is a chance to fundamentally address powerful equity issues for every student regardless of conditions. The accountability is daunting. Since over one-half of all students to be tested under NCLB are in grades five to eight, the middle grades will be a defining factor of the legislation's success. Further, it has the potential to exacerbate the "volatile mismatch" between practices and student needs. This alone can jeopardize the middle grades of the last decade.

Furthermore, the current definition and stipulation of what constitutes a "highly qualified teacher" for the middle school runs the risk of undermining the progress made in creating small learning communities and small teams, integration across content specializations, and teacher preservice preparation for the middle grades. The stakes for middle grades could not be higher. It is shaping up as a pivotal moment in the movement's history:

> Even where mild, tentative efforts have been made to change how students are taught and tested, many of the reforms subsequently get rolled back ... Look at the middle school movement, a long, overdue attempt to turn the

hell that is junior high school into a more supportive, developmentally appropriate place for young adolescents. Today that movement is on the defensive as champions of the old school succeed in their quest for even tougher standards, more testing and a return to high school style instruction. (Kohn, 1999, p. 9)

And this statement was made prior to the NCLB Act! When the current economic conditions are factored into the equation, it can induce a sense of panic that the decades of effort and advancement will be stopped in its tracks. In many communities across the country, decisions are being made to dismantle programs and eliminate proven practices not because they did not work, but because budgets necessitate slashing out anything but the barest of essentials.

The dual pressures of federal legislation and several financial hardships are tightening the squeeze on middle grades at precisely the moment in its history when it was set to have "break out" season. So the second century of middle grades education begins with yet another significant turning point in its history.

MIDDLE GRADES: THE CENTURY AWAITS

The work of improving the outcomes for young adolescents is far from complete. Even in the best of times and circumstances, the familiar trends through the decades deserve vigilance. The quality of the teachers involved with middle grades matters; proven practices that make good sense for adolescent learning do get good results when done well; strong academics are paramount but not at the expense of personalization; and leaders with know-how are needed to bring the life to the middle grades schools our students need. These trends are vital today just as they were before and will be tomorrow.

Yet policymakers and leaders will be well advised to be attuned to the future trends for the entire area of education and not let the political climate force them to be too reactionary or narrow of vision. For middle grades educators, it is not sufficient to stay true to the movement's developmental roots and key issues alone. The advancement of middle grades education in the next several decades will require that advocates evolve the field beyond the previous trends. Then middle grades will be a valued commodity in the educational spectrum.

If futurists are remotely close in their predictions, trends broader than the impact of current federal legislation will influence educational directions for the long-term in the 21st century:

Emphasis on high-stakes testing will decline as middle-class families become disenchanted because their youngsters aren't doing well on them. High stakes testing may be peaked now. The middle class is turning away from them (Good, 1999).

Those interested in "uniformizing" educational experiences seem more interested in equipping children with the trappings of intellect than with offering any real intellectual substance (Posner, 2002, p. 317).

As NCLB unfolds, adjustments and modifications in the legislation are sure to happen. There will be corrections made for the unintended outcomes and affects. There will be the opportunity to influence those modifications for the benefit of middle grades education so the ultimate effect of having all children succeed can be accomplished without abandoning the middle grades core philosophies and practices.

This is precisely where middle grades can lead the way for all other levels of education. Its culture of reform has included the habit of questioning conventional practices and taking risks to innovate and endorse more cutting-edge practices around organization, curriculum and instruction. The nature of ten-to-fifteen-year-olds demands no less from its educators. In large part the reason the middle school movement has been the longest running grassroots movement is that middle grades teachers experience first-hand, often painfully, how ineffective traditional practices can be. A bounding class of seventh graders increases one's search for better strategies and techniques for learning.

The young adolescent learner is the ever-present barometer and compass to the future. At some point almost all 10 to 15-year-olds experience the physical, intellectual, and socioemotional changes and growth spurts that prepare them for adulthood. It is true that societal shifts and demands place different pressures upon each generation; however it is surprising how the general qualities of young adolescence remain remarkably constant over the decades.

It is that focus on the clientele that predicated the call for changes a century ago. Middle grades education of the future will do what it has wanted to do and has been trying to do for most of the last century. It will show how to break out of the confines of traditional assumptions about schooling, curriculum, time, grade level groupings and achievement (Spady, 2000) and move beyond piecemeal, tinkering types of reform. The past decades have been the antecedent to the future.

> Once you have stopped trying to fit your ideas, words and possibilities into the boxes that have defined schooling and reform for the past century, you'll find it's remarkably exciting to discuss learning. (Spady, 2001, 53)

There is nothing more exciting than creating the climate, structures and framework for young adolescent learning. The future context for learning is changing as education undergoes major shifts. Students will face the effects of changing demographics: the old will outnumber the young, the country will be a nation of minorities; social-intellectual capital will be of primary economic commodity; and technology will speed up all of life's communications capabilities (Good, 1999; Marx, 2001). According to Morgan, Matranga, Peltier, and Hill (1998) "The use of technology will not be seen to be as critical an issue as it is today because technology will be so pervasive as to be institutionalized (p. 341).

Technology makes globalization a fact of the future. To give American students the competitive global advantage, current educational structures need to be "flattened" so real decisions are made by teachers attuned to their students; students need to have more control over their education; educational experiences need to foster creativity and entrepreneurial skills; and curriculum must also emphasize human relation skills and de-emphasize testing.

> In our zeal for standardized testing, we are subjecting our children to stress-ful situations that are unnatural in the real world . . . how useful is the infor-mation found on these tests for students who will need to succeed in the Global Village. (Nordgren, 2002, p. 320)

Narrow, test-driven instruction has the potential to sort students, propel-ling some to first-class citizenship, while relegating others to the bottom of the economic and social heap. But by broadening our educational goals and our instructional strategies, we will not only enhance student academic performance but also create healthy, self-fulfilled, active citizens to respect themselves and others, serve their communities, and safeguard the planet (Ames, 2003, p. 38).

Good, in *Future Trends Affecting Education* (1999), projected a shift in pri-orities in education away from systems of high compliance, time-driven, labor intensive, subject knowledge, rote learning and memorizing with a focus on academic weaknesses of students to educational practices and sys-tems which are based upon high achievement, results driven, capital inten-sive, process knowledge orientation or learning to learn with a focus on academic strengths of students. These trends will mean the education sys-tem is moving toward more balance between:

From ...	Toward ...
School time	Learning anytime, anyplace
Teacher-centered	Student-centered
Textbook funds	Education resource funds
One pace for all	Different rates and styles of learning
Building	Multiple access points for learning
Mass instruction	Personalized instruction

Forecasters say that the most critical skills for future life will be those of adapting and innovating, communicating effectively, thinking critically, solving problems and collaborating (Sparzo, Bruning, Vargas, & Gilman, 1998). The skill shortage of the future will be the earnings differential between skilled and unskilled workers, and this will raise the premium of education (Carnevale, 2001). Assets will be not just what you know. A valued commodity will be social capital: who you know and how well you connect with team members and other collaborators (Marx, 2001).

Even as "cyberschooling" becomes more mainstream, it is predicted that classroom teachers will remain the backbone (Good, 1999).

> Real, not virtual relationships are what school has over e-mail, Internet, the screen and the radio. Schools that serve our collective social purposes need to exploit real relationships by being genuine communities—small enough so everyone is well known and diverse enough so we're bound to come to know people very different from ourselves. (Meier, 2003, p. 19)

> Teachers will emerge as facilitators of learning and they will work in places where staff are given more time for planning, collaborating and learning than in the past—where staff will be engaged in ongoing evaluation and reshaping of the curriculum and instruction to meet the needs of a diverse student populations. (Gaskins, 2000, p. 132)

A press for personalization rather than a system driven by uniformity is emerging (Marx, 2001). In fact, as the learning experience becomes more individualized, it will be less tied to a location; yet the schooling experience will actually gain in value.

> Schooling will continue to be one of the pivotal processes in our society through which people come together in sustained, face-to-face social interactions. The quality of these human interactions will contribute significantly to how young people see and appreciate rich, diverse cultural context and establish important enduring social connections throughout their lives. (Mahiri, 2000, p. 132)

The middle grades learning experience of tomorrow may be the big "new" transition period in life's development—the time of schooling which moves the location of learning from school-based (at one location primarily) to a combination of learning environments including experiences where students and faculty are engaged in learning anytime, anywhere at virtual or off-site locations. The nature of young adolescents is naturally a time of maturing and striving for independence while craving interaction and social connections. Middle grades schools can capitalize on the convergence of future modes of education and student maturation needs by segueing students from highly structured learning experiences to widely flexible settings in multiple forms in preparation for the more independent learning experiences of the later grades. By the time the students of tomorrow proceed to the next tier of schooling, the foundation has to be set. Middle grades students will have to demonstrate the prerequisite academic skills, but also the habits of mind and adaptability skills, to handle the fast-paced, fluid demands of both advanced schooling and adult life.

In the middle grades schools and classrooms of the future, teachers and students will come together in many varied groupings and the duration of those experiences will be far different than the schooling experience currently known. True flexible scheduling will likely replace the day-by-day, hour-by-hour rigid requirements of today. Standards will be reached through a vast array of customized learning experiences ranging from individual to small group to larger group opportunities, thereby ensuring that individual students receive enough support to reach high levels of learning. The length of the teacher/student relationships will extend over a greater amount of time so the role of teacher as guide and facilitator is optimized. The ultimate difference will be that all students will not be in the same building everyday to do the same type of uniform learning with the same set of students year after year. The lines between school and the real world will blur as more come to realize that there's "much more learning of value to be found outside the school curriculum than in it" (Spady, 2000, p. 52). More discretion will be applied as educators determine which techniques should be used that will enhance the learning experiences for young adolescents. It is likely that some unifying function of schooling will remain. "Schooling is an essential part of an advanced society and the work of teaching and learning that goes on in schools are vital" (Sparzo et al., 1998, p. 7).

Middle grades education and its literature already speak widely about what futurists say it will take to nurture and create the productive citizen and worker of tomorrow.

> Much of what needs to be done is already here: interdisciplinary teaching, applications of cognitive research, instruction for multiple intelligences, a focus on teaching thinking and reasoning skills, a commitment to helping students turn information into knowledge, planning backward from outcomes we'd like to see (Marx, 2001, p. 8–9).

This "new" set of prerequisite skills for other levels dot the landscape of middle grades already. As *Turning Points 2000* cautions, it is not the lack of knowledge or know-how that continues to hinder our progress, what is possible is known. Often it is the will and leadership.

A focused lens about exemplary middle grades education exists to garner the will and elevate the leadership to new dimensions and challenges of the future. The vision statement of the National Forum to Accelerate Middle Grades Reform sets three interrelated, equally balanced goals that give the guidance as well as provide the flexibility to respond appropriately with multiple and emerging trends. Tomorrow's high performing schools must reach harmony around academic excellence, developmental responsiveness, and social equity in order to fulfill the ultimate goal of high quality schooling for each and every middle grades student.

Since a "one size fits all" model for middle grades of the future is an unrealistic scenario, the best way to talk about what the future of middle grades education will look like is to generate questions for inquiry. To move forward, the middle grades community has to raise questions, consider many possibilities, examine and create new strategies, and think far beyond the current "School Box." The manifesto, *Speaking with One Voice*, closed with questions about academic purpose, desired levels of performance and outcomes for students; actions to ensure universal achievement; procedures for classroom grouping assignments; methods for having students learn more eagerly, extensively and deeply; intentional strategies for changing curriculum, pedagogy and school services to improve academic outcomes; and outcomes to hold ourselves accountable for attaining the results we desire (Lipsitz et al., 1997, p. 540).

Rigorous inquiry is not an easy habit to perfect but it is extremely necessary to start building the responsive, effective learning experiences for the next century. We have a long history of tinkering with the boxes, calling the tinkering "reform" but leaving the boxes fundamentally unchanged (Spady, 2000). Although this has been said before, the rapid advancements in science and technology in the coming years will break the grip of business as usual in our schools. It has already started. The time is right to generate many questions around the goals of academic excellence, social equity and developmental responsiveness as well as those of school structures that support learning. The process of self-inquiry, scanning the futures horizon, data gathering, and consensus building about the viability of practices of the future is endemic of an organization with a healthy future.

To get the conversation started, a sampling of the kinds of questions which will together move both the vision and criteria of middle grades and the demands for the schooling experience of the future forward may be ones such as:

- How are we engaging our students in meaningful, high quality learning now and where can we yet go? To what extent are we getting all our students to use their minds well? How can we do more than attain standards through rich learning experiences?

- How can the learning be best accomplished? Where does it make sense to learn around central themes and big questions? Which learning requires individualization? What is accomplished most effectively as a large group or a small group, in seminar format or as an entire team? How can we vary when and where we come together to learn? What advantages are there in bringing the classroom routinely into the community? What needs to be done in specific locations beyond the regular school building? What advantages do our students gain from a flexible learning environment? What segments of our program need the unity of spirit that comes from gathering together regularly?
- Where can students do more independent work through technological learning stations they access at home? How do the individual learning styles and strengths of students determine their best learning arrangements and allow them to receive the support they need? What and when are the aspects of our program that need the face-to-face interactions and time to make meaning from what they are learning?
- As technology becomes more dominate, how will the learning experience be facilitated by teachers in the best interest of various students?
- How would students' progress evolve if small sets of teachers had responsibility for the same set of students over multiple years?
- How can we do individual diagnosis and arrange for tutorial assistance that leads to increasingly complex work?
- How do we balance adolescent needs for structure with opportunities for a variety of learning systems?

Savvy faculty, middle grades leaders, policymakers, districts and school board members, parents, and students will use the National Forum Schools to Watch Criteria, *This We Believe*, reports of future trends and other sources of information as catapults for inquiry and projection into the future.

CONCLUSION

The future of middle grades education lies in our ability to question and think critically beyond what is now to what needs to be in the times to come. The journey of middle grades is composed of one destination after another from decade to decade.

It is also critical to remember that reform is never completed, because everyone continually changes, and everyone continually learns, experiencing fresh insights from practice, from research, and from the synergy of teachers, administrators, students, parents and other inquiring together. (Darling-Hammond, 1997, p. 337)

High performance learning communities keyed toward the future engage in rigorous inquiry without defensiveness. The purpose is not to determine if a good or poor job has been done, but rather to look for ways to be most effective, responsive, and in turn, decide what skills and competencies will be best suited for the next generation of learners. Absolutes do not exist. The future of middle grades needs to build upon its core beliefs, goals, and practices but with the lens on the whole, new world to come. Policymakers will need to bring middle grades issues to the forefront more often and draw upon the resources that its teachers and students can provide for others.

The future really speaks of hope for middle grades education, and the contributions it can provide. After a century of trying to convince a slow-churning, educational system that our way of thinking about the education of young adolescents makes best sense, the movement can be encouraged that all the predictions about what is important for preparing students for the next century are within our reach. Over time the practices and traditions valued by the establishment have put obstacles in our way even when data suggested otherwise. The trends of the future will actually grease the pathway for the middle grades movement to accelerate. There is remarkable congruence between what is projected and middle grades practices. True reform and changes will move both upwards and downwards from the middle across the educational spectrum, and the long sought after sense of legitimacy for the middle grades will happen.

Our first century of middle grades education is almost over, but our work remains boldly in front of us. It is not enough just "to keep it" any longer. We must make our work finally live up to the greatest aspirations of the vision even in these times of greatest pressures.

REFERENCES

Ames, N. (2003). To truly educate. *Principal Leadership, 3*(7), 35–38.

Academy for Educational Development. (1993). *Middle grades education in an era of reform: Proceeding of a seminar series.* New York: Author.

Berliner, B. (1997). *What it takes to work together: The promise of educational partnerships.* San Francisco: WestEd.

Brand, C. F., & Johnson, K. P. (2002). Forces of change: Schools in the new century. *Comtemporary Education, 72*(1), 32–38.

Carnegie Council on Adolescent Development. (1989, June). *Turning points: Preparing American youth for the 21st century.* The Report of the Task Force on Education of Young Adolescents. New York: Carnegie Corporation of New York.

Carnevale, A. (July 27, 2001). The future of education, employment, and training policy: A conversation with Tony Carnevale. Washington, DC: American Youth Policy Forum.

Council of Chief State Officers. (1992). *Reform in middle grades education: Current status, future directions.* Washington, DC: Author.

Darling-Hammond, L. (1997). *The right to learn: A blueprint for creating schools that work.* San Francisco: Jossey-Bass.

Dickinson, T. S., & Butler, D. A. (2001). Reinventing the middle school. *Middle School Journal, 33*(1), 7–13.

Eichhorn, D. H. (1966, 1987). *The middle school.* Columbus, OH: National Middle School Association and National Association of Secondary School Principals.

Epstein, J. L., & Mac Iver, D. J. (1990). *Education in the middle grades.* Columbus, OH: National Middle School Association.

Felner, R. D., Jackson, A. W., Kasak, D., Mulhall, P., Brand, S. & Flowers, N. (1997). The impact of school reform for the middle years: Longitudinal study of a Network engaged in *Turning Points*-based comprehensive school transformation. *Phi Delta Kappan, 78*(7), 528–550.

Gaskins, I. W. (2000). What will classrooms and schools look like in the new millennium? *Reading Research Quarterly, 35*(1), 132–134.

George, P. S., & Malinka, R. M. (1977). *The middle school: A look ahead.* Fairborn, OH: National Middle School Association.

Good, D. G. (1999). *Future trends affecting education.* Denver, CO: Education Commission of the States.

Gruhn, W. T., & Douglass, H. R. (1947). *The modern junior high school.* New York: Ronald Press Co.

Irvin, J. L. (Ed.). (1992). *Transforming middle level education: Perspectives and possibilities.* Boston, MA: Allyn & Bacon.

Jackson, A. W., & Davis, G. A. (2000). *Turning points 2000: Educating adolescents in the 21st century.* New York: Teachers College Press.

Kohn, A. (1999). *The schools our children deserve: Moving beyond traditional classrooms and "tougher standards".* New York: Houghton Mifflin.

Kronley, R. A. & Handley, C. (2003). Maturing investments: Philanthropy and middle grades reform. Portland, OR: Grantmakers for Education.

Lipsitz, J., Mizell, M. H., Jackson, A. W., & Austin, L. M. (1997). Speaking with one voice: A manifesto for middle-grades reform. *Phi Delta Kappan, 78*(7), 533–540.

Lounsbury, J. (1991). *As I see it.* Columbus, OH: National Middle School Association.

Lousnbury, J. (Ed.). (1984). *Perspectives: Middle school education.* Columbus, OH: National Middle School Association.

Mahiri, J. (2000). What will be the social implication and interactions of schooling In the next millennium? *Reading Research Quarterly, 35*(3), 420–424.

Marx, G. (2001). 10 trends for tomorrow's kids. *Education Digest, 77*(8), 4–10.

Meier, D. W. (2003). Becoming educated: The power of ideas. *Principal Leadership, 3*(7), 16–19.

Mizell, M. H. (2002). Shooting for the sun: The message of middle school reform. New York: Edna McConnell Clark Foundation.

Morgan, A. D., Matranga, M., Peltier, G., & Hill, G. C. (1998). What issues will confront public education in the years 2000–2020? Predictions of chief state school officers. *The Clearing House, 71*(6), 339–341.

National Middle School Association. (1995). *This we believe: Developmentally responsive middle level schools.* Columbus, OH: Author.

No child left behind act of 2001, Pub. L. No 107-110, 115 Stat. 1425 (2002).

Nordgren, R. D. (2002). Globalization and education: What students will need to know and be able to do in the global village. *Phi Delta Kappan, 84*(4), 318–321.

Oakes, J., Quartes, K. H., Ryan, S., 7 Lyston, M. (2000). *Becoming good American schools: The struggle for civic virtue in education reform.* San Francisco: Jossey-Bass.

Posner, D. (2002). Education for the 21st century. *Phi Delta Kappan, 84*(4), 316–317.

Spady, W. G. (2000). Breaking out of the box. *American School Board Journal, 187*(9), 52–53.

Sparzo, F. J., Bruning, R., Vargaas, J. S., Gilman, D. A. (1998). Education problems for the 21st century Part I: The purpose of schooling. *Contemporary Education, 70*(1), 5–13.

Appendix

SCHOOLS TO WATCH CRITERIA

National Forum to Accelerate Middle-Grades Reform

Guiding criteria of academic excellence include:

- Expecting all students to meet high academic standards
- Providing clear picture of what students should know and be able to do with the instruction, curriculum and assessment reinforcing this picture of student learning
- Having students learn important concepts and skills
- Using a variety of methods to help students master standards and assess their progress
- Ensuring students have enough time and chances to learn
- Securing extra help and support
- Engaging school staff members in continuous improvement of their knowledge and skills

Guiding criteria of developmental responsive includes:

- Creating a sense of belonging for all members of the community
- Getting help for students with difficulties and their families
- Using a variety of engaging activities where students are encouraged to explore their interests and be creative
- Covering topics relevant to students' lives and interests
- Helping students make exciting connections across different subjects
- Offering many varied activities and programs to develop and expand their interests and expand their competencies
- Having students involved in real decisions
- Having partnerships with families and communities where students both receive services and give to their communities
- Offering programs and activities during and after school

Guiding criteria of social equity includes:

- Expecting high-quality work from every student and making sure students produce it
- Taking different approaches to learning and showing what they have learned
- Improving curriculum, teaching and assessment is on-going
- Having every student involved in challenging classes and high-level learning activities
- Having students learn about their own and others cultures

- Knowing every student well is a priority of the school and each student is appreciated and respected
- Making certain all families are involved in the school
- Recognizing contributions of all students
- Having teachers and staff coming from many backgrounds
- Finding ways to keep suspension rates low and engaged learning time high

Guiding criteria of support for school improvement includes:

- Inspiring vision and excellence that is shared and drives constant improvement
- Leading with school improvement in mind
- Expecting everyone to be learning including the school's many partners
- Providing high quality help to teachers so the vision is possible
- Holding itself accountable for results
- Viewing barriers as challenges not problems
- Preparing, recruiting and mentoring teachers who share the vision
- Incorporating families and community members as full partners in the improvement efforts

(*www.schoolstowatch.org*, STW criteria)

ABOUT THE AUTHORS

Nancy Ames is Vice-President and Director of the Center for Family, School, and Community at Education Development Center, Inc. Ms. Ames is a founder of the National Forum to Accelerate Middle-Grades Reform, a unique alliance of middle-grades leaders dedicated to improving academic and developmental outcomes for all students. Based on her experience with 16 urban school systems in Indiana, she co-authored *Changing Middle Schools: How to Make Schools Work for Young Adolescents*. A leader in comprehensive school reform, she is also co-author of *School Reform Behind the Scenes: How ATLAS is shaping the future of education.*

Vincent A. Anfara, Jr. is Associate Professor of Educational Administration and Policy Studies at The University of Tennessee, Knoxville. He received his Ph.D. in educational administration from the University of New Orleans in 1995. Before entering the professorate, he taught for 25 years in both middle and high schools in Louisiana and New Mexico. He is the author of numerous articles on middle school advisory programs, middle grades reform, and the middle level principalship. He is the coauthor of *From the Desk of the Middle School Principal: Leadership Responsive to the Needs of Young Adolescents* (with K. Brown, 2002). In 2003, he coauthored *Research and Resources in Support of This We Believe* (with Andrews, Hough, Mertens, Mizelle, & White). Currently he is the president of the American Education Research Association's Special Interest Group, Middle Level Education Research, and Chair of the National Middle School Association's Research Committee.

James A. Beane is Professor in the National College of Education at National-Louis University. He is author of *Curriculum Integration: Designing*

Reforming Middle Level Education: Considerations for Policymakers, pages 251–256
Copyright © 2004 by Information Age Publishing
All rights of reproduction in any form reserved.

the Core of a Democratic Education, Affect in the Curriculum: Toward Democracy, Dignity, and Diversity, and *A Middle School Curriculum: From Rhetoric to Reality;* co-author of *Self-Concept, Self-Esteem and the Curriculum, Curriculum Planning and Development, The Middle School and Beyond,* and *When the Kids Come First: Enhancing Self-Esteem at the Middle Level;* co-editor of *Democratic Schools;* and editor of the 1995 ASCD Yearbook, *Toward a Coherent Curriculum.* In addition he has written forewords and chapters for many books and articles for a variety of professional journals. He has spoken at numerous international, national, state, and local conferences, has been a consultant for educational projects in the U.S. and elsewhere, and served in various capacities for several professional associations. In 1997 he received the John H. Lounsbury Distinguished Service Award from the National Middle School Association

Thomas S. Dickinson is Professor of Education at DePauw University in Greencastle, Indiana. He is on a two-year leave of absence from his tenured position at Indiana State University where he will resume his duties as Professor of Education in the fall of 2004. Dr. Dickinson has taught at the college and university level in North Carolina, Illinois, Georgia, and Indiana. A former editor of *Middle School Journal* for the National Middle School Association, he is the author of numerous books, chapters, and articles on middle school education. One of the latest books he edited is *Reinventing Middle Schools.*

Nancy M. Doda began her career as a middle school Language Arts teacher in a Florida middle school acknowledged as an exemplary, model middle school. Nancy is Associate Professor in the National College of Education at National-Louis University's Northern Virginia/Washington, DC campus where she teaches in the Department of Elementary/Middle Level Teacher Preparation. Early in her career as a middle school teacher, she authored a regular column for the *Middle School Journal* entitled "Teacher to Teacher", which became an NMSA monograph. Dr. Doda co-edited *Transforming Ourselves, Transforming Schools: Middle School Change.* She served five years as a member of the NMSA Board. She has spoken at numerous international, national, state, and local conferences and has been a consultant for education projects in the U.S. and elsewhere. In recent years, she served as a charter member of the National Forum to Accelerate Middle-Grades Reform and currently serves on that Forum. In 2001 she received the John H. Lounsbury Distinguished Service Award from the National Middle School Association.

Stephanie Hirsh is the Deputy Executive Director of the National Staff Development Council. Her role involves directing the work of the Staff Development Leadership Councils (SDLCs)., grassroots groups focused on the adoption of policies that advance staff development at the local and state levels. She is also responsible for organizational partnerships, fund development, and supporting the Council's agenda in the policymaking arena. Dr. Hirsh has co-authored three manuals published by NSDC: *School Improvement Planning Manual, Keys to Successful Meetings, and NSDC's Standards for Staff Development: Trainer's Guide*. She has written numerous journal articles. Her book, *A New Vision for Staff Development*, written with Dennis Sparks was co-published by the Association for Supervision and Curriculum and NSDC. Prior to her position with the council, she completed 15 years of district and school-based leadership positions.

J. Howard Johnston is Professor of Education at University of South Florida in Tampa, Florida. Dr. Johnston has received numerous honors and awards, including the Gruhn-Long Award for Lifetime Service to Middle Level Education from the National Association of Secondary School Principals. In 2003 he received the John H. Lounsbury Distinguished Service Award from the National Middle School Association. Dr. Johnston has been the keynote speaker at two National Middle School Conferences and many state conferences. He is an author of numerous books, monographs, journal articles and chapters in edited books on middle school education. His current research agenda is standards-based middle school reform, productive student behavior, and technology and school reform.

Deborah Kasak is the Executive Director for the National Forum to Accelerate Middle-Grades Reform. The National Forum is an affiliation of the country's most prominent associations, foundations, researchers, and practitioners, united to speak in one voice about needed improvement in the middle grades. Previously, she was the executive director of the Association of Illinois Middle Level Schools for eight years. Nationally, AIMS is regarded as one of the most active and innovative middle level associations. She helped create the Illinois Middle Grades Network. She oversaw the operation of one of the first regional centers for the National Turning Points Design Model, a reform model with New American Schools. She was actively involved with the middle grades self-study process and collaborated with staff at the Center for Prevention Research and Development at the University of Illinois, Urbana-Champaign. Deborah served as president of the National Middle School Association in 2001–2002. She has presented widely on all aspects of middle grades development.

John H. Lounsbury began teaching in 1948 and 35 years later retired as Dean of the School of Education at Georgia College & State University. After retirement the School of Education was named the John H. Lounsbury School of Education. That retirement was merely a technicality as he maintains a full schedule dealing with his special interest—middle level education. After 14 years as editor of *Middle School Journal* he headed the association's venture into publishing books and has produced over 100 books. He is known for his commitment and insistence that educators face the most significant, philosophical, value-laden questions. Dr. Lounsbury has presented all over the country as part of his effort to make the educational experiences of young adolescents more than mere schooling. The National Middle School Association named its most prestigious award after John H. Lounsbury.

Ken McEwin is Professor of Curriculum and Instruction at Appalachian State University, Boone, North Carolina. He is a former sixth grade teacher and principal, and has extensive experience as a consultant. He is author of numerous professional publications that focus on middle school education. He is a member of the National Forum to Accelerate Middle-Grades Reform. The National Forum is an affiliation of the country's most prominent associations, foundations, researchers, and practitioners, united to speak in one voice about needed improvement in the middle grades. He helped to draft the National Forum's policy statement on Middle Grades Teacher Preparation. He is a recipient of the National Middle School Association John H. Lounsbury Distinguished Service Award and the North Carolina Middle School Association Distinguished Service Award.

David A. Payton is Supervisor of the New York State Education Department's Middle-Level Education Program. He is a 20-year veteran of the Department, with prior experience in public schools, Boards of Cooperative Educational Services (BOCES), and post-secondary institutions. During his tenure, New York State, working with partners such as the Statewide Network of Middle-Level Education Liaisons and the New York State Middle School Associate, has developed two middle-level policy statements (1998 and 2003), translated State policy into an implementation guide titled *Essential Elements of Standards-Focused Middle-Level Schools and Programs*, conducted research on best practice in the middle grades, and established middle-level education as a State priority. Dr. Payton is also a member of the National Forum to Accelerate Middle-Grades Reform.

Tracy Smith is Assistant Professor of Curriculum and Instruction at Appalachian State University, Boone, North Carolina. She teaches and advises in the undergraduate and graduate middle level teacher preparation programs at Appalachian. Dr. Smith is a former middle school language arts and social studies teacher. She is a respected consultant and author of professional publications focusing on teaching expertise and middle level teacher preparation and licensure.

Sandra L. Stacki is the Middle-Level Coordinator in the Department of Curriculum and Teaching at Hofstra University in New York, a Board member for the New York State Association of Teacher Education, and a member of the Statewide Network of Middle-Level Education Liaisons. She works with preservice undergraduate and graduate students as well as doctoral students. Along with middle-level courses, she teaches courses on curriculum change, perspectives on educational practice, gender issues, qualitative research, and international/comparative education. Her research interests include teacher development and empowerment, gender, teaming, policy analysis, and qualitative and feminist research in both national and international contexts. With co-author Jeannette Stern, she teaches an intensive middle-level summer session at Hofstra University. They have formed an informal partnership to provide university study and practical experience at the middle school for pre-service students.

Jeannette Stern is currently the New York Middle School Association president (NYSMSA), the principal of Wantagh Middle School, and a member of the Statewide Network of Middle-Level Education Liaisons. She has been a middle-level educator in the Wantagh school district for over 30 years. With co-author Sandra Stacki, she teaches an intensive middle-level summer session at Hofstra University. They have formed an informal partnership to provide university study and practical experience at the middle school for preservice students.

Sue Swaim is the Executive Director of the National Middle School Association (NMSA). The Association is headquartered in Columbus, Ohio with a satellite office in Washington, DC. NMSA has over 30,000 members and 58 affiliate organizations throughout the United States and beyond. It is the only national and international association that focused solely on the education and well-being of young adolescents, ages 10 through 14. Ms. Swaim has been very active in middle level education as a teacher, principal, educational consultant and professional association officer. She has been a primary consultant to numerous school districts and keynote speaker at middle level conferences and institutes nationally and internationally. She is a past president of the National Middle School Association and past president and a past executive director of the Colorado Association of Middle Level Education.

Sue C. Thompson is Assistant Professor in the Urban Leadership and Policy Studies in Education Division at the University of Missouri, Kansas City. She has been a middle school teacher, principal, and director of middle level education. She serves on the National Forum to Accelerate Middle Grades Reform and is Chair of the National Middle School Association's Urban Issues Task Force. She co-edited *Transforming Ourselves, Transforming*

Schools: Middle School Change, as well as written journal articles about middle level education. She has been a primary consultant to numerous school districts. Her research interests include middle school reculturing, leadership, and issues of race/ethnicity, class and gender as they relate to social equity and democratic schools.

Ron Williamson is Associate Professor of Educational Leadership at Eastern Michigan University. He is co-chair of the National Forum to Accelerate Middle-Grades Reform and was formerly Executive Director of the National Middle School Association. Until 1994 he was a middle school principal and Executive Director of Curriculum and Instruction in Ann Arbor, Michigan. *Phi Delta Kappan* cited two of Dr. Williamson's publications as essential core readings for middle level educators. In addition, he has published two books on scheduling to improve student learning.